Birds of the Sudbury River Valley–

An Historical Perspective

By Richard K. Walton

Published by the Massachusetts Audubon Society
Lincoln, Massachusetts

First Edition

ISBN 0-932691-00-5

For A.W.W.

CONTENTS

Acknowledgments

Introduction viii

PART I — THE LAND AND THE NATURALIST

Chapter 1 . . . . . New Beginnings: The Sudbury River Valley 1635-1800. . 1

Chapter 2 . . . . . The River Meadows 8

Chapter 3 . . . . . Henry David Thoreau 12

Chapter 4 . . . . . The Woodlands and the Railroads 20

Chapter 5 . . . . . 19th Century Pressures on the Birdlife 28

Chapter 6 . . . . . William Brewster 31

Chapter 7 . . . . . Ludlow Griscom 38

Chapter 8 . . . . . The Urbanization of the Valley 43

Chapter 9 . . . . . Allen Morgan: Preserving the Land 47

Chapter 10 . . . . . The 1980s: Promise and Peril 55

PART II — THE JOURNALS

A Season of Hope 59

The Spring Migration 66

The Nesting Season 76

Late Summer Wanderings & The Fall Migration 82

The Winter Season 91

PART III — THE CHECKLIST

Species Accounts 100

Appendix A - Valley Birdlife: Seasons and Habitats 187

Appendix B - Concord Christmas Count: 1960-1983 189

Notes and Sources 203

Index 214

Photographs and Illustrations

Cover . . . . Marsh Wren, watercolor by John Sill

Chapter 1 . . . . . . 17th Century Map of The Sudbury River Valley - from William Wood's *New England's Prospect* reproduced by permission of The Houghton Library, Harvard University

Chapter 2 . . . . . . Sudbury River Meadows, by Alfred Wayland Cutting (1860-1935) - courtesy Wayland Public Library

Chapter 3 . . . . . . Henry David Thoreau, from a daguerreotype by Benjamin D. Maxham (1856) - courtesy Thoreau Lyceum

Chapter 4 . . . . . . Boston & Maine Steam Engine, Passing Walden Pond - courtesy Thoreau Society
Barrett's Mill - courtesy Concord Free Public Library

Chapter 6 . . . . . . William Brewster - courtesy Concord Free Public Library

Chapter 7 . . . . . . Ludlow Griscom - courtesy Massachusetts Audubon Society

Chapter 8 . . . . . . Sudbury River Valley at Framingham, A.S. MacLean, Landslides, Lincoln, MA

Chapter 9 . . . . . . Allen Morgan, photograph by R. Walton
Nine Acre Corner, Landslides
Sudbury River Valley, North from Route 20, Landslides

Map . . . . Leslie Cowperthwaite

ACKNOWLEDGMENTS

Without the support of two organizations, this book would not have become a reality. First, I want to express my gratitude to the Sudbury Valley Trustees for their initial help that, in part, allowed me to begin the process of gathering data for this book. Allen H. Morgan, in particular, has been a source of encouragement and assistance. The Massachusetts Audubon Society has been supportive throughout the process, and it was the special interest that the society's president, Dr. Gerard A. Bertrand, took in the project which brought it to fruition.

The author would particularly like to thank F. Gregg Bemis whose generous support made publication possible.

I especially want to thank Richard A. Forster for his invaluable assistance. Dick Forster was always accessible and willing to share his considerable knowledge of Sudbury River Valley birdlife. I also want to thank James Baird for his help with the manuscript, but more especially for his willingness to add the duties of editor to his already busy schedule.

I am indebted to John Hines, Jr. and Wayne Petersen for their comments and suggestions on the species accounts, to Wayne Hanley for reading Part I, to Ann McGrath of the Thoreau Lyceum for reading the chapter on Thoreau, and to Susan Emmons for her assistance with the Christmas Count data.

I am grateful to several organizations for permission to use various passages in this book. I am especially indebted to the Concord Free Public Library for permission to use the Jarvis manuscript, to the Harvard University Press for permission to reprint parts of William Brewster's *October Farm* and *Concord River* and Ludlow Griscom's *The Birds of Concord*, to the Museum of Comparative Zoology, Harvard University for permission to publish parts of William Brewster's journals, and to the Peabody Museum of Salem, Massachusetts for granting permission to publish parts of Ludlow Griscom's journals. My thanks go to Ruth P. Emery, Richard A. Forster, David L. Garrison, Allen H. Morgan, Wayne R. Petersen and Betty Porter for their journal accounts.

I want to thank the staffs of the Concord Free Public Library, the Sudbury Public Library, the Wayland Public Library, the Museum of Comparative Zoology of Harvard University and the Peabody Museum of Salem, Massachusetts. In particular, my thanks go to Marcia Moss and Joyce Woodman of Concord's library and Ann Blum of the MCZ's library.

Thanks go as well to Charlotte Smith for typing much of the manuscript and to Leslie Cowperthwaite for her typing and map design chores.

Last, but not least, I want to thank my family for their help, encouragement and forbearance. Adelaide Walton has been involved in almost every aspect of this work. Her support and many hours of toil are truly appreciated.

INTRODUCTION

The Sudbury River Valley* holds a unique place in ornithological history. For the past 150 years naturalists have been at work in the Valley recording facts about the birdlife. A succession of field notes, journals and publications constitutes a chronicle unsurpassed in North America. An important strand of natural history has been woven from these records.

Intertwined with this tradition has been history of a different sort. The cultural history of this area has been one of pioneering, farming, revolution, industrialization, war, population explosion and suburbanization.

The realities of the natural world have affected the social history; civilization has altered the natural world. This interrelationship between nature and culture provides one perspective for investigating the history of the Sudbury River Valley.

Here spring floods and politicians, plows and poets, condominium developers and conservationists have come together. Their interactions have led to change in the Valley.

For the present-day student of nature an understanding of these changes fosters a broader perspective on the natural history of this area. A familiarity with the land history and the works of the earlier naturalists enhances current studies.

We are, in the 1980s struggling to reach a balance between the demands for uncontrolled growth and those needs fulfilled through the preservation of the land. This has not always been so.

---

* The Sudbury River forms a part of the SuAsCo basin. This larger watershed is defined by the drainage area of the Sudbury, Assabet and Concord Rivers and their feeder brooks. Two of these rivers, the Sudbury and the Assabet, arise near the Cedar Swamp in the town of Westborough, Massachusetts. The Assabet, following a more northerly course, travels from Westborough through Northborough, Marlboro, Hudson, Stow, Maynard and Acton and then into Concord. The Sudbury begins its course in an easterly direction out of Westborough into Southborough, Cordaville, Ashland and Framingham where it turns in a more northerly direction as it flows through Wayland and Sudbury, past Lincoln, and into Concord. In Concord these two rivers join to become the Concord River. From this confluence the river's course is generally northeast and forms the boundary between Bedford and Carlisle. From there it flows into Billerica, Chelmsford, Tewksbury and Lowell. In Lowell, the Concord joins the Merrimack River on its path to the Atlantic Ocean. In all, the SuAsCo basin drains an area of approximately 400 square miles.

The focus of this book is that section of the Sudbury and Concord river valley that includes the towns of Concord, Sudbury and Wayland. This was the first section of the river valley to be settled and has been the traditional center of natural history studies in this area. Although what I will call the "Valley" is somewhat representative of other locales along these rivers and of inland sites in general, enough local differences exist, even in other areas along the Sudbury River, to caution against the inclination to draw parallels too finely. Each area is characterized by a unique interaction of natural and cultural history.

PART I — THE LAND AND THE NATURALIST

Chapter 1

> . . . land that is left wholly to nature, that hath no improvement of
> pastorage, tillage, or planting, is called, as indeed it is, 'waste,' and we
> shall find the benefit of it amount to little more than nothing.
>
> John Locke

The valley of the Musketaquid in eastern Massachusetts was the home of the
Pawtuckett Indians in the seventeenth century. Here tribal members hunted
in the forest, raised corn in upland fields and set their weirs in slow moving
streams. The rivers were their passageways for migrations to and from the
coast. Contact with the tidal colonies brought the Pawtuckett cotton cloth,
hoes, brassware and copper goods; it also brought plague and smallpox. By
the 1630s more than three-quarters of the local Indian population had
perished. The English colonists were quick to expand the frontier, and in
1635 the General Court cleared the way for the first inland settlement in
Massachusetts.

> It is ordered that there shall be a plantation att Musketaquid, and that
> there shall be 6 miles of land square to belonge to it . . . and the name
> of the place is changed and here after to be callcd Concord.

Concord was the wilderness. Edward Johnson's* colorful description of the
pioneers' initial journey to the Sudbury River Valley provides a contemporary perspective of the frontier.

> The land they purchase of the Indians, and with much difficulties
> travelling through unknowne woods, and through watery swamps, they
> discover the fitnesse of the place; sometimes passing through the
> thickets, where their hands are forced to make way for their bodies
> passage, and their feet clambering over the crossed trees, which when
> they missed they sunke into an uncertaine bottome in water, and wade
> up to their knees, tumbling sometimes higher and sometimes lower.
> Wearied with this toile, they at the end of this meet with a scorching
> plaine, yet not so plaine, but that the ragged bushes scratch their legs
> fouly, even to wearing their stockings to their bare skin in two or three
> hours. If they be not otherwise well defended with bootes or bushkins,
> their flesh will be torne. Some of them being forced to passe on without
> further provision, have had the bloud trickle downe at every step. And
> in the time of summer, the sun casts such a reflecting heate from the
> sweet ferne, whose scent is so strong, that some herewith have beene
> very near fainting, although very able bodies to undergoe much
> travel . . .
>
> Their further hardship is to travell sometimes they know not whither,
> bewildered indeed without sight of sun, their compasse miscarrying in
> crouding through the bushes. They sadly search up and down for a
> known way, the Indian paths being not above one foot broad, so that a
> man may travell many dayes and never find one . . .

*See Notes and Sources for bibliographic information.

> This intricate worke no whit daunted these resolved servants of Christ
> to go on with the worke in hand; but lying in the open aire, while the
> watery clouds poure down all the night season, and sometimes the driv-
> ing snow dissolving on their backs, they keep their wet cloathes warme
> with a continued fire, 'till the renewed morning gives fresh opportunity
> of further travell . . .

The catalogue of difficulties continues in Johnson's account. Bread was
scarce and meat practically unobtainable, "unlesse they could barter with
the Indians for venison or rockoons." Their work was "like the labours of
Hercules never at an end." The environs and the natives were unfriendly.
The situation of the pioneers " . . . was much aggravated by continuall
feare of Indians approach, whose cruelities were much spoken of . . . "

There were, however, several positive aspects to the pioneers' existence. The
fishing was good, the corn bountiful, and the church fellowship allowed the
settlers to suffer in company.

On the other side of the Atlantic, curiosity about the New World was
widespread. William Wood, perhaps the first Englishman to visit the Sudbury River Valley, returned home with maps and news of the new lands.
The publication of his *New England's Prospect* in 1634 provided practical
advice for the would-be pioneer, favorable accounts of living conditions,
and vivid descriptions of new and strange beasts.

> Every man likewise must carry over good store of apparel; for if he
> come to buy it there, he shall find it dearer than in England. Woolen
> cloth is a very good commodity and linen better . . .

> For the country, it is as well watered as any land under the sun, every
> two families having a spring of sweet water betwixt them, which is far
> different from the waters of England, being not so sharp but of a fatter
> substance and a more jetty color. It is thought that there can be no bet-
> ter water in the world. Yet dare I not prefer it before good beer as some
> men have done, but any man will choose it before bad beer, whey, or
> buttermilk. Those that drink it be as healthful, fresh, and lusty as they
> that drink beer . . .

> The ounce or wildcat is as big as a mongrel dog. This creature is by
> nature fierce and more dangerous to be met withal than any other
> creature, not fearing either dog or man. He useth to kill deer, which he
> thus effecteth: knowing the deer's tracts, he will lie lurking in long
> weeds, the deer passing by he suddenly leaps upon his back, from
> thence gets to his neck and scratcheth out his throat. He hath likewise a
> devise to get geese, for being much of the color of a goose he will place
> himself close by the water, holding up his bob tail, which is like a goose
> neck; the geese seeing this counterfeiting goose neigh to visit him, who
> with a sudden jerk apprehends his mistrustless prey. The English kill
> many of those, accounting them very good meat. Their skins be a very
> deep kind of fur, spotted white and black on the belly.

Englishmen were tempted by these tales of virgin country and fascinated
with the accounts of wild animals. Once across the Atlantic, however, col-
onials quickly lost their curiosity. Basic necessities and land became the major concerns of pioneers intent on establishing inland settlements along the

The South part of Nevv-England, as it is Planted this yeare, 1634.

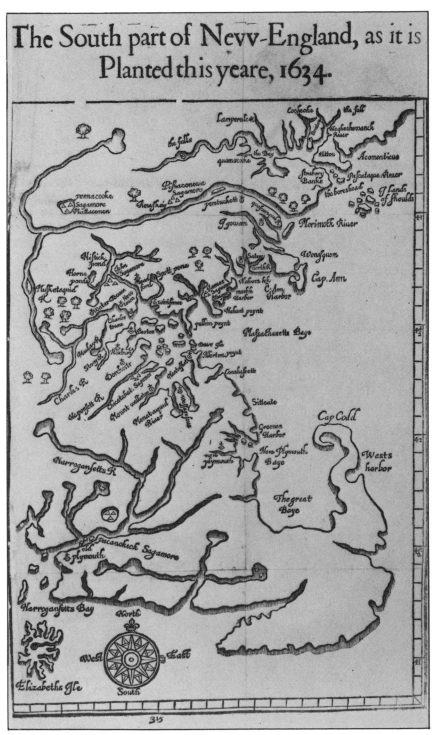

William Wood's 17th century map including Musketaquid River.

Sudbury River Valley. A crusadelike Puritan mission set out to "save" the land as well as the soul; the frontier wilderness was perceived as a hostile, ungodly place ripe for conversion by cultivation. As Roderick Nash points out in his discussion of colonial attitudes: "The driving impulse was always to carve a garden from the wilds; to make an island of spiritual light in the surrounding darkness. The Puritan mission had no place for wild country." The settlers had little interest in studying either sweet ferns or "rockoons." More than two centuries would pass before a plea for wilderness would be heard from this part of the world.

The traditional image of the frontier is one of primeval forest stretching from seacoast to prairie. It was, however, the absence of such forest that attracted the colonists to the area along the rivers. As early as 1645, laws were passed in the Sudbury settlement to protect the large trees that remained on the common lands. Lemuel Shattuck's *The History of the Town of Concord* and Alfred Hudson's *The History of Sudbury, Massachusetts* provide a picture of the first colonial settlements in the Sudbury River Valley.

Concord

The situation of the place, though then considered far in the interior and accessible only with great difficulty, held out strong inducements to form an English settlement, and early attracted the attention of the adventurous Pilgrims. Extensive meadows, bordering on rivers and lying adjacent to upland plains, have ever been favorite spots to new settlers; and this was peculiarly the character of Musketaquid. The Great Fields, extending from the Great Meadows on the north to the Boston road south, and down the river considerably into the present limits of Bedford, and up the river beyond Deacon Hubbard's, and the extensive tract between the two rivers, contained large quantities of open land, which bore some resemblance to the prairies of the western country. These plains were annually burned or dug over, for the purposes of hunting or the rude culture of corn. Forest trees or small shrubbery rarely opposed the immediate and easy culture of the soil. And the open meadows, scattered along the borders of the small streams, as well as the great rivers, and in the solitary glens, then producing, it is said, even larger crops and of better quality, than they now do, promised abundant support for all the necessary stock of the farm-yard. These advantages were early made known to the English emigrants.

Sudbury

The country about Sudbury at the time of its settlement was largely covered with heavy timber. That tar making was, to an extent, an early occupation indicates that these trees were, many of them, pines. But probably not one of them now remains; the rapid growth and early decay of these trees, and their fitness for building purposes, causing them to disappear long since. A solitary pasture oak, left here and there for a landmark or serviceable shade, is about all that remains of those old monarchs of the wood. But, notwithstanding there was formerly so much timber land, we are not to suppose the country was one unbroken forest; on the contrary, it was interspersed with clearings; and the fact that in those first years the town was choice of its timber, and passed stringent laws concerning it, indicates that these clearings were considerable . . . The cleared spaces were occasioned by both natural and artificial causes. The Indians, by setting fires, cleared places for their planting grounds and sunny spots for their homes. The natural openings were the broad, beautiful meadows on the river and brooks.

A remarkable feature of these forests was their freedom from underbrush. The early settlers could traverse large portions of them on horseback and meet with few obstacles, except the streams and swamps. In places the forests were kept clear by means of the annual fires which the Indians set to facilitate transit and the capture of game.

The animal populations inhabiting the streams, the river meadows and the forests were diverse and plentiful. From the settlers' perspective, these creatures were a potential source of food or fur, a threat to their safety, or a pestilence. Early accounts of wildlife stress economics rather than appreciation or understanding. Hudson's summary of the early fauna expresses this viewpoint.

The country afforded fine ranges for wild animals, and was well stocked with game, which made it an attractive hunting ground for the Indians. Deer reeves were annually chosen by the town for years after the settlement, and wolves were considered such a pest that a bounty was set upon them. Prior to 1646, ten shillings were offered apiece for them; and repeatedly laws were enacted for the destruction of these forest marauders. Bears found favorite resort among the highlands of Nobscot and Goodman's Hill . . .

Beaver pelts were an article of merchandise through a large part of the Musketahquid country. Wild fowl were abundant. Turkeys strutted with stately tread in the lowlands by the meadow margins, and large flocks of waterfowl frequented the streams and made their nests on their sedgy borders. Pigeons were plentiful, and grouse enlivened the shrubbery of the numerous swamps. The supply of fish was ample, including salmon, alewives, shad and dace.

Shattuck's account of the natural history of the Concord region includes the following description:

The principal *quadripeds* found here, at the first settlement of the town, were bear, moose, wolf, deer, fox, otter, beaver, muskrat or musquash (*mus zibithicus*), marten, etc., etc. Wolves were many years very troublesome in killing calves and sheep, and rewards were offered for destroying them. The fur-trade here was once very important. As early as 1641, a company was formed in the colony, of which Major Willard of Concord was superintendent, and had the exclusive right to trade with the Indians in furs and other articles . . . The solitary ponds, rivers, and meadows in Concord, were peculiarly the favorite resorts of the beaver and other amphibious animals . . .

The *Birds* have no peculiar locality in this town. The most troublesome to the inhabitants have been the black bird, which frequent the low meadow in great numbers, the crow, and the jay. Rewards were paid for the heads of the two latter kinds.

Concord's early town records document the settlers' attempts to control undesirable species.

1672 - and that incorigment be given for the destroying of blackbirds and jaies

January ye 13th 1706. Then Jme Davis of Concord produced ye head of a grown wolf, so that the s^d wolfe ears was cut out of by Sam^{ll} Chandler one of the constables of s^d Town in the presence of one or more of ye selectmen of this Town according to law, for wch he was pay^d by Sam^{ll} Chandler constable

January 7, 1737/8. Then pay^d by an order to Mr. Joseph Barrett Town Treasurer to Mr. Jonathan Miles for one grown wildcat by him killed in or near the Town of Concord ye sum of twenty shillings in full - 01-00-0

Other records reflect the economic importance of local natural resources.

1715 . . . propounded whether the selectmen of Concord be hereby impowered to petition ye General Court in the name and the behalfe of s^d Town of Concord for the removing the mill dam at Belericah which is Judged to be a very great hendrance to ye fishes coming up Concord River for ye relife of ye Inhabitants of the s^d Town and other Towns above them on ye sam River Voted on the affermative

1727-1728 - voted that John Bateman, Ephraim Brown, John Holdin junr, John Hunt, Jonathan Ball, John Fox and Daniel Holdin, have liberty to set a ware across Concord River (for the catching of fish in the season thereof) for the space of five years next, provided they obtain license from the Court of General Sessions of the peace for the same, and pay into the Town Treasury for the use of the Town the sum of five pounds a year

During the first half-century of colonial settlement, relatively little change took place in the landscape of the Sudbury River Valley. Pioneers were content to pasture their cattle on the river meadows and plant grain in upland fields that had been used for decades by the Pawtuckett. The harvest barely supported the farmer and his family. As Shattuck points out, conditions were difficult:

The uplands which the first planters selected for cultivation, proved to be of a poor quality; and the meadows were unexpectedly much overflowed with water. All the fish and other manure which were applied to enrich the sand hills east of the village were useless. These were causes of great disappointment and suffering.

Original land grants were divided and redivided; additional tracts were petitioned for and received. By the turn of the century, sons were eager to have their own acreage. Natural river meadow openings and Indian agricultural plots were not enough; more land needed to be cleared. With gathering momentum the landscape began to change.

Information compiled by Robert Gross gives us an idea of the quantity and character of land clearing in Concord during the 1700s. Figures for the two decades preceding the Revolutionary War show that improved land increased by 45 percent. This new farmland was not the result of expansion or acquisition; the number and size of farms remained stable during this period. The increase does indicate major changes on existing properties. The agricultural category that increased the most during the prewar years was pasturage (+91 percent). To make space for new pasture, woodlot acreage was reduced. As farmland increased and agricultural methods improved, a surplus resulted. The first crop raised for market was livestock. By 1771, 80 percent of Concord's farmland was in meadow and pasture, but already the land was losing its ability to support the grazing herds. Continuous planting of grain in upland fields had depleted and eroded the mediocre soil. Overgrazing inevitably led to poorer land. Robert Gross has characterized the farming approach of this period as "an intensive agricultural regime, where the farmers saved on labor by exploiting the land."

Leisure time was a rare commodity for the overworked farmer. That there was no systematic accounting of even the common mammal and bird species present during the first two centuries of settlement is not surprising. We are left with those few references to bounties paid, permits granted, and deer reeves assigned, as well as the nineteenth century histories such as Shattuck's and Hudson's. We can surmise that as the settlements gradually spread, large predators such as bears and wolves withdrew, and gamebird populations, including turkey and grouse, declined.

Howard Russell has suggested that during the earliest years of the settlements, predator numbers and flocks of granivorous birds actually may have increased due to a ready supply of domesticated livestock and new grain sources. Certainly by the eve of the revolution original animal populations were much reduced. Trapping, hunting, bounties and especially land clearing had taken their toll. Whatever primeval forest did exist receded westward and northward.

The hopes and challenges of the New World, the roots and rocks in every field, left little time for concerns with land depletion or wildlife inventories. The goal of the pioneers was land they could call their own; their survival depended on subduing the land and making it work for them. Each stone in every stone wall stands as a monument to the settlers' determination to prevail. Beavers and wolves, spring floods and forests, Indians and Kings all had to be overcome. The plow and the musket served the farmer well.

Townsend Scudder, in his chapter, "This Founding Enterprise," characterizes this new holder of real estate. The pioneer was proud and said with passion:

> This is my land . . . free of all rents, all feudal fees and fines. Here I can add further acres; clear more tillage. This earth I can leave to my sons.

Chapter 2

"good for nothing in its natural state . . . "

Elijah Wood, Jr.

The reality was that successive generations could not be supported by the land. Many young men and women were forced to leave family farms. Those that remained and inherited the farms were faced with mediocre land, a lack of basic tools, and an overwhelming diversity of tasks. By the end of the eighteenth century, the depleted land would no longer support grazing herds. New cash crops were needed; the answers were wood, grain and hay. Throughout the first half of the nineteenth century, deforestation gained momentum as woodlot after woodlot was chopped down and taken to mill. The land was cleared and plowed, fields of timothy, clover and oats were planted, and the harvest sold at market. Between 1801 and 1850, more than 2,000 acres of woodland were cut in Concord alone. At the end of this period only 10 percent of the town had forest cover.

To make even more room for meadow, wetlands were drained and reclaimed. The Concord Farmers Club held its first meeting on March 27, 1852. The topic for discussion was "Reclaiming Wet Lands." At the March 26, 1857, meeting of the club, Elijah Wood, Jr., was the featured speaker.

> We have in this country millions of acres of waste land, good for nothing in its natural state, but which by thorough draining, and cultivation, can be made as productive as the best bottom land in the West . . .
>
> Benefactors in agriculture are those that make two spears of grass grow where only one grew before, and this effect is produced more by draining . . .
>
> Improvement now must be the order of the day, or we are bankrupt.

Wood goes on to explain that expenses are high, labor dear, and "constant cropping has worn out the upland . . . " The solution was to reclaim and make profitable the wetlands. Another Concord citizen interested in recovering more land was Henry F. French, father of Daniel Chester French, President of Massachusetts Agricultural College (later the University of Massachusetts), and a self-described "progressive farmer." French published *Farm Drainage* in 1859. This 382-page book describes in detail the history, benefits, methods and materials of land reclamation. Drainage in general is treated as an ideal way to create improved land. Drainage of swamps was seen not only as a boon to the farmer, but also as an improvement sure to enhance the health and well-being of the community.

> Frogs and snakes find in these swamps an agreeable residence, and wild beasts a safe retreat from their common foe. Notoriously, such lands are unhealthful, producing fevers and agues in their neighborhood, often traceable to tracts no larger than a very few acres.

Henry French, like many present-day water wizards, held out great hope for ultimately controlling the vagaries of natural cycles.

> The day will come, when on our Atlantic coast, the ocean waves will be stayed, and all along our great rivers, the Spring floods, and the Summer freshets, will be held within artificial barriers, and the enclosed lands be kept dry by engines propelled by steam, or some more efficient or economical agent.

The publication of French's book was timely. Water control, especially along the Sudbury River, was of immediate concern to the farmers of the Valley. The river meadows were threatened. Original claims on the Concord and Sudbury Rivers were valued according to the acreage of their meadow grass. Early tax assessments were based on river meadow holdings. By the middle of the nineteenth century, however, many of these tracts were flooded permanently and lawsuits were being prepared. Like the salt marsh hay of the coastal zone, the river meadow grasses provided fodder for fattening livestock and draft animals. Howard Russell summed it up this way.

> . . . cattle were essential not for milk (the colonist drank little of it) but for beef; and in any case, far less for beef than for motive power: traction. No truck or tractors then; no big Flanders horses, only small south-England nags that today would be considered large ponies. It was oxen that furnished all the power for clearing and plowing; and oxen have to be fed: grass and hay. So hay marsh was vital.

The problem was the river level. As early as 1636, Concord residents had petitioned the court for help in dealing with the natural spring flooding of the meadows. Although this annual event was an inconvenience, flood waters generally receded within several weeks, and the farmer once again had access to his valuable hay crop. By the end of the eighteenth century, however, changes were taking place that ultimately would alter the ecology of the river valley and destroy the meadows. Colonial mill dams at Billerica were the initial problem. They increased the effects of the natural flooding cycle by retarding normal drainage upstream. In the 1790s, dam heights at Billerica were increased to provide additional water power for the mills, to assure an adequate water supply for the Middlesex Canal, and to make the Concord-Sudbury a navigable waterway. Fifty years later, at the other end of the Valley, holding reservoirs were established to provide a water source for Boston. The system was then in place to control the rate of flow of the Sudbury and the Concord. The mill interests owned and operated the reservoirs at the headwaters of the Sudbury. Laurence Richardson relates what happened next.

> Now they (the mill owners) could store the water when the river was high and let it down during dry spells. And they did, but it kept the meadows from draining off so the farmer could get his hay and cranberries. The farmers complained again to the legislature but got no relief.

The litigation came to a head in 1860. The following testimony was presented by the petitioners.

> Sixty-five years ago the meadows were perfectly accessible to the heaviest teams, up and down the river to its brink, and immense loads for three and four cattle were hauled from them without the slightest difficulty from slumping. Such teams were habitually driven across the

Sudbury River Meadow by Alfred Wayland Cutting (1860-1935).

stream, at certain points, when not loaded, and occasionally when they were. But from about the year 1804, when the canal proprietors had made two additions to the height of their dam, and had opened the canal for travel and transportation, the meadows became so soft as to be impassable for teams, except in times of extreme dryness, and then only for light ones, and in particular parts. Since the last addition to the dam, thirty years ago, these lands have been, with slight exceptions, inaccessbile not only to teams, but to grazing cattle, which used to get plenty of fresh fall feed, - a great resource for the farmers every season, but especially when the pastures and other uplands were parched by drought. The hay crops were abundant and very valuable, for although they could not, in general, be considered equal to the best English hay, yet this forage had properties and peculiarities which caused it to be sought for far and near. There was no farm produce in so great demand . . .

The farmers' loss was economic; meadowland values dropped from $100 to $5 per acre. The ecological changes resulted in river meadow grasses being replaced by more water tolerant species; button-bush, bur-reed and cattail. These changes, in turn, affected animal populations.

The first half of the nineteenth century was also a time of commercial development in the Sudbury River Valley. In 1828, the millpond in the center of Concord was drained, the Milldam Company formed, and business lots offered for sale. In the 60 year period between 1790 and 1850, the total number of commercial buildings in Concord doubled. All along the Assabet River primitive colonial mills were being improved. A textile factory was built in Concord, a powder mill in Acton, and at Assabet Village A. Maynard and W.H. Knight were establishing a business that by the end of the century would become the largest woolens industry in the country. In 1830, 600,000 pounds of bog iron ore was mined from a swamp in Sudbury and rafted down river to the Chelmsford forge. Wayland, originally part of Sudbury, was incorporated in 1835. By mid-century, the combined populations of Concord and Sudbury totaled 3,827.

During this period most Valley farmers were gradually moving away from the ideal of self-sufficiency. The expanding market economy offered a way to get out from under the endless tasks that were the price of independence. The Sudbury River Valley, its farmers, tradesmen and shopkeepers "had entered the world of modern capitalism." Pioneer-settlers, intent on subsistence, were replaced by agrarian reformers intent on higher yields. Fur-traders made way for Milldam entrepreneurs and Anglo-Saxon labor was supplemented by Irish and Italian immigrants. The wilderness was fast disappearing.

Chapter 3

"in wildness is the preservation of the world . . . "

Henry David Thoreau

Henry David Throeau was not optimistic about the "modern" world. In fact, he described the condition of his fellow citizens as desperate. Thoreau agreed with Johnson's earlier characterization; the work of the Valley farmer was Herculean.

> The twelve labors of Hercules were trifling in comparison with those which my neighbors have undertaken . . .

> How many a poor immortal soul have I met well-nigh crushed and smothered under its load, creeping down the road of life, pushing before it a barn seventy-five feet by forty, its Augean stable never cleaned, and one hundred acres of land, tillage, mowing, pasture, and woodlot.

The case for civilization and progress was being made, for better or worse, all about him. Thoreau's response to the natural world would be the antithesis of the Puritan farmers'. Instead of struggling to make improvements on the land, Thoreau would accept it as it was. He summarized this position in an 1850 essay entitled "Walking."

> I wish to speak a word for Nature, for absolute freedom and wildness, as contrasted with a freedom and culture merely civil, - to regard man as an inhabitant, or a part and parcel of Nature, rather than a member of society. I wish to make an extreme statement, if so I may make an emphatic one, for there are enough champions of civilization: the minister and the school committee and every one of you will take care of that.

Thoreau's conception of wilderness was as much the expression of a philosophical requirement as it was a description of an ideal natural world. Wilderness was a source for inspiration and study; it was the medium of both philosophy and natural history.

As a transcendentalist-philosopher, Thoreau saw the natural world as a symbol or metaphor that expressed higher truths. The better we understand nature (wilderness), the greater our chances to experience ultimate truths.

As a naturalist, Thoreau was willing to ask if nature might not be a proper and useful area of study by and for itself.

> Are we to be put off and amused in this life, as it were with a mere allegory? Is not nature, rightly read, that which she is commonly taken to be the symbol merely?

The transcendentalist and the naturalist, the philosopher and the scientist represent different sides of Thoreau that are, at times, reconciled but often in conflict. When the poet prevails, we catch mere glimpses of the flora and fauna; Thoreau is reaching for something, more spiritual -

> March 4, 1840. I learned today that my ornithology had done me no service. The birds I heard, which fortunately did not come within the

scope of my science, sung as freshly as if it had been the first morning of creation, and had for background to their song an untrodden wilderness, stretching through many a Carolina and Mexico of the soul.

When the naturalist speaks, the observations and descriptions seem an end in themselves.

May 12, 1855. Watched a black and white creeper from Bittern Cliff, a very neat and active bird, exploring the limbs on all sides and looking three or four ways almost at once for insects. Now and then it raises its head a *little,* opens its bill, and, without closing it, utters its faint *seeser, seeser, seeser.*

If Thoreau's attitude towards science was at times ambiguous, his preference for fieldwork over laboratory science was clearcut. He chose to learn from personal experience, observation and direct contact with the natural world. His distaste for lifeless specimens and clinical descriptions is a repeated theme.

March 15, 1860. A hen-hawk sails away from the wood southward. I get a fair sight of it sailing overhead. What a perfectly regular and neat outline it presents! an easily recognized figure anywhere. Yet I never see it represented in any books. The exact correspondence of the marks on one side to those on the other, as the black or dark tip of one wing to the other, and the dark line midway the wing. I have no idea that one can get as correct an idea of the form and color of the under sides of a hen-hawk's wings by spreading those of a dead specimen in his study as by looking up at a free and living hawk soaring above him in the fields . . .

Some, seeing and admiring the neat figure of the hawk sailing two or three hundred feet above their heads, wish to get nearer and hold it in their hands, perchance, not realizing that they can see it best at this distance, better now, perhaps, than ever they will again. What is an eagle in captivity, screaming in the courtyard? I am not the wiser respecting eagles for having seen one there. I do not wish to know the length of its entrails.

His inclination was to embrace the living world on its own terms.

Dec. 15, 1856. The hooting of an owl! That is a sound which my red predecessors heard here more than a thousand years ago. It rings far and wide, occupying the spaces rightfully, - grand, primeval, aboriginal sound. There is no whisper in it of the Buckleys, the Flints, the Hosmers who recently squatted here, nor of the first parish, nor of Concord Fight, nor of the last town meeting.

Thoreau was a gifted naturalist with a wide range of interests. Early in his career he collected reptiles, mammals and fish for Louis Agassiz of Harvard. One fish species, the striped bream, was unknown when Thoreau collected it at Walden Pond. The natural history of ponds and the ecology of forest succession were also subjects of his investigations. Botany was of special interest, and Thoreau spent many hours in the field studying both the common and the rare plants of the Concord area. Ray Angelo, in his *Botanical Index to the Journal of Henry David Thoreau,* concludes that while it was not Thoreau's intent to advance systematic botany, "his observations and collections in Concord represent, perhaps, the most complete survey of a New England township's flora up to that time.'' A note from the journal of Ralph Waldo Emerson indicates Thoreau's involvement.

> May 21, 1856. Yesterday to the Sawmill Brook with Henry. He was in search of yellow violet (*pubescens*) and *menyanthes* (Buck-bean) which he waded into the water for; and which he concluded, on examination, had been out for five days. Having found his flower, he drew out of his breast pocket his diary and read the names of all the plants that should bloom this day, May 20; whereof he keeps account as a banker when his notes fall due; *Rubus triflora* (Dwarf raspberry), *Quercus* (Oak), *Vaccinium* (Blueberry), etc. The *Cypripedium* (Lady's slipper) not due till tomorrow. Then we diverged to the brook, where was *Viburnum dentatum,* Arrow-wood.

Richard Eaton, in his *A Flora of Concord,* gives the following evaluation of Thoreau the botanist:

> In retrospect, and to judge only from Journal entries, Thoreau the Naturalist begins to compete with Thoreau the Philosopher in 1852, to the latter's evident distaste. By 1857 botany has achieved intellectual status and is emotionally acceptable. Considering his lack of adequate optical instruments, his lack of professional guidance and professionally annotated herbarium material for purposes of comparison, his taxonomic competence seems to have developed rapidly to a remarkable degree. His capacity for keen observation both in the field and at the desk, and his careful attention to the need for accuracy were contributing factors in achieving the status of a good amateur botanist.

Thoreau's ornithological studies in the Sudbury River Valley began a tradition that has continued for 150 years. Although he was not inclined to organize data in a systematic way, Thoreau did record an accurate picture of much of the birdlife in the Valley. Perhaps of even more significance was his approach to studying the birdlife. In an era when ornithology primarily was concerned with cataloguing and describing, Thoreau's interests foreshadowed future concerns with field identification, behavior and ecological relationships.

Present-day field identification technique has evolved from the work of Ludlow Griscom and Roger Tory Peterson. Griscom made the case that field identification was not only possible but also could be consistently accurate. Furthermore, it offered an alternative to collecting (shooting) each bird to be studied. Peterson developed a system of representing birds, at the species level, by identifiable field characteristics. In her work *Thoreau on Birds,* Helen Cruickshank raises the possibility that Thoreau may have had some indirect influence on the Peterson system. Certainly Thoreau was concerned with similar problems, as the following passage indicates.

> Sept. 18, 1858. I notice that the wing of the peet-weet (Spotted Sandpiper), which is about two inches wide, has a conspicuous and straightedged white bar along its middle on the under side for half its length. It is seven eighths of an inch wide and . . . it produces that singular effect in its flying that I have noticed. This line, by the way, is not men-

tioned by Wilson,* yet it is, perhaps, the most noticeable mark of the bird when flying . . .

May 25, 1853. I quarrel with most botanists' description of different species, say willow. It is a difference without a distinction. No stress is laid upon the peculiarity of the species in question, and it requires a very careful examination and comparison to detect any difference in the description. Having described you one species, he begins again at the beginning when he comes to the next and describes it *absolutely,* wasting time; in fact does not describe the species, but rather the genus or family; as if, in describing the particular race of men, you should say of each in its turn that it is but dust and to dust it shall return. The object should be to describe not those particulars in which a species resembles its genus, for they are many and that would be a negative description but those in which it is peculiar, for they are few and positive.

Thoreau's close attention to bird behavior is another focus of his field studies. Behavior is not only a valuable aid to identification but also a key to the daily and seasonal activities of birds.

March 10, 1852. Heard the phoebe note of the chickadee today for the first time. I had at first heard their *day-day-day* ungratefully, - ah! you but carry my thoughts back to winter, - but anon I found that they too had become spring birds; they had changed their note. Even they feel the influence of spring.

May 4, 1855. Sitting in Abel Brooks's Hollow, see a small hawk go over high in the air, with a long tail . . . It advanced by a sort of limping flight yet rapidly, not circling nor tacking, but flapping briskly at intervals and then gliding straight ahead with rapidity, controlling itself with its tail. It seemed to be going a journey. Was it not the sharp-shinned, or *Falco fuscus*?

Nov. 26, 1859. I see here to-day one brown creeper busily inspecting the pitch pines. It begins at the base, and creeps rapidly upward by starts, adhering close to the bark and shifting a little from side to side often till near the top, then suddenly darts off downward to the base of another tree, where it repeats the same course. This has no black cockade, like the nuthatch.

Dec. 18, 1859. I see three shrikes in different places to-day, - two on the top of apple trees, sitting still in the storm, on the lookout. They fly low to another tree when disturbed, much like a bluebird, and jerk their tails once or twice when they alight.

Contemporary interest in ecological relationships and environmental conditions expresses concerns that are similar to those raised by Thoreau a century and a half ago. He was aware of the importance of understanding the relationships among living things and the consequence of ignoring such relationships.

May 17, 1853. He who cuts down woods beyond a certain limit exterminates birds.

---

*Alexander Wilson, author of *American Ornithology* (1808-1813), one of first comprehensive guides to American birds.

Henry David Thoreau, from a daguerrotype by Benjamin D. Maxham (1856).

Thoreau's belief in the inherent value of the natural world was a minority opinion in the nineteenth century. Thoreau saw himself not above nature, but as a part of the natural world. He was concerned about the prevailing attitude that enshrined man as the exploiter of nature. Thoreau believed that the natural world was threatend by progress and materialism out of control. Thoreau saw a different set of needs for mankind.

> April 15, 1852. How indispensable our one or two flocks of geese in spring and autumn! What would be a spring in which that sound was not heard? Coming to unlock the fetters of northern rivers. Those annual steamers of the air.

Aldo Leopold has expressed this position for the twentieth century.

> Like winds and sunsets, wild things were taken for granted until progress began to do away with them. Now we face the question whether a still higher 'standard of living' is worth its cost in things natural, wild, and free. For us of the minority, the opportunity to see geese is more important than television, and the chance to find a pasqueflower is a right as inalienable as free speech.

At times Thoreau marshalled his insights into ecological dynamics to support his outcries against the abuses of the natural world by his fellow men. At other times, Thoreau was simply interested in understanding the animals' specific relationships, requirements and interactions.

> March 30, 1859. See on Walden two sheldrakes, male and female, as is common. So they have for some time paired. They are a hundred rods off. The male the larger, with his black head and white breast, the female with a red head. With my glass I see the long red bills of both. They swim at first one way near together, then tack and swim the other, looking around incessantly, never quite at their ease, wary and watchful for foes. A man cannot walk down to the shore or stand out on a hill overlooking the pond without disturbing them. They will have an eye upon him. The locomotive-whistle makes every wild duck start that is floating with the limits of the town. I see that these ducks are not here for protection alone, for at last they both dive, and remain beneath about forty pulse-beats, - and again, and again. I think they are looking for fishes. Perhaps, therefore, these divers are more likely to alight in Walden than the black ducks are.

> May 12, 1856. I see, in the road beyond Luther Hosmer's, in different places, two bank swallows which were undoubtedly killed by the four days' northeast rain we have just had.

> April 22, 1859. When setting the pines at Walden the last three days, I was sung to by the field sparrow. For music I heard their jingle from time to time . . . It would seem as if such a field as this - a dry open or half-open pasture in the woods, with small pine trees scattered in it - was well-nigh, if not quite, abandoned to this one alone among the sparrows. The surface of the earth is portioned out among them. By a beautiful law of distribution, one creature does not too much interfere with another. I do not hear the song sparrow here. As the pines gradually increase, and a woodlot is formed, these birds will withdraw to new pastures, and the thrushes, etc., will take their place . . .

In the process of analyzing the works of Thoreau, it is often tempting to look for causes, for this man was an advocate; to look for progressive insights, for this man was a prophet. In the meantime, we may lose sight of the side of Thoreau that was most human, most at home with himself as a fellow being among equals in the natural world. There is a lyrical joy about Henry David Thoreau as he goes forth into a world he loves. His friend and companion Ralph Waldo Emerson has left us this sketch.

> May 21, 1856. There came Henry with music-book under his arm, to press flowers in; with telescope in his pocket, to see the birds, and microscope to count stamens; with a diary, jack-knife, and twine; in stout shoes, and strong grey trousers, ready to brave the shrub-oaks and smilax, and to climb the tree for a hawk's nest. His strong legs, when he wades, were no insignificant part of his armour.

Thoreau's journals give the details.

> March 20, 1855. Trying the other day to imitate the honking of geese, I found myself flapping my sides with my elbows, as with wings, and uttering something like the syllables *mow-ack* with a nasal twang and twist in my head; and I produced their note so perfectly in the opinion of the hearers that I thought I might possibly draw a flock down.

> Jan. 30, 1841. Fair Haven Pond is scored with the trails of foxes, and you may see where they have gambolled and gone through a hundred evolutions, which testify to a singular listlessness and leisure in nature.

> Suddenly, looking down the river, I saw a fox some sixty rods off, making across to the hills on my left. As the snow lay five inches deep, he made but slow progress, but it was no impediment to me. So, yielding to the instinct of the chase, I tossed my head aloft and bounded away, snuffing the air like a fox-hound, and spurning the world and Humane Society at each bound. It seemed the woods rang with the hunter's horn, and Diana and all the satyrs joined in the chase and cheered me on. Olympian and Elean youths were waving palms on the hills. In the meanwhile I gained rapidly on the fox; but he showed a remarkable presence of mind, for, instead of keeping up the face of the hill, which was steep and unwooded in that part, he kept along the slope in the direction of the forest, although he lost ground by it. Notwithstanding his fright, he took no step which was not beautiful. The course on his part was a series of most graceful curves. It was a sort of leopard canter, I should say, as if he were no-wise impeded by the snow, but were husbanding his strength all the while. When he doubled I wheeled and cut him off, bounding with fresh vigor, and Antaeus-like, recovering my strength each time I touched the snow. Having got near enough for a fair view, just as he was slipping into the wood, I gracefully yielded him the palm. He ran as though there were not a bone in his back, occasionally dropping his muzzle to the snow for a rod or two, and then tossing his head aloft when satisfied of his course. When he came to a declivity he put his fore feet together and slid down it like a cat. He trod so softly that you could not have heard it from any nearness, and yet with such expression that it would not have been quite inaudible at any distance. So, hoping this experience would prove a useful lesson to him, I returned to the village by the highway of the river.

Oct. 8, 1852. P.M. - Walden. As I was paddling along the north shore, after having looked in vain over the pond for a loon, suddenly a loon, sailing toward the middle, a few rods in front, set up his wild laugh and betrayed himself. I pursued with a paddle and he dived, but when he came up I was nearer than before. He dived again, but I miscalculated the direction he would take, and we were fifty rods apart when he came up, and again he laughed long and loud. He managed very cunningly, and I could not get within half a dozen rods of him. Sometimes he would come up unexpectedly on the opposite side of me, as if he had passed directly under the boat. So long-winded was he, so unweariable, that he would immediately plunge again, and then no wit could divine where in the deep pond, beneath the smooth surface, he might be speeding his way like a fish, perchance passing under the boat. He had time and ability to visit the bottom of the pond in its deepest part. A newspaper authority says a fisherman - giving his name - has caught loon in Seneca Lake, N.Y., eighty feet beneath the surface, with hooks set for trout. Miss Cooper has said the same. Yet he appeared to know his course as surely under water as on the surface, and swam much faster there than he sailed on the surface. It was surprising how serenely he sailed off with unruffled bosom when he came to the surface. It was as well for me to rest on my oars and await his reappearance as to endeavor to calculate where he would come up. When I was straining my eyes over the surface, I would suddenly be startled by his unearthly laugh behind me. But why, after displaying so much cunning, did he betray himself the moment he came to the surface with that loud laugh? His white breast enough betrayed him. He was indeed a silly loon, I thought. Though he took all this pains to avoid me, he never failed to give notice of his whereabouts the moment he came to the surface. After an hour he seemed as fresh as ever, dived as willingly, and swam yet farther than at first. Once or twice I saw a ripple where he approached the surface, just put his head out to reconnoitre, and instantly dived again. I could commonly hear the plash of the water when he came up, and so also detected him. It was commonly a demoniac laughter, yet somewhat like a water-bird, but occasionally, when he had balked me most successfully and come up a long way off, he uttered a long-drawn unearthly howl, probably more like a wolf than any other bird. This was his looning. As when a beast puts his muzzle to the ground and deliberately howls; perhaps the wildest sound I ever heard, making the woods ring; and I concluded that he laughed in derision of my efforts, confident of his own resources. Though the sky was overcast, the pond was so smooth that I could see where he broke the surface if I did not hear him. His white breast, the stillness of the air, the smoothness of the water, were all against him. At length, having come up fifty rods off, he uttered one of those prolonged unearthly howls, as if calling on the god of loons to aid him, and immediately there came a wind from the east and rippled the surface, and filled the whole air with misty rain. I was impressed as if it were the prayer of the loon and his god was angry with me. How surprised must be the fishes to see this ungainly visitant from another sphere speeding his way amid their schools!

I have never seen more than one at a time in our pond, and I believe that that is always a male.

Chapter 4

What is the railroad to me?

I never go to see

Where it ends.

It fills a few hollows,

And makes banks for swallows,

It sets the sands a-blowing,

And the blackberries a-growing,

but I cross it like a cart-path in the woods

I will not have my eyes put out and my ears spoiled

by its smoke and steam and hissing.

Henry David Thoreau

Like it or not, the new reality of the second half of the nineteenth century was the railroad. The Fitchburg line through Concord was completed in 1844. During the next three decades, rights-of-way were cleared, ties cut, and track laid for additional lines. By 1873 four railroads crisscrossed Concord. The Framingham and Lowell hauled freight and passengers up and down the Sudbury River Valley. Locomotive boilers were wood-fired and year after year, thousands of cords of wood were supplied by Valley forests.

Paradoxically, the railroads were to play a large part in both the destruction of local forests and ultimately in the return of the woodlands. By mid-nineteenth century, the Valley landscape was, like much of New England, open, rolling country; meadow, field and pasture seamed together by stone walls. The occasional woodlots were exceptional timbered islands scattered here and there across the land. Unimproved land - marshes, swamps and bogs - also supported some timber, but even these stands of wood were threatened by the needs of the railroads.

At the same time that these railroads were reducing New England's remaining forests, they were also opening up the way west. In combination with the Erie Canal, the Boston and Albany line was a key link to new acreage in the west, expansive, rich, well-drained land that was ideal for growing grain. A new generation of pioneers began to settle and farm the western frontier. Ultimately, the New England farmer could not compete, at least not in the grain or livestock business. By the 1860s the "period of abandonment" was well under way. Many farmers, particularly those owning poor-soil farms in upland locations, simply latched the door behind them and left. While some families moved west, others migrated to manufacturing centers that were developing around large mill towns. Slowly the woodland acreage in the Valley began to increase.

The deforestation of the landscape in the nineteenth century had not been equaled since the last glacial era. Then the ice sheets had removed all vegetation from the face of the land. Ten thousand years ago as the last glacier retreated, the plants slowly returned. Into an uneven land of drumlin and esker, outwash plain and lake bottom, kettle-hole and terrace crept the

Boston & Maine Steam Engine, Passing Walden Pond.

pioneer plants. Vegetation that had survived in areas south of the glacier's edge gradually spread northward. Eventually, forest types included birch, beech and maple, the core of the northern hardwoods as well as oaks, hickories and chestnuts, the typical sprout hardwoods of central New England. These deciduous trees and conifers including hemlock and pine, forested the lands of the Sudbury River Valley. Throughout the ensuing thousands of years, forests grew, matured, and reached climax stage. Disasters such as fires and hurricanes, insect and bacterial blight, along with natural competitive forces caused continuous change in the forest. Just a century and a half before the first settlers arrived in the Valley, a great storm destroyed large portions of the forest. During the following 150 years the woodlands grew back. It was this growth that dominated the landscape of the seventeenth century.

Attempts to document the exact nature of this precolonial forest have been frustrated by the scarcity of competent firsthand accounts and the subsequent wholesale woodcutting. One reliable observer, Peter Whitney, described the primeval forest in 1793 at Petersham, a town 50 miles west of the Valley.

> On the highlands the growth of wood is oak, more chestnut, and a good deal of walnut* of later years. In the swamps and lowlands, there is birch, beech, maple, ash, elm, and hemlock.

Recent research on the composition of the Concord forests indicates that oaks (*Quercus* sp.) were the predominant hardwood, while pitch pine was the characteristic conifer. Local soil conditions, as well as the Indian practice of burning-over areas for agricultural purposes, favored these fire resistant species.

Whatever the exact proportions, the colonists had little use for the forest — at least while it remained standing. Some wooded areas provided marginal foraging for livestock, but the farmers' first needs were for acreage in tillage and pasture; this meant less forest. Once the trees were felled, they were put to various uses. Larger trees became saw logs that furnished lumber for house, shed and barn. Smaller stock and slash was used for cordwood. Before outside markets became accessible, the farmer piled and burned excess wood. The ashes were gathered and processed into potash, a ready source of fertilizer. When sawmills opened up markets for timber, the woodlots provided the farmer with a welcome source of capital. Cordwood was sold for fuel, and the choice oak and pine was marketed to shipbuilders. Local timber supplied stock for everything from barrels and boxes to pencils and matchsticks. America was, as Donald Worster has said, living "in an age of wood." The forests were an expendable resource, used with little thought for the future. In 1841 a state agricultural report contained the following statements: "Very little if any wood is standing, which is not comparatively recent. The original forests have long since disappeared." George Emerson's *Report on the Trees and Shrubs Growing Naturally in the Forests of Massachusetts* (1846) paints a bleak picture of this woodland economy.

---

*"Walnut" was used to refer to both walnut and hickory.

Barrett's Mill, Concord.

The effects of the wasteful destruction of forest-trees are already visible. A very large portion of the materials for ship-building, house-building, and manufactures, in the towns along the coast, are now brought from other States . . . The same thing is taking place, almost imperceptibly, in all parts of the State. Every mechanic who works in wood looks every year more and more out of the State for his materials. . . .

By mid-century Thoreau saw that exploitive practices threatened the soil as well as the forests.

Walking afterward on the hill behind Abel Hosmer's overlooking the russet interval, the ground being bare where the corn was cultivated last year, I see that the sandy soil has been washed far down the hill for its whole length by the recent rains combined with the melting snow, and it forms on the nearly level ground at the base very distinct flat yellow sands with a convex edge contrasting with the darker soil there. Such slopes must lose a great deal of soil in a single spring, and I should think that there was a sound reason in many cases for leaving them woodland and never exposing and breaking the surface.

Hudson's *History of Sudbury* (1889) provides details of the forest history in his town.

The soil of Sudbury has, from its settlement, been abundantly productive in its timber lands, of which it has always possessed many acres. The principal trees are the oak, pine, chestnut, walnut, maple, white birch and spruce with here and there a popular, elm and hemlock. The first three are the most abundant, and, until recently, many acres were covered with them . . . Large quantities of cordwood, mostly pine, were, about forty years ago, carried by ox-team to the railroad and factories at Saxonville, and the lanes and yards of the Sudbury saw-mills were piled with hundreds of large logs to be sawn into boards.

Massachusetts Census figures for yearly cordwood production in four Valley towns indicate how this resource was exploited.

CORDWOOD PRODUCTION

YEAR	CARLISLE	CONCORD	SUDBURY	WAYLAND	TOTAL
1845	2,126	3,862	4,128	2,746	12,862
1855	1,500	3,000	1,377	534	6,411
1865	770	1,217	—	686	2,673
1875	2,522	3,474	2,727	1,556	10,279
1885	1,068	1,803	2,327	944	6,142

During this period, the average production for these four towns was 7,673 cords per year. This represents 3,836,500* board feet of lumber or enough annually to build a six-foot high wooden wall across the state of Massachusetts from Boston to Pittsfield. In addition to the cordwood, the mills in these four towns produced, on the average, 721,000 board feet of construction-grade lumber each year. This frenzied harvest continued for half a century.

*The usual conversion formula is 2 cords per 1000 board feet.

Another index of land use is the proportion of woodland relative to total town acreage. Early valuation and tax records as well as nineteenth century census data provide the figures for the Town of Concord.

CONCORD WOODLANDS*

YEAR	ACREAGE	% OF TOWN
1786	3,401	28
1801	3,641	27
1821	3,264	23
1840	1,944	13
1850	1,487	10
1865	3,859	25
1875	3,460	30
1885	4,920	34
1895	3,079	28
1905	7,065	46

By the 1850s the deforestation was virtually complete. Up and down the Valley, from Westborough to Lowell, the primeval forest had been eliminated. Most woodlots had been cut and recut every twenty to thirty years. Surprisingly the forest had one more cash crop to offer. As the upland meadows and pastures gradually were let go, many old fields grew back in forests of white pine, which often included pure stands of valuable, clear timber. Predictably, and systematically, beginning in about 1880, these woodlands were clear-cut. These were the "great woods" of the turn of the century, not primeval, but second-growth forest made possible by the farmers' judicious clearing.

In 1890 one more wooded hillside was going on the block. Davis' Hill rises from the west bank of the Concord River opposite the present site of the Great Meadows empoundments. William Brewster, then a resident of Cambridge, had decided to purchase Davis' Hill in order to save the "large and venerable" trees from the woodcutter's axe. Brewster was well acquainted with the Sudbury River Valley. For more than two decades he had hunted, canoed and studied the natural history of this area. In the summer of 1886 he stopped at Sudbury to enjoy one of the few remaining stands of "virgin" forest. Brewster's journal account recalls a scene that was rare even in his day.

> 1886
>
> July 19
>
> This is the first time that I have done more than drive through these remarkable woods and they are well worth a brief description. The wood road passes between two clusters of the largest trees. That on the right or western side comprises some fifty white pines, oaks (*Q. alba*) and maples (*A. ruber*) all of unusually large size with trunks rising almost without a lateral branch from 20 to 50 ft. The ground beneath is perfectly free from undergrowth and being rich and damp supports a luxurious growth of *Impatiens fulva* Spotted Touch-me-not and ferns

---

*Changes in Concord's aggregate acreage account for the inconsistent relationship between percentages and acres as expressed in the chart. Acreage increased from 12,235 in 1786 to 15,433 in 1905.

(chiefly the cinnamon fern). The wide spaces between the ground and the canopy of foliage high above was filled with a subdued light, almost as dim and restful to the eye as twilight.

The other grove on the opposite (eastern) side of the road is composed almost exclusively of white pines, some fifty in all, the largest and finest that I have ever seen. They stand rather close together in places, in others scattered about the slope of the land rising from the swamp below and the sandy level above. Many of them are fully 3 ft. in diameter, one or two perhaps nearly 4 ft. Their trunks taper but slightly for the first 50 ft. and the lowest living branches are usually at from 30 to 45 ft. above the ground. Several trees must reach a total height of fully 100 feet. The ground beneath is dry and more or less covered with huckleberry and other undergrowth. The open spaces are densely carpeted with *Mitchella* Partridgeberry, *Pyrrhula* Shinleaf? etc.

The history of the forest in the Sudbury River Valley, since its formation in the postglacial era, has been one of change. During the relatively brief period between the 1630s and 1900, however, that change was traumatic. The woodlands literally were cleared off the land. As they grew back, they were cut and recut. These pressures on the forests were not relieved until the railroads opened the lands farther west. But by then it was too late, at least for the primeval woodlands.

Fourteen special trees grow in a corner of the Carlisle State Forest. They form a scattered grove of white pine and hemlock that are remnants of the primeval forest in the Sudbury River Valley. The largest pine is over 130 feet tall; its trunk diameter is almost 3 feet. These giants seem strangely out of place in a Valley forest. But there they stand, living evidence, not so much of what might have been but rather of what remains.

The same railroads that opened a western frontier provided better access to local markets. The Valley farmers that remained, survived and even prospered because they were willing to change their agricultural emphasis. Dairy herds increased and by the mid-1880s Concord alone shipped 2,500 gallons of milk daily. Fruits, including apples, cherries, pears and plums, were cash crops shipped by rail to big-city customers. Potatoes, asparagus and cucumbers also were grown for export. In 1875, 100,000 bunches of Valley asparagus were sold at market. Trains took produce out and brought back the latest farm equipment. In the early years of the twentieth century, a farmer with a gas tractor could plow in one hour the same field that would have taken his eighteenth century ancestor four days of labor. Greenhouse farming was another innovation, one which lengthened the season and provided choice vegetables.

Railroads also supported the growth of industry and factories. On the Assabet River, Damon Mill processed cotton and produced textiles; a bucket factory used native wood for staves; and the Waring Hat Factory shipped finished products to Boston shops. In the Cochituate section of Wayland, a locally important shoe manufacturing industry developed during the period from the 1850s through the 1880s. The Bent Company was the largest of several firms and by 1880 had a work-force in excess of 300 laborers. Many of the shoes and boots produced in Wayland ended up in Boston stores.

Farm produce and factory products were not the only things that the big cities wanted from the Sudbury River Valley. In 1872 Boston obtained permission from the state to divert water from the Sudbury River to augment the city's water supply. At times during the ensuing two decades the rate of flow of the Sudbury was reduced to almost nothing. A malaria scare in 1894 caused the state board of health to investigate the conditions of the rivers and wetlands in the Valley. Laurence Richardson, in *Concord River*, reports its findings.

> It was found that the City of Boston was taking all the Sudbury River water above Framingham, most of the year, except the 1,500,000 gallons per day they were obliged to release and that this would continue until another source for Boston was available, and into this comparatively small amount of water released, there was discharged at Saxonville "a considerable quantity of water polluted in the process of scouring wool and washing cloth . . . rendering it foul for a long distance below the village. In the drier portions of the year, this pollution is noticeable to the eye . . . six miles down the river."

The pollution of the Assabet River was even worse. One hundred ten thousand gallons of sewage was being discharged daily from the Concord Reformatory. Farther upstream, factories dumped wool-scouring waste, process soap, and more sewage.

Several of Thoreau's worst fears were becoming realities. The rivers were polluted and diverted; the forests were cut and recut. Nobody seemed willing to ask or answer the questions Thoreau had posed decades before.

> What are the natural features which make a township handsome — and worth going far to dwell in? A river with its water-falls — meadows, lakes — hills, cliffs or individual rocks, a forest and single ancient trees — such things are beautiful. They have a high use which dollars and cents never represent. If the inhabitants of a town were wise they would seek to preserve these though at a considerable expense.

Chapter 5

Changing economic realities during the latter half of the nineteenth century led to several positive changes in the landscape. The westward expansion made possible by the railroads relieved much of the pressure on lands in the East that had been exploited for more than two centuries. By the 1880s coal and anthracite were replacing wood as energy sources for railroads and residences. This in turn initiated the regrowth of some woodland acreage. The richer soil of the river valleys was preferred for vegetable farming, and many of the upland fields were "let go" and began the natural process of field-to-forest succession. The cultivation of fruit trees began to cover denuded pastures and hillsides.

These old-field and orchard habitats provided ideal territory for a variety of wildlife species. William Brewster was among those who understood and appreciated the benefits of such areas.

> May 12
> 1886
>
> The apple trees were snowy domes of blossoms which scented the air with their delicate fragrance and among which countless bees droned and hummed. The orchard was framed on every side by a setting of the tenderest green with every now and then a touch of salmon red, marking the position of a solitary maple with its clusters of winged seeds. Three Brown Thrashers were singing at once in different directions, their varied notes drowning the weaker voices of the Warblers and Sparrows. Every now and then however, the song of a Chestnut-sided Warbler or a Black & White creeper would rise above the din; and in the distance I occasionally caught the *zee dee dee* of a Golden Winged Warbler, or the ringing notes of a Field Sparrow. A Grouse was drumming in some Oak woods across the turnpike and a pair of Downy Woodpeckers sounding their call taps in the tops of some tall Chestnuts. Then there were Towhees, Song Sparrows, Robins and Flickers joining their voices to the chorus . . .

The birds that caught Brewster's attention were also of interest to other citizens of the Valley. During the seventeenth and eighteenth centuries large mammal predators and smaller fur-bearing species were reduced greatly by extensive hunting and trapping. By the nineteenth century the bird populations had become the target of these activities. Threats to the bird life ran the gamut from child's play to big business. Edward Jarvis described a Valley tradition of the 1800s.

> . . . election day was held in high prominence by the boys . . . They looked forward to it, with fondness and yet with anxiety, lest the weather should be unfavorable to out of door sports. A large part expected to go hunting birds in the woods and fields or fishing in the ponds and rivers.
>
> The bird hunting was the most attractive and exciting. Most of the boys 14 and over, owned or borrowed guns and powder horns and flasks and shot and pouches. These were prepared for a day or days before, and early, on the election day, they went forth on their cruel and wanton amusement. My brother Francis owned a gun, Charles and I borrowed.

Our father furnished us with money to purchase ammunition, apparently cheerfully. . . .

With some rude discrimination, the birds were divided and classed according to their supposed value, each having its assigned rank. The crow was considered the highest, afterward the hawk and down to the smallest, and eggs which were counted lowest. Each hunter was to go to his work, in his own way and place and kill as many as he could and also rob all the nests of their eggs. In the afternoon all were to assemble with their ill-gotten trophies at some appointed place. The only one I ever attended was on the 9 acre corner road. . . .

There the birds of each side were laid in separate heaps and sorted out, and their individual and collective value determined. . . . That (side) which had the most was considered the winner. . . . Fortunately for the morals and sensibilities of boys and youth, election day, with its corrupting and demoralizing influences occurred but once a year, and in 1821 ceased entirely.

It is interesting to note that Jarvis was concerned only with the corrupting and demoralizing influence this tradition might have on the hunters; he expressed no regrets for the hunted. His recollection that such activities ended in 1821 is incorrect. Thoreau mentions seeing a Scarlet Tanager on an election day string of birds as late as 1854. This "holiday" was celebrated on the last Wednesday in May, the height of the nesting season for many species.

Hunting for sport was not just child's play. Before 1817 hunting was permitted in any season and no bag limits were set. The Valley had its share of hunters who concentrated on grouse, snipe and woodcock. E. H. Forbush, the first Massachusetts State Ornithologist, recounted the exploits of one such hunter.

There is a story current among old gunners in Concord, Mass., that years ago one man won a wager that he could kill fifty Wilson's Snipe in an hour or two with a limited number of shots.

Such unrestricted hunting eliminated several bird species that had been common in the Sudbury River Valley. Brewster, writing in his *Birds of the Cambridge Region*, recounts the final chapter of the Wild Turkey in the Valley.

At Concord, less than ten miles further inland, the species had not become wholly extinct at the beginning of the past (19th) century. The late Steadman Buttrick of that town, a keen lover of field sports and a man of undoubted veracity, who died in 1874, used to delight in narrating how, when a boy, he had made repeated but invariably fruitless expeditions in pursuit of the last Wild Turkey that is known to have lingered in the region about his home. He often saw the bird, a fine old gobbler, but it was so very wary that neither he nor any of the other Concord gunners of that day ever succeeded in getting a fair shot at it. It was in the habit of roosting in some tall pines on Ball's Hill whence, when disturbed, it usually flew for refuge into an extensive wooded swamp on the opposite (Bedford) side of Concord River.

Market gunning was big business in the latter half of the nineteenth century. Although a majority of this slaughter in Massachusetts took place on the coast, commercial netting did occur in the Valley. Forbush, writing in 1905, described the plunder of the market hunters.

> Within thirty years, tons of Passenger Pigeons have stood in barrels in the Boston market, and men now living can remember when the eastern markets were glutted with Quail and Prairie Chickens.

Although such quantities seem unimaginable, Thoreau was witness to the sizable Passenger Pigeon business in Concord.

> On a white oak beyond Everett's orchard by the road, I see quite a flock of pigeons; their blue-black droppings and their feathers spot the road. The bare limbs of the oak apparently attracted them, though its acorns are thick on the ground. These are found whole in their crops . . . I hear that Wetherbee caught ninety-two dozen last week.

Brewster noted one of the last big fall flights of these birds through the Valley. The year was 1871.

> I was in the Maine woods at the time, but on my return was assured by game dealers in the Boston markets and by reliable sportsmen of my acquaintance that the birds had been very numerous everywhere and that "thousands" had been killed. At Concord and Reading old pigeon trappers had even used their long neglected nets with some success.

High fashion and interior decoration also took their toll on wildlife during the nineteenth century. Thrushes, tanagers and orioles were as common on ladies' hats as they were in woodlands and orchards. Not content to leave nature outside, many homeowners were bent on establishing their very own museums. Ludlow Griscom, writing in *The Birds of Concord,* described this costly fad.

> Every town supported a taxidermist, and every village four corners had a sporting goods store, which displayed stuffed birds in its window cases. These people paid money to boys and men who brought birds in, the cash value varying from five cents to one dollar, depending on size and rarity. It was part of the taste of the Victorian Era to have stuffed birds as mantlepiece decorations. Everybody had stuffed ducks, hawks, owls, and a group of brightly colored little birds on some kind of paper rock or tree, covered with a bell-jar. There were beautiful little creations, like a fire screen on which was fastened a snowy owl with wings fully extended. Chipmunks, squirrels, foxes, and woodchucks grinned at you from the dining-room walls. When your pet canary or poll parrot died you had it stuffed; some people preserved their dogs and cats. There was a good living in taxidermy, but it was hard on the wildlife.

By the final decades of the century there was growing concern for the remaining wildlife. Excessive hunting, thoughtless profiteering, and continued destruction of habitat had to be controlled. A small group of naturalists and conservationists were beginning to raise their voices. In the forefront of this movement was William Brewster.

Chapter 6

William Brewster was born in Wakefield, Massachusetts, on July 5, 1851. He grew up in Cambridge in a house on Brattle Street. Cambridge in the middle of the nineteenth century still had a rural flavor and was bordered by farms, fields, marshes and ponds. The Brewster property had its own barn with an assortment of animals. The barnyard, fields and marshes were the playgrounds for young Will, Frenchy (Daniel Chester French) and Dick (Richard Dana). The boys and Jack (Brewster's "full-blooded cur") spent many long days wandering and exploring in their own little wilderness. Years later Brewster recalled a familiar scene of his youth—Fresh Pond.

> I remember many of the experiences of those years as vividly as if they had happened only yesterday. It was necessary to be early on the ground,—or rather water,—and, as we lived nearly a mile from the pond, we were accustomed to start an hour or more before daybreak and to make our way, as best we could in the darkness, to the place where our boats were kept. Sometimes we followed Vassall Lane, stumbling over its deep ruts and other inequalities of surface, but when there was a moon we often struck directly across the open fields, skirting the marshy spots and passing the dimly outlined forms of recumbent cows sleeping under the wild apple trees. There were few sounds save the drowsy creaking of crickets in the dew-laden grass, the faint lisping notes of migrating Warblers or Sparrows coming from the starry heavens above us, or the distant barking of alert watch dogs . . .
>
> For a time the pond remained shrouded in a gloom so deep that one could scarce trace the circles left by the rising fish or the silvery furrows that the muskrats were forever ploughing from point to point across the shallow coves. Every now and then the wailing of a Screech Owl came from some grove or orchard in our rear, or the hoarse *quawk* of a Night Heron out of the darkness directly overhead. Invisible and for the most part nameless creatures, moving among the half-submerged reeds close by the boat, or in the grass or leaves on shore, were making all manner of mysterious and often uncanny rustling, whispering, murmuring, grating, gurgling and plashing sounds. With the first unmistakable signs of daybreak the crowing of cocks might be heard in every direction in the distance. Shortly afterwards Song and Swamp Sparrows began stirring and chirping, or even singing a little, in their grassy or leafy covers near the water's edge; Rails called among the reeds; Wilson's Snipe darted past, uttering their rasping *scaipes*; while the harsh rattle of Kingfishers and the musical *peet-weet-weet* of Spotted Sandpipers came at frequent intervals from various places along the shore. All the while the warm flush in the east had been deepening and spreading until, in this direction, the entire heavens, from the horizon to the zenith, were aglow with rose and crimson, and the calm surface of the pond shining with reflected light. Everywhere the sky had as yet changed but little, and the water, as well as land, remained shrouded in gloom nearly or quite impenetrable to human eyes.

When he was ten years old, Brewster learned to use a shotgun. On many of his trips afield, he hunted wildfowl and upland game. Young Brewster also had a passion for collecting birds, nests and eggs. Early it became apparent

William Brewster

that he and a few of his companions were serious about their bird studies. French's father had a copy of "Nuttall"* and Brewster's dad gave William a copy of "Audubon's Ornithology."** The boys learned taxidermy and "studied (Nuttall and Audubon) with a thoroughness which would have put us at the head of our classes if applied to our school books."

Brewster had prepared for Harvard but impaired eyesight prevented him from continuing his formal education. He found reading and close-up study impossible at times when he was a young man. Fortunately his distance vision was acute and his close-range vision improved with age. Perhaps it was as compensation for this handicap that Brewster developed an impressive memory and keen hearing. Henry Henshaw in his memorial to Brewster gives the following account:

> His hearing was extraordinarily acute, and his ability to recognize the notes of birds at a distance and amid other and confusing sounds was little less than marvelous, and far exceeded that of anyone I ever knew. Along with this phenomenal hearing went a good memory for bird notes and songs, the study and analysis of which always greatly interested him.

With the college option gone, Brewster agreed to a trial period at his father's bank. Both Brewsters soon realized tht this was not to be Will's niche. He was now free to devote all his energies to natural history. It turned out to be a good choice. Thirty years after Brewster's death, Ludlow Griscom offered the following appraisal.

> Having spent some thirteen years in studying Brewster's field work and records, it is my humble opinion that he was one of the greatest and most naturally gifted field ornithologists that America has ever produced.

Brewster's initial trips to the Valley took place in the late 1860s. Both hunting trips and expeditions for the purpose of adding to his growing bird collection brought Brewster to this area. He often visited the French family at their farm on the Sudbury River. In 1886 Brewster and his wife took rooms at the Manse in Concord. Their stay lasted from April through October. Brewster's journal records his first look around.

> 1886
> April 27
> We moved to Concord this morning having taken the Old Manse for the summer . . .

> During the short time I was able to spend along the river bank and in the orchard this morning, I saw several *Dendroica coronata* (Yellow-rumped Warblers) and a little company of Goldfinches. In the old Elms near the bridge a Nuthatch (*Sitta carolinensis*) was cork-screwing about and *hanking* loudly. A pair of Downy Woodpeckers were also hammering on the dead limbs. In the boathouse a pair of Pewees (Phoebes) had a finished but empty nest, a Muskrat was swimming from place to place

*Thomas Nuttall was professor of natural history at Harvard and author of *Manual of Ornithology of the United States and Canada* (1832-1834).

**John James Audubon was author of *Ornithological Biographies* (1827-1839): a series of life histories of the bird species illustrated in his major work, *Birds of America*.

uttering his peculiar whining cry. Red-wings were singing over the green meadows and Bluebirds warbling.

This extended visit to Concord was the beginning of a permanent relationship between Brewster and the Sudbury River Valley. The Brewsters also spent the following summer at the Manse. Within three years they would purchase their own place just north of the Concord village on Monument Street. Like Thoreau before him, Brewster was inclined to travel much in Concord. Henshaw recalled that:

> With all the world open to him he liked best to follow well beaten paths and to revisit year after year the scenes and localities already endeared to him by familiarity and association. This explains in part why he spent so much time in Concord . . .

These travels kept Brewster in the field almost continuously. In the evening he would sit down and patiently write up field lists and journal accounts. Brewster's journals contain literally hundreds of pages of careful observations and detailed descriptions.

1886
June 11

A gray dawn, the sky clearing and the sun shining out at about 5:30 A.M. Remainder of day clear and hot.

Arose at day-break and was off in my boat at exactly 4:30. Spent about two hours along the banks of Great Meadow and then paddled on without stopping, past Ball's Hill, and nearly to Billerica Bridge. I had intended to go below the bridge, but hearing the song of a *Parula* in the woods on the West side of the river, I landed, crossed the meadow and found myself in an extensive tract of fine old timber, mixed hardwoods and pine, with at least one black spruce.

Birds proved to be more numerous here than I have found them elsewhere this season. On every side the woods rang with their songs. Naturally I was in no rush to leave and I spent three or four hours there.

Besides the *Parula* catalogued above I heard another ♂ and saw its mate tugging at the scattered tufts of Usnea, evidently collecting material for its nest, although I failed to follow it. The *Blackburnian* was in full song and doubtless breeding. The Solitary Vireos must have had a nest for the ♀ was about today. It seemed quite like the Maine woods to hear these three birds singing in the same neighborhood.

I found an *Ovenbird's* nest with 4 eggs far advanced and a *Hummingbird's* with two in a similar condition. As usually, the ♀ betrayed her treasures by over-anxiety attracting my attention by her humble-bee like buzzing overhead. The nest was on the dead branch of a small black oak . . .

Brewster found writing to be arduous and painstaking. He confided to Daniel French that many a sentence was the result of "constant erasure and revision." It is ironic that Brewster, a man with a vision handicap, should exhibit such a genius for detailed observation and that his natural, graceful prose should result from such a torturous process.

In all, Brewster filled over 40 journal volumes, as well as his field lists, annual diaries, and catalogues of collected specimens. Charles Batchelder's bibliography of Brewster's published papers contains some 360 separate entries. A review of these publications shows Brewster's preference for fieldwork over laboratory ornithology. His works, as Frank Chapman recalled, "relate to living rather than to dead birds, to faunal and biographic, rather than to systematic ornithology." Brewster's contributions were both literary and scientific. When *Concord River* (1937) was published after Brewster's death, it was reviewed in the *New York Times*. The following is an excerpt from that review:

> Lucky Concord to have been so lovingly chronicled. To the local writing of Emerson, Thoreau, Alcott, Sanborn, Channing and Hawthorne, the bird journals of William Brewster must now be gratefully added . . . Concord has been gloriously appreciated.

After purchasing the Davis' Hill property in 1890, Brewster acquired the Ball's Hill land, the John Barrett farm and the Ritchie Place—in all, 300 acres that he called October Farm. From the mid-1890s until his death in 1919, Brewster spent increasing amounts of time in Concord.

Below Ball's Hill on the bank of the Concord River he built a cabin, boathouse and landing. He often spent the night there, rising early to begin his field trips by canoe up and down the river from Carlisle to Sudbury. Included among his companions were the noted ornithologists Frank Chapman and Edward Howe Forbush.

> 1892
> October 6
>
> To Fairhaven by boat with C(hapman), starting at 10 A.M. and getting home about dark. I had a very hard row as far as Clamshell Hill, beyond which we sailed, using an umbrella for this purpose. We landed at Conantum and lunched at the foot of Lee's Cliff under a pine where the sun lay warm on the carpet of freshly fallen needles (the white pines have nearly finished shedding) and scarce a breath of the chill wind reached us. A few crickets were chirping feebly and a small yellow butterfly was driven by the wind across the Bay . . .
>
> This was a Hawk day. I saw seven Sharp-shins, two Cooper's, three Marsh Hawks, one Pigeon Hawk, two Red-shouldered and one Red-tailed Hawk. With the exception of one of the Red-shoulders, which was perched on a tree, all these birds were flying, not in any one direction but scaling, soaring in circles, or beating up against the strong wind, by short vertical tacks, now rising to meet the blasts or to gain sufficient elevation to skim off for a half mile or more on a gentle incline towards earth. Of course it was a migratory flight—a Hawk wave which had rolled down to us from the north but, as already stated, the birds were not apparently prosecuting their southward journey when seen by me. Nor was there any indication that they were looking for food. They seemed rather to be roaming aimlessly over the country and sporting with the high winds . . .

Henry Thoreau also had watched and described the hawks over Fairhaven Bay. For Thoreau a flight of hawks presented an opportunity to draw an analogy. The "unfettered freedom" of a hawk might be more important to Thoreau as a symbol than as a point of natural history. Thoreau is often concerned with the meaning behind the event. Although Brewster read and admired his predecessor's writing, for the most part, his style was to avoid the interjection of human values. Brewster focuses on the event itself.

One of the great joys in William Brewster's life was the October Farm. He and his crew spent countless hours planting, trimming, landscaping and trail cutting. Vistas were planned expressly to show off old and noble trees. Although part of the land was farmed by a tenant, the crops were intended for wildlife as much as for market. As could be expected, Brewster kept careful track of the animal residents. It bemused him that, over the years, all his improvements on the land did not result in an increase in the number of bird pairs that nested on his property. Each year the familiar species would take up residence on the same territories. As he grew older, Brewster spent less time wandering the Valley and more time on his October Farm. His appreciation for this place never lessened.

Brewster often traveled beyond Concord. Besides annual visits to the Lake Umbagog region of Maine, where he had his own camp, Brewster journeyed to the southern and midwestern states on several occasions. He did fieldwork on the Gulf of St. Lawrence, the Bay of Fundy and in Trinidad. Brewster also made three trips to England and it was on one of these that he made the acquaintance of Rudyard Kipling.

Added to all these travels was Brewster's prodigious amount of organizational work. He was founder of the Nuttall Ornithological Club, first president of the Massachusetts Audubon Society, president of the Massachusetts Fish and Game Commission, and a founder of the American Ornithologists' Union. These organizations were models for ornithological pursuits, including research, scholarship and protective legislation. As a member of the Committee on Bird Protection of the AOU, Brewster was a pioneer in wildlife conservation. The efforts of this and other groups resulted in state and federal legislation that defined hunting seasons, set bag limits and protected outright many species of birds.

Sadly, many of the areas Brewster loved were destroyed during his lifetime. The wilderness of the Umbagog was slowly overrun, the Fresh Pond marshes of Cambridge were partly filled, and even in Concord the last of the "great woods" were decimated by gypsy moths and brown tails. Still Brewster returned to Concord. He came back to look, to listen and to write. In the end it was still the familiar, commonplace scenes of the Valley that he most enjoyed. There was nothing extraordinary about William Brewster's last day in Concord; yet for him it was perfection.

1919
May 14

Cloudless, windless and of summerlike warmth, the day was simply perfect as befitted one which brought the very highest perfection of blossoming apple orchards and fields carpeted with golden dandelions. When I awoke at daybreak a Great Crested Flycatcher was calling in the orchard. At breakfast time and later a rare-voiced Wood Thrush was singing in the run. Besides these there were our usual Oriole, Phoebe, Bobolink, Purple Finch, etc.—altogether a glad choir of delightful bird music. I spent most of the afternoon in an armchair supervising work on the flower beds. Left the farm in a Ford car at 11.10.

Brewster died in Cambridge on July 11, 1919.

In his lifetime Brewster was not just a respected ornithologist. To many of his contemporaries, he was also a model human being. Soon after his death the eulogies began to flow. Characterizations such as "generous", "kindly", "gentlemanly", and even "perfect" were not uncommon in these accounts. It can be said without exaggeration that William Brewster was not only highly respected by those who knew him, but also well loved.

Chapter 7

The landscape of the Sudbury River Valley continued to change in the first half of the twentieth century. Of the changes that took place in the forest habitats, some were positive. After the harvest of the old field pine, and with the exception of the occasional firewood cutting, many woodlands were allowed to grow back. The extent of this regeneration is evident in figures for the towns of Concord, Sudbury and Wayland: woodland in these areas increased from 41 percent of the total acreage in 1905 to 50 percent in 1951. Other changes, however, in the form of two natural disasters, adversely affected the forests during this period. In the first decades of the century, a fungus blight spread throughout New England and destroyed virtually all of the American chestnut trees. These valuable trees were common in the Valley before the blight but exist now only as short-lived, debilitated root-sprouts. In September 1938 a hurricane tore through the Valley, devastating a majority of the mature white pines as well as many deciduous trees. A few of these wrecked woodlands are still in evidence.

Farmlands declined only slightly during the first half of the century. By 1951, agricultural areas in the three towns accounted for approximately one-third of the total acreage. Two world wars had created large markets for agricultural produce, and Valley farmers enjoyed the profits from their increasingly mechanized dairy and vegetable businesses.

Half-way through the twentieth century, Ludlow Griscom, writing in *The Birds of Concord* (1949), described the Sudbury River Valley as "definitely a rural area (where), barring the town and village centers and their immediate vicinity, no substantial increase in population has taken place in a century." Actually the population of the area was slowly increasing. The combined populations of the towns of Concord, Sudbury and Wayland had increased 72 percent from 9,105 in 1900 to 15,626 in 1950. But Griscom's basic impressions were correct; this was still a rural area. At midcentury Sudbury was a country town with a population of fewer than 2,600 people; diagonal parking still occurred in the Concord village; and Wayland supported.large dairy herds. It was this rural scene that would provide the setting for the next chapter in the ornithological history of the Valley.

Ludlow Griscom was the premier field ornithologist of the first half of the twentieth century. Born in New York City in 1890, his family was wealthy, educated and well traveled. By the time Griscom was old enough to decide on a career, he could include among his choices the foreign service (he was fluent in five languages and could read ten others), concert piano and ornithology. Griscom's choice was ornithology.

As a young boy in Central Park, Griscom had developed a system of identifying birds in the field by recognizable characteristics. His method was reliable and consistent; his skill was exceptional. The traditional field ornithologists of the time, accustomed as they were to observing birds either across a gun-sight or as specimens in the hand, were more than impressed by young Griscom's abilities. Throughout his lifetime Ludlow Griscom would continue to impress.

Ludlow Griscom

After receiving a prelaw degree from Columbia University in 1912, Griscom redirected his education towards ornithological pursuits. By 1915 he was awarded an M.S. from Cornell University, where he had studied with Arthur A. Allen, America's first professor of ornithology.

Griscom's professional career was divided between New York and Boston. Between 1917 and 1927 he worked at the American Musuem of Natural History under Frank M. Chapman, Curator of Birds. Chapman, one of the most influential ornithologists of his time, was author of *Handbook of Birds of Eastern North America* (1895). As a member of the Linnaean Society, Griscom met and rubbed elbows with many of the best naturalists in the New York City area. It wasn't long before he was holding court in this influential forum. Griscom's genius for split-second identification, encyclopedic memory and engaging manner brought him quickly to the throne. In 1927 Ludlow Griscom was elected president of the Linnaean Society. Roger Tory Peterson in a memorial article wrote: "Ludlow was our God and his *Birds of the New York City Region* published in 1923 became our Bible. We could recite chapter and verse and even adopted his inflections when we pronounced a bird to be 'unprecedented' or 'a common summer resident.'" The cult of Ludlow Griscom, with its cliches ("That's just a weed bird"—"Put it down to ignorance, incompetence, and inexperience"—"Any velvet?") and mannerisms, was well established.

In 1927 Griscom accepted the post of assistant curator of ornithology at Havard's Museum of Comparative Zoology. For the next three decades he would dominate Massachusetts' field ornithology. Griscom began making trips to the Sudbury River Valley in 1928. It was natural that he should develop an interest in this area. Brewster, who had guided bird studies in Massachusetts for half a century, had been active in the Valley less than a decade before; his field notes, journals and collections were at the MCZ.

In 1935 Griscom began to analyze Brewster's Concord data. It was a monumental task that he worked at over a period of thirteen years. At the end of this time Griscom was impressed not only with the quantity but the quality of Brewster's work. In 1949 Griscom published *The Birds of Concord*. This work is not simply a checklist of local birds but rather a comprehensive look at the ornithology of the Sudbury River Valley. Included in this book are a detailed analysis of Brewster's work, a discussion of factors affecting bird populations, and facts about bird biology. Griscom uses specific examples of birdlife in the Valley to elucidate more general theories and ideas. H. I. Fisher in his review published in *The Auk* sums up Griscom's focus in *The Birds of Concord:* "The book represents one of the first attempts to deal quantitatively with localized populations of birds over long periods of time." One intent of the work was to demonstrate the relationships between these population trends and various ecological changes. In this matter Griscom was not entirely successful. Fisher's review summarizes the problem: "Although the area has been studied more intensively, in quantitative fashion, and over a longer period of time than any other region of North America, the data presented show how woefully inadequate and incomparable is our numerical information." When sufficient data were not on hand, Griscom replaced them with personal impressions. His impressions of historical changes and ecological factors were, at times, unfounded. To put these criticisms in perspective, it should be realized that in these efforts Griscom was breaking new ground. He was outlining an ecological framework for the study of bird populations. The problems he raised, if not the solutions, are ones that are still being actively researched. Ironically, Griscom's impressions are also a strength of the book when applied to discussions of contemporary status and distribution of birds. Griscom, perhaps more than anyone else in his era, knew the birdlife of eastern Massachusetts. His knowledge and expertise illuminate many of the species accounts in *The Birds of Concord.* In that book Brewster's data are summarized and compared to the field work done by Griscom and his contemporaries. Specific localities, dates and numbers of birds provide present day and future naturalists with an indication of the historical status of many species.

— 46 —
HOODED MERGANSER

Lophodytes cucullatus (Linnaeus)

Formerly a regular transient, fairly common in spring, uncommon in fall; declining to very rare; once more fairly common, and a recent breeding record.

1880-1893. Of regular occurrence at Concord, flocks seen on five occasions in the spring of 1893 (Brewster)

1895-1917. Only three records at Concord (Brewster)

1905 on. Virtually unknown at Wayland and Sudbury (Maynard)

1935-1948. Increasing, recorded every spring and fall from 1938 on in small numbers, maximum 20 in a day

1947. Nests in one of the Wood Duck boxes at the Great Meadows Refuge, the third breeding locality in the state

Other remarks in the species accounts provide interesting facts about the birdlife.

There is no known better place in Massachusetts for the Rusty Blackbird than the Concord Region. While common enough in spring, flocks of 100 birds are quite exceptional. Actually there are two populations. An early spring group passes through in March, arriving exceptionally in early February (sic), in late springs from late March to early April, after which the migration appears to be concluded. Without exception it recommences after a hiatus of nearly a month, and small flocks of Rusties pass through again in early May. Two different subspecies may prove to be involved. I have been familiar with this fact for 40 years over the whole northeast. No such separation can be made in the fall.

An especially interesting field study published in *The Birds of Concord* was the Heard's Pond breeding-bird census. In 1945 Griscom and members of the Old Colony Bird Club censused an area of marsh, river meadow, agricultural field and forest in Wayland. The data summary includes a species list, habitat reference, estimates of numbers of breeding pairs and a brief "comments" section. This study provides an historical basis with which to compare future studies. *The Birds of Concord* established an ornithological benchmark for local naturalists. The contemporary status of the various bird species was defined within an historical framework. Furthermore, Griscom encouraged (sometimes provoked) his readers to consider a multitude of cultural and environmental factors when studying the birdlife.

Ludlow Griscom added an important chapter to the tradition of bird study in the Sudbury River Valley. His work in the Valley was, however, a small part of a distinguished career. Included among his publications is *Birds of Massachusetts* (1955). Written with Dorothy Snyder, this has been a standard reference for over a quarter of a century. His professional studies in Mexico and Central America led to several innovative and scholarly publications. Griscom also took on his share of organizational commitments. He had leading roles in both the National and Massachusetts Audubon Societies and the Boston Society of Natural History. Griscom was president of the Nuttall Ornithological Club and in 1956 he was elected president of the American Ornithologists' Union.

The last ten years of Ludlow Griscom's life were difficult. A series of strokes left him partially paralyzed and confined to a wheelchair. This did not dampen his enthusiasm. He made trips to Mexico in 1956 and Africa in 1958. Still energetic after the African adventure, he would write: "I was allowed only one big day trip in Essex County and we had only 131 (species) for the day."

Ludlow Griscom returned to the Sudbury River Valley shortly before his death. He came in a wheelchair to see a very special bird. A Hawk Owl had been found at Concord in December of 1958.

The Hawk Owl was Ludlow Griscom's last "life bird." He died in Cambridge on May 28, 1959, shortly after the peak of the spring migration.

The legacy of Ludlow Griscom is one of excellence in field ornithology. He developed a fledgling pastime into a popular and professional pursuit.

Chapter 8

When we walk, we naturally go to the fields and woods: what would become of us, if we walked only in a garden or a mall?

Henry David Thoreau

Ludlow Griscom noted a pattern emerging in the first half of the twentieth century. There was, he said, a growing population of people purchasing residences in the country: " . . . men of some means, often commuting to Boston for business or professional pursuits. They could afford to pay taxes on a substantial acreage, took pride in owning some decent-looking woodland and a good stand of pines . . . " This had, he said, created improved habitats and was beneficial to many bird species. In typical Griscom style, he went on to venture a projected scenario: "If the present high costs of living and the tremendous taxes continue much longer, these estates will be liquidated, and the timber cut once more." In fact, the cost of living did rise and the taxes did increase, with the onslaught of suburbanization. The decades of the 50s, 60s, and 70s would once again alter the face of the land in the Sudbury River Valley.

The changes that took place in this era were significant ones. The structure of land-use in the Valley was altered in a basic manner. Traditional agricultural use was based on a relatively small number of land owners controlling large acreages. The wealth of the farmer and the value of the land derived from the products of the land. During the eighteenth and nineteenth centuries, many of the Valley's sons and daughters were forced to move on.

This situation was reversed in the 1950s as suddenly there seemed to be room for everyone. The great influx of people who moved into the Valley following World War II had no intention of working the land. Their wealth was based on "services to be rendered." Their ties to the land were tenuous at best, their professions often highly mobile. All that this population required was living space. They would, often as not, ply their "wares" outside the Valley. The automobile made this possible. To be sure, some prospective buyers wanted more land than others, but no one was in the market for tillage, pasture and meadow. An urban land-use pattern was developing.

The numbers tell the story. Combined population figures for the towns of Concord, Wayland and Sudbury show the relatively slow growth during the first half century.

YEAR	POPULATION	% CHANGE PRECEDING DECADE
1900	9,105	
1910	9,747	+7
1920	9,517	-2
1930	11,596	+18
1940	13,231	+14
1950	15,666	+18
1960	30,411	+94
1970	43,493	+43
1980	42,955	-1

Sudbury River Valley at Framingham.

The irruption takes place in the 50s and 60s. This population growth was not distributed evenly among the three towns. Sudbury's population increased a phenomenal 420 percent, Wayland's by over 200 percent, and Concord's by not quite 90 percent.

Another indication of the magnitude of the change can be found in the residential construction statistics. At the beginning of this period, in 1949, the combined number of residential dwellings in Concord, Sudbury and Wayland was fewer than 4,000. In the following three decades a building boom resulted in close to 9,000 new single family homes in these three towns. The rural character of much of the Valley was rapidly becoming urbanized.

During the first half of the twentieth century the population density of the three towns nearly doubled. In the decades of the 50s and 60s the numbers doubled again and by 1970 came close to being three times the 1950 figure.

YEAR	POPULATION	DENSITY / SQUARE MILE*
1900	9,105	137
1950	15,666	237
1960	30,411	459
1970	43,493	657
1980	42,995	649

Along with population growth and residential development, came the attendant service industries. Both private businesses and public facilities burgeoned. Town centers began to spread out, new convenience retail areas were developed, and ultimately that archetype of urban design — the shopping mall — began to appear.

How did these demographic changes affect the land? Fortunately, we have an accurate index of this change: the McConnell-Cobb Map-Down Project. In this study two sets of aerial photographs were taken at a twenty-year interval (1951-1971). The maps were analyzed and the data categorized by land-use type. A comparison of the two sets of data in conjuction with earlier Massachusetts Agricultural Census information gives a good indication of change in this century.

We already have seen that forest acreage was increasing over the first half of the century. In the decades of the 50s and 60s the forest essentially held its own (a slight decrease of 817 forest acres for the three towns is indicated). Woodland acreage in 1971 accounted for 48 percent of total acreage. There is also evidence that the forest was maturing during this period. In the 1950s a majority of the woodlands analyzed were described as "young" forest (less than 40 feet tall). By the 1970s this situation was reversed and the majority of the woodlands were characterized as "older" (41 feet or more). Although comparable data are not available for the decade of the 1970s, a slightly reduced population and a decrease in housing starts relative to the

*Total Land Area: 66.22 Sq. Miles

two preceding decades indicate a fairly stable situation. The nineteenth century pattern of cutting the woodlands every twenty to thirty years, or whenever a harvestable crop had grown in, had been altered. The Sudbury River Valley now has a substantial and maturing forest cover.

It has been the agricultural land that has borne the brunt of urban development. At the beginning of the century (1905) agricultural lands accounted for 42 percent of the total acreage of Concord, Sudbury and Wayland. By mid-century the total had slipped to 31 percent of the combined acreage. During the period of greatest growth (1950s and 1960s), half of the remaining agricultural land was lost to urban development. Construction costs were naturally cheaper on the cleared and graded farmland, and as demand increased, land values soared. Agricultural markets could not compete with the rewards offered by the developers. Back to back neighborhoods grew on the pastures; acres in tillage were seeded with townhouses; and cornfields were replaced by condominiums. On many acres at least the last crop had been planted. Six thousand one hundred seventy-four acres of farmland were lost to the three towns between 1951 and 1971. At the end of this period barely 16 percent of the total land was farmed. The last decade has seen further decreases in agricultural land. Although the figures are not exactly comparable to the McConnell-Cobb data, the 1977 Open Space Plans from these towns indicate a combined farmland acreage of 3,847. This represents barely 11 percent of total area. At present real-estate markets and certain taxing structures threaten a portion of these remaining few acres.

As prime farmland acres were reduced, pressure increased on "unimproved" lands. The nineteenth century tradition of filling wetlands was revived as a solution to twentieth century real estate needs. Hundreds of acres of marsh and swampland were filled and developed. In the mid-1950s a plan was being devised to fill the river meadow at Sudbury.

Chapter 9

January 7, 1955

The towns in the Sudbury Valley are expanding so rapidly that I am sure that the marshes will be destroyed within my lifetime if prompt action is not taken. Already, marsh land is being bull-dozed out and filled with gravel in order to build more houses.

Letter from Allen Morgan to C. Russell Mason

Allen Morgan was born in Waltham, Massachusetts, on August 12, 1925. Within two years his family moved to Wayland. Looking back on the scenes and circumstances of his youth, Morgan recalled: "This particular piece of property had been cultivated until about 1926—the apple and pear trees still were producing lavishly, and the fields were entirely open; indeed, Wayland in the early mid-1930s was still essentially a farming community. My father, when he purchased our home in 1927, was one of the pioneers of a new age: the businessman-commuter from Boston."

In this rural setting Allen Morgan began to develop an interest in natural history. An early fascination with insects led to the study of birds. By the time he was eleven years old, Morgan had begun to keep a regular journal of his field trips. His involvement with the natural world was stimulated by friends and nurtured by teachers. David Garrison, one of Allen Morgan's teachers at the Mount Prospect School, considered the arrival of the first spring Phoebe an important part of the curriculum. Weekend birding trips around Waltham, through the Valley and even to the Peregrine eyrie on Mt. Tom were standard fare for Garrison's boys. Alexander (Sandy) Bergstrom, who would later go on to a distinguished career in ornithology, was a constant companion of Morgan's. The boys were filled with enthusiasm and spent little time indoors. It was Sandy who sent Allen a special-delivery letter from Cambridge. Could Allen get a ride into the Mount Auburn Cemetery as soon as possible? A Prothonotary Warbler had been found!

Morgan also had the good fortune to come under the guidance of Ludlow Griscom. "It was my great privilege almost immediately to journey afield on such expeditions with Ludlow Griscom. Only those fortunate enough to have known this remarkable gentleman in his prime can appreciate what an enormously stimulating and exciting experience this was." This relationship lasted over twenty years. During this period Morgan birded with Griscom throughout Massachusetts. Their trips through the Valley, Essex County and Cape Cod often resulted in new field records. More than once the student delighted his mentor by collecting a particularly interesting species. It was Allen Morgan who brought Ludlow Griscom to Concord to see the Hawk Owl.

As is the case with most avid birders, Allen Morgan spent a good deal of time chasing the rare species and the migrational movements at the coast: "Unfortunately my early observations carried me where chance and whim dictated—usually where the largest number of birds could be found." By 1948, however, Morgan's journal indicates a determination to make exact counts, and in 1949 he established systematic routes in the Heard's Pond

Allen H. Morgan

area of Wayland. This census, which Morgan repeated in the early 1960s, included segments on both land and river. The data is published in "Barometer of Change." This article, which Morgan wrote in 1965, discusses the changes in both the birdlife and the land of the Sudbury River Valley. The efforts of the preservationists at the beginning of the century, said Morgan, had resulted in an increase in bird numbers by the 1930s and 1940s. During the postwar urbanization boom, however, conditions began to turn around for many species. Morgan said: "The list of 'common' Sudbury Valley birds in the period 1935 to 1950 that have either totally disappeared or so markedly declined as now to be classed as uncommon or rare, is impressive indeed." During the period of residential construction, many field bird species declined. As much of the Valley landscape changed, one area remained relatively stable.

> —the River itself, and the extensive open marshes and wooded swamps along it . . . virtually all of this extensive flood plain remains intact —the habitat has not changed in terms of the gross impact of civilization: it has not been filled with gravel or trash, and the same marshes and wooded swamps are still present.

The preservation of this area was due, in large part, to the efforts of Allen Morgan and the Sudbury Valley Trustees.

Sudbury Valley Trustees, Inc., was incorporated on November 27, 1953. Its founders " . . . a group of seven Wayland residents, included a geographer, an insurance salesman, a lawyer, a city planner, a local real-estate man, an amateur ornithologist and a telephone-company executive. They shared a common love for the natural and aesthetic amenities of the Valley and a common feeling that something must be done to save them before intensive development took place." The original charter included among its goals scientific study and natural history education, as well as land acquisition and preservation. The first step in achieving these goals was the purchase of a ten-acre section of river marsh. Bought for less than ten dollars an acre in 1954, this marsh-land is south of the Old Stone Bridge on the historic Oxbow section of the Sudbury River.

Allen Morgan and the SVT soon became involved in political maneuvering that would have far-reaching effects on the Sudbury River Valley. In March 1950 several Massachusetts state boards had issued the "Report of the Sudbury Valley Commission." This document presented a regional approach to planning for the future in the Valley. Morgan summed up the report a month after it was issued; " . . . while it may not be ideal from any single viewpoint, still it is an excellent reconciliation of the opposing interests of the farmer, sportsman, ornithologist, and the citizen who likes to see the countryside preserved in its natural state." The commission's studies included the watershed's historical and legislative background, sanitary conditions, zoning and recreation. Part of the report focuses on defining the natural resources of the Valley. Aspects of the flora and the fauna are summarized by numerous contributors, including Ludlow Griscom and Richard Eaton. The report makes several specific recommendations intended to preserve and protect these resources. On the positive side it urged the conservation of undeveloped lands, particularly along the rivers, from Framingham to Billerica. More controversial was the report's suggestion to study the feasibility of major physical alterations to the riverways. Flood control measures, including dredging, channelizing and the installation of 'control works' were suggested.

One year later, in 1951, the engineering features of the report were defined by the Department of Public Work's Turner Plan. Fortunately, at that time the Turner Plan was not deemed cost effective. In 1955, however, flood damage by Hurricane Diane added impetus to the growing demands for artificial control systems. Certain private and commercial interests in the Valley felt they would be best served by such projects. The SUASCO Corporation was formed to promote this approach. An alternative view was suggested by Allen Morgan and the SVT. In April of 1956 Judge Robert Walcott, president of the Massachusetts Audubon Society, devoted the "President's Page" of *The Bulletin* to this debate.

> Two recent publications are illustrated by two very different points of view. The Sunday *Globe* of February 19, 1956, had nearly a page urging support of a project of the Suwasco Corporation, which has a bill on which a hearing has already been given, directing the Commonwealth to acquire the banks of the Assabet and Sudbury rivers to 'improve' the same by straightening the channels of the river and filling their marshy banks; also to lower or wholly remove the Talbot Dam at Billerica and to install dams on tributary brooks with the aim that less water remain at each side of the river in the marshes bordering the river, and the rivers would more quickly empty themselves into the Merrimac River at Lowell . . . Allen Morgan, clerk of Sudbury Valley Trustees, Inc., has issued, in their *Newsletter* of January 12, 1956, one of the best short statements on flood control considerations, which I think will be enthusiastically endorsed by our members and by those interested in the preservation of the natural landscape and in the retention of conditions favorable to our fauna and flora which will not endure gravel fill and buildings but need moist earth and vegetation. He wrote:
>
> 'Often we hear people complain bitterly of the annual flooding of the marshes and adjoining lowlands, stating that if only something could be done to drain the entire valley quickly, great benefits would be realized in terms of the elimination of annual damage to property located on the flood plain itself, and increased acreage (popularly described now as wasteland without value of any sort) would be made available for farming, home and industrial development.
>
> 'We feel that it is most important to remind everyone of some very basic facts: The disastrous floods of the Ohio, Mississippi, Missouri, Sacramento and Naugatuck River Valleys (to mention but a few) are the direct result of this sort of land reclamation where marshes and ponds were drained to create more farmland, and where forests were destroyed at the same time.
>
> 'Really serious and destructive flooding (such as that recently experienced in Connecticut and Western Massachusetts) occurs when a river does not have a flood plain or natural basin of marshes and lowlands to catch the water, store it, allow it to sink into the ground (providing us incidentally with a fine supply of drinking water) and release the excess gradually without great damage downstream.'

Looking south from Nine Acre Corner Concord with the river in flood.

Looking north from route 20 Wayland with the river in flood.

Morgan quickly began to get his message across. As early as October 1956 he could report to the SVT membership that " . . . it is becoming generally recognized that the solution to the problem (of flood control) is not as simple as merely digging a ditch, lining it with concrete and running off the water as fast as possible." When the SUASCO Watershed Work Plan was published in August 1958 a more enlightened view prevailed.

A 1960 Water Resources Commission suggested that further studies be made of ways to preserve and protect the Valley's wetlands. Charles H.W. Foster, commissioner of natural resources, was directed to complete this work. The SVT took on the job of "liaison between his (Foster's) department and the local communities." The trustees organized meetings that brought together town agencies, interested individuals and state officials. The outcome of these efforts was a regional "Plan for the Preservation of the Wetlands in the Sudbury and Concord Rivers." A new group with the SuAsCo appellation, but of a decidedly different makeup from its predecessor, was also beginning to lend its efforts to the "Wetlands Plan." The SuAsCo River Basin Group of the League of Women Voters became involved in gathering and publicizing information about the plan. After considerable political maneuvering, the enabling legislation was finally passed by the Massachusetts Legislature in April 1961. As a result of this act, land preservation proceeded on the federal, state and local level. The Great Meadows National Wildlife Refuge presently owns and manages close to 3,000 acres of land along the Sudbury and Concord Rivers (much of which was originally secured by the SVT). The state has acquired 392 acres that it continues to manage in the Pantry Brook area of Concord and Sudbury. At the local level, many towns in the Valley have gone ahead with programs to conserve land along feeder tributaries and in upland situations.

During the decades of the 1960s and 1970s the SVT continued to acquire land through gifts and outright purchase. At the present time the trustees hold approximately 600 acres of river meadow, marsh and upland in the towns of Westborough, Framingham, Wayland, Concord and Sudbury. The SVT is continuing to work towards the preservation of natural resources in the Sudbury River Valley.

Throughout this period Allen Morgan was a guiding force behind the SVT. It was also during the 60s and 70s that Morgan ran the Massachusetts Audubon Society. During his tenure there he transformed the Society from an organization that appealed mainly to naturalists into a broadly based forum for environmental awareness and education. Morgan hired a staff that included James Baird and William H. Drury, Jr. They in turn studied and defined important environmental issues, including pesticide use and wetlands protection. Morgan also brought to the MAS another man who could explain these problems and issues to the public. For almost two decades, Wayne Hanley transcribed the technical jargon of environmental assessments into narrative the layperson could understand and appreciate. The important part that the Society played in raising the environmental consciousness of a wide range of citizens was due, in large part, to the leadership efforts of Allen Morgan.

In 1980 Morgan returned to work full-time for the SVT and the Natural Resources Defense Council.

No one person or organization has been responsible for the preservation of the Valley's rivers, meadows and marshes. Indeed, they are still at risk. The positive efforts that have occurred in the last thirty years have been a joint effort and represent the will of many citizens. The fact remains, however, that it was Allen H. Morgan who ultimately mobilized and directed that will.

Chapter 10

During the last three decades many positive changes have taken place in the Valley. Perhaps the foremost has been a growing awareness on the part of many citizens of environmental conditions. More and more individuals are convinced, as Allen Morgan has noted, that the quality of their living experience is a reflection of the quality of the environment. Many of these individuals have become directly involved with efforts to preserve and protect the natural resources of the Sudbury River Valley. From grassroots efforts such as the one mounted to pass the Bottle Bill to individual decisions to grant conservation restrictions on private property, a sensitized citizenry has moved to promote a sounder environment.

Important legislation has been enacted and advocacy groups established that help to protect and monitor environmental conditions. At the local level floodplain zoning, and protection of wetland watersheds has been instituted in many towns. Wayland in the early 1960s became one of the first towns in the state to enact bylaws for the protection of river and wetlands habitats. Since that time many Valley towns have followed suit. Massachusetts laws, including the Wetlands Protection Act (1963) and the Wetlands Restriction Act, have provided a framework for local action. State laws passed in 1957 enabled towns to establish Conservation Commissions. This action in combination with the Self-Help Act of 1960 encouraged many communities to set aside considerable acreage. At present the towns of Concord, Sudbury and Wayland have preserved over 2,000 acres through this process. Private land trusts, working towards similar goals, have obtained many additional pieces of land. Federal legislation, including the National Environmental Policy Act and the Clean Water Act, have also established guidelines for natural-resources protection. Unfortunately, the interpretation and enforcement of federal legislation is subject to the whims of the presiding administration.

A recent state plan—the Agricultural Preservation Restriction (APR) program—establishes a procedure that is helping to maintain the farming segment of our local communities. At present, over 200 acres in Sudbury and 14 acres in Concord are permanently preserved by this plan.

Several private organizations are also actively seeking to preserve local natural resources. The SuAsCo Watershed Association, Inc., the third organization to bear the SUASCO acronym, seeks to promote the development and maintenance of clean water in the watershed. The New England Rivers Center and the Thoreau Group of the Sierra Club are also working towards river preservation.

Large portions of the Sudbury River Valley are now in a fairly stable condition. Forest habitats are maturing and major portions of the rivers and wetlands are protected locally. The urbanization boom has slowed and many residential acres are, with age, increasingly able to provide suitable habitat for a suburban wildlife population. In general, a working balance seems to have been reached between the forces urging development and those advocating preservation. .

Nevertheless, clear and present dangers still threaten the natural resources of the Sudbury River Valley. While several of the problems are close by and readily apparent, others are either unseen or to a large extent outside the control of local forces. A few of these threats are potentially catastrophic.

The latest chapter in the river history involves the Metropolitan District Commission (MDC). The MDC is obliged to provide water to member communities within a fifteen-mile radius of the State House. Because this is the most densely populated area in the state, demand for water is increasing and threatens to exceed present supplies (mostly from the Quabbin Reservoir System). The MDC is presently studying two plans that would divert water from the upper Sudbury River. The first plan proposes to draw down 22 million gallons per day (mgd), the second, 45 mgd.

The effects of such diversions are not exactly clear. We do know that the rate of flow of the Sudbury is already minimal. At some level of diversion the rate would be so low as to cause the riverbed to silt over. If this happens the river will die. All plant and animal communities associated with the river and wetlands would be affected; many would be extirpated. Diversion of any amount would increase the percentage of nutrients relative to the total volume of water. This would accelerate the growth of algae, which in turn would reduce the levels of available oxygen in the river. At some point fish and other aquatic life would begin to die. Toxic pollutants, somewhat diluted by present volumes of water, would become more concentrated. The MDC suggests that it would monitor any diversion and not permit negative conditions to develop. It allegedly would divert water only during flood-crest periods. Yet the history of natural resources abuses suggests something else. When push comes to shove, basic human need is an argument used to override all other considerations. MDC district customers certainly don't have a vested interest in the Sudbury River Valley. Water for drinking, cooking and even washing the family car is of immediate consequence for them.

The management system within the MDC water district is another troubling factor. The MDC now has little control over how (or how much) member districts use the water resource itself. One estimate of water loss due to leaks within the system is 40 percent. Any diversion under present conditions literally would be pouring water down a bottomless hole.

The studies now underway are based on MDC projections of future water needs. Although the basic demographic statistics underlying their needs assessment have been questioned, the planning goes on. Legally the MDC could divert all but 1.5 mgd. This would mean the end of the Sudbury River Valley as we know it.

Another potential hazard, and one whose source is far from the Valley, is the phenomenon known as acid rain. A growing body of evidence indicates that pollutants such as sulphur and nitrogen, which are emitted from the large, fossil-fuel burning plants of the industrial Midwest, end up being deposited on the ecosystems of the Northeast. The airborne particles are drawn out of the atmosphere by rain or snow and cover the forests, fields and river basins downwind. Although the National Academy of Sciences has recommended reducing the volumes of emissions as a way of controlling the effects of acid rain, at present considerable political resistance to remedial efforts exists. The economic interest of one group (the Midwestern industrial institutions) seems to prevail. In the meantime, local natural habitats are absorbing increasing amounts of these destructive compounds.

The deliberate introduction of toxic compounds into the environment is another subject for concern. Considerable progress has been made with regards to the most dangerous group of insecticides, the chlorinated hydrocarbons. By 1969 the use of DDT and most of the related persistent insecticides was severely restricted. Many of these compounds, which accumulate in the ecosystem and are life-threatening to vertebrates and invertebrates, are now banned. The temptation still exists, however, to resort to pesticides of various kinds as controls on pests such as mosquitoes and gypsy moths. By definition, pesticides destroy living organisms. Their use needs to be monitored carefully.

The hazard that represents the most clear and present danger to local ecosystems is the threat posed by industrial wastes and byproducts. Extremely poisonous elements and chemical compounds have been introduced into the environment through careless and improper disposal techniques.

At present the Massachusetts Department of Environmental Quality Engineering (DEQE) has identified two sites in this watershed that are of immediate concern. The Nyanza site on the upper Sudbury River is a source of chemical wastes, including mercury. Soil and groundwater contamination has resulted and "concern has also been expressed over the possible migration of wind-blown mercury laden particulates from exposed 'heavy metal' sludges." The W. R. Grace wastewater site on the Assabet River has been responsible for the contamination of a municipal water supply. Leaks and spills from various industrial processes at Grace have been reported over several years. The cost of dealing with these and other sources of contamination will be high. The cost of avoiding such problems would be even higher.

Finally, the threat of a nuclear holocaust must be added to the list of potential hazards. Although there is something absurd about considering such devastation as it relates to this valley or that, perhaps a local focus will give us hold on a problem that seems so awesome as to defy definition. While it is true, as Gerard Bertrand, President of Massachusetts Audubon Society, has said, that "we cannot avoid the specter of an environmental crisis so devastating that it would alter all life on earth forever," it is also difficult to deal with the problem in these terms. At the global level, nuclear war is truly a specter. Perhaps if we can manage to think about a force that would destroy our river meadows, raze the Valley forests, exterminate the Wood Ducks, and in an instant obliterate our way of life, we will be moved to act. Perhaps each of us can focus on one small, well-loved aspect of the Valley and consider all the possibilities, including the nuclear ones. Then we must each do something.

PART II — THE JOURNALS

Tradition and a sense of place are the constant companions of the naturalist in the Sudbury River Valley. Even for the casual visitor, there is an awareness of Thoreau's sojourns and perhaps of Brewster's fieldwork in our area. To the initiated, each meadow, farm and bend in the river takes on added meaning.

In fall as I lean back against the granite outcroppings of the Fairhaven Cliffs, below me is the hillside where Thoreau chased the fox. Across the river at Martha's Point, Brewster and Bolles hooted for owls. Upriver at Nine Acre Corner I stand in line to count the snipe. In front of me are Thoreau, Brewster, Maynard and Griscom—and many others.

Both men and events have woven this tradition; the commonplace: a spring flight of Ring-necked Ducks, the courtship cries of Red-shouldered or Red-tailed Hawks, and raucous flocks of blackbirds; and the unusual: the mysterious song of the "night warbler", the confounding "Kicker", an invasion of southern herons, and a Hawk Owl. And on and on—for it is an appreciation for the everyday, an appetite for the unusual, and a curiosity about the unknown that characterize the naturalist.

Our great fortune in the Valley is that many of her naturalists have written down their observations and experiences. Their differing perspectives of similar events and their own unique experiences enrich this tradition.

Perhaps because of the diversity of natural phenomena, the student of nature seeks to order, categorize, define and classify. We want to know when the Wood Thrush will arrive and when begone. We measure and chart these comings and goings with all due precision—and yet it is the unexpected that brings a gleam to our eyes and often a strong desire to share.

The journal entries that follow share this Valley tradition.

A Season of Hope

There are beginnings in a February snowstorm. A flock of Snow Buntings, feeding nervously amid the frozen clods of earth and corn stubble, suddenly rise and, flashing black and white, wheel to the east and then to the north. They will follow the edge of winter on their way to the high Arctic. Behind them they leave the promise of spring.

And then one day the breeze comes from the southwest, the chill goes out of the air, and Mourning Doves sing.

This is a season of hope—a time to look forward. The events themselves are often subtle and unspectacular: skunk cabbage pushing through the soil, a muskrat on the ice, or a pair of goldeneyes in the river channel. Often it is the light we notice first—a brightening of the willows or a lengthening of the day. These happenings turn our thoughts toward spring and the beginning of a new cycle.

But while our sights may be set on spring, the realities of this season are something else. The return of the waterfowl and blackbirds often occur amidst snowstorms and chilling winds. One fine day followed by ten more days of winter—and no little frustration. We endure this halting progress and with persistence find the Killdeer, the Woodcock, and the Phoebe. Their presence gives us hope, their songs delight.

Even the storms themselves provide some joy. They detain the Fox Sparrow and we are treated to his song—so seldom and briefly heard. And then one night a warm rain comes. The Wood Frogs sing and the salamanders move. In the morning we see a warbler or two and in the afternoon a butterfly—April is here.

February 2, 1892
Concord. Cloudy and warm. Snow storm in late P.M.

To Ball's Hill at 10 A.M. driving down with George and, for the first time since my illness, taking lunch and spending the day.

The morning was delightfully soft and warm without a breath of wind, the sun peeping through a thin curtain of clouds at intervals. The road was muddy and the snow melted rapidly on the northern slopes.

On reaching Holden's I got out of the buggy and cut across the intervening fields and wood lots directly for Ball's Hill. The first bird I saw was a fine old Red-tailed Hawk soaring over the woods on Holden's Hill. Soon after entering these woods I heard a Chickadee giving the flock notes at regular intervals. On reaching Ball's Hill I found a large flock (I counted 43 birds and certainly missed some) of Tree Sparrows in the bushes on the edge of Bensen's cranberry meadow. There was a Downy Woodpecker with them. One of the Tree Sparrows was in nearly, if not quite, full song when I first came within hearing and afterwards when I was following the flock either the same or another male sang a dozen times more making the woods ring with the wild, sweet strain...

W.B.

February 4, 1955

Wayland—Dick Stackpole phoned me at the office at 10 a.m. in great excitement to report an adult male Barrow's Goldeneye in the river rapids at Erwin's Farm. I left work at 3 p.m., arrived at the farm at 4:00 where we found:

Blacks	128
Mallard	6
Pintail	2 females
Pied-billed Grebe	1
American Goldeneye	8
Barrow's Goldeneye	1 male

A beautiful bird—fully adult, feeding actively in the open channel side by side with drake Americans. Fine look—studied shape of head, purple color, crescent of white on the head, and of course the dark wing with white spots. First record for the Sudbury Valley and first good record inland in Massachusetts per L.G. Very Fancy!

A.H.M.

February 12, 1950

Wayland—a beautiful day, clear and cloudless all morning with temperature to 43 degrees, wind N.W. Gradually becoming overcast in the afternoon and colder. River entirely open, marshes generally frozen...

List:

Black Duck	3	Blue Jay	15
Red-shouldered Hawk	1	Crow	75
Rough-legged Hawk	1	Chickadee	15
Pheasant	1 male	White-breasted Nuthatch	2
Herring Gull	2	Starling	8
Flicker	1	English Sparrow	6
Northern Horned Lark	6	Goldfinch	350
Prairie Horned Lark	1 singing	Junco	3
		Tree Sparrow	20

A.H.M.

February 13, 1965

Sudbury Valley—River Road to Nine Acre Corner

Rough-legged Hawk	15 (1 dark phase, 14 light phase)
Common Crow	135
Eastern Bluebird	1
Northern Shrike	1 (immature)

R.A.F. and W.R.P.

March 1, 1854

As for the birds of the past winter: I have seen but three hawks,—one early in the winter and two lately; have heard the hooting owl pretty often late in the afternoon. Crows have not been numerous, but their cawing was heard chiefly in pleasanter mornings. Blue jays have blown the trumpet of winter as usual, but they, as all birds, are most lively in springlike days. The chickadees have been the *prevailing* bird. The partridge common enough. One ditcher tells me that he saw two robins in Moore's Swamp a month ago. I have not seen a quail, though a few have been killed in the thaws. Four or five downy woodpeckers. The white-breasted nuthatch four or five times. Tree sparrows one or more at a time, oftener than any bird that comes to us from the north. Two pigeon woodpeckers, I think, lately. One dead shrike, and perhaps one or two live ones. Have heard of two white owls—one about Thanksgiving time and one in midwinter. One short-eared owl in December. Several flocks of snow buntings for a week in the severest storm, and in December, last past. One grebe in Walden just before it froze completely. And two brown creepers once in middle of February. Channing says he saw a little olivaceous-green bird lately. I have not seen an *F. linaria*, nor a pine grosbeak, nor an *F. hyemalis* this winter, though the first was the prevailing bird last winter.

H.D.T.

March 3, 1981
Partly cloudy—wind: n.w. 15-20, 35 degrees

At the Great Meadows today at 1:45 I saw 3 Bald Eagles—all birds were immatures. They moved in from the northern-most pool and soared around the tower for several minutes. Twice one bird chased another and made mock dives. The ice is completely out and there is a sizable fish kill in the pools.

R.K.W.

March 4, 1859
What a perfectly New England sound is the voice of the crow! If you stand perfectly still anywhere in the outskirts of the town and listen, stilling the almost incessant hum of your own personal factory, this is perhaps the sound which you will be most sure to hear rising above all sounds of human industry and leading your thoughts to some far bay in the woods where the crow is venting his disgust. This bird sees the white man come and the Indian withdraw, but it withdraws not. Its untamed voice is still heard above the tinkling of the forge. It sees a race pass away, but it passes not away. It remains to remind us of our aboriginal nature.

H.D.T.

March 10, 1979
Rain and fog most of the day—a raw 40 degrees.

Nine Acre Corner: 15 Pintail, 2 Widgeon, 1 Ring-necked Duck, many Redwings and the seaons's first Grackles.
GMNWR: The lower pool is mostly ice free—ducks included: 3 Hooded Mergansers, 2 Widgeon, 1 Common Merganser, and 1 Green-winged Teal.
Concord Center, Monument Square: 70+ Cedar Waxwings and 1 Bohemian Waxwing feeding on hawthorne berries.
Hawthorne Lane: my first Killdeer (3) of the season (I also heard at least one individual at Nine Acre Corner).
Sherman Bridge: first Pied-billed Grebe of the season.

The local population of Mallards has increased greatly in the last few days; many Canada Geese (300+) are also on hand.

R.K.W.

March 11, 1859

I see and hear a red-wing. It sings almost steadily on its perch there, sitting all alone, as if to attract companions (and I see two more, also solitary, on different tree-tops within a quarter of a mile), calling the river to life and tempting ice to melt and trickle like its own sprayey notes. Another flies over on high, with a *tchuck* and at length a clear whistle. The birds anticipate the spring: they come to melt the ice with their songs.

H.D.T.

March 11, 1939

Wayland Region—Snow-covered ground; largely ice-covered river. About 25 degrees (10 degrees at 7 a.m.); light snow by 6 p.m.; wind very light.

We tried to cover all the open water holes...The most open water was at the head of Hurd's Pd...

Winter Finches were a feature of the day, turning up everywhere. In a field near Hurd's...was a flock of 200 Finches, roughly 100 Goldfinches, 80 Redpolls, 20 Purple Finches, and 2 Siskins. We struck Robins once, a big flock in cedar and juniper cover...

Conspicuous by their absence were:

> Bluebird
> Starling
> Rusty Blackbird
> Grackle
> Cowbird
> Redwing

List:

Black Duck	150		Chickadee	15
Mallard	5		White Nuthatch	3
Blue-winged Teal	2		Red Nuthatch	2
Wood Duck	6		Robin	14
Ring-necked Duck	9		English Sparrow	several
Canvasback	1		Meadowlark	2
Am. Goldeneye	34		Red-wing	7
Am. Merganser	30		Purple Finch	54
Accipiter (cooperi?)	1		Redpoll	112
Red-shouldered Hawk	2		Siskin	2
Herring Gull	4		Goldfinch	175
Flicker	1		Junco	10
Downy Woodpecker	3		Tree Sparrow	35
N. Horned Lark	58		Fox Sparrow	1
(Prairie)	2	alleged	Song Sparrow	5
Blue Jay	5		Crow	10

D.L.G.

March 13, 1966

Cloudy and misty all day with a light East wind and 30⁰ temperature. About 2-4'' of snow on the ground.

Dick (Forster) and I made our first stop at River Road in Wayland. On the river we had a pair of Gadwall with several Canada Geese. The hawks here were quite remarkable. They were perched in trees all along the far and near shores of the river, as well as some in the air over the Broad Meadows in Sudbury. At least 3 Rough-legs were here (one melanistic), along with 2-3 Red-tails. One Red-tail was very dark on the back—like a dark Rough-leg—however, when it perched we could see the typical light breast area. The bird was unique in my experience, but I don't feel the bird was a true melano, although it certainly was abnormally dark. Just an example of the extreme variation in Buteos.

Another Rough-leg in Concord helped prove that this sudden rise of the S.V. Rough-leg population must be due to some spring movement. The S.V. is nice in that it enables one to really observe this species increase as spring approaches. The idea of the S.V. being a good locality in which to see the species is actually a contradiction to the premise set forth by Griscom (*Birds of Concord*).

At Great Meadows 3 Rusty Blackbirds, a singing Meadowlark, 3 Ringnecks, and a Baldpate were of note.

W.R.P.

March 13, 1979

Cloudy, 45 degrees, wind gusty—20 mph from s.w.
Woodcock are back in the meadow below the house. At 6:00 p.m. after walking the ridge, I waited for a while in the meadow. I watched one individual in its flight display and peenting. It seems to me these early birds spend some time patrolling the general area before beginning their evening flights. Later in the season they seem to peent, "launch", and land in a more confined area.

Other dates for Woodcock arrivals in this meadow:

2/24/76	3/19/80
3/14/77	—
3/28/78	3/22/82
3/13/79	3/15/83

R.K.W.

March 15, 1852

A mild spring day . . . The air is full of bluebirds. The ground almost entirely bare. The villagers are out in the sun, and every man is happy whose work takes him outdoors . . . I lean over a rail to hear what is in the air, liquid with the bluebirds' warble.

H.D.T.

March 17, 1858

Ah! there is the note of the first flicker, a prolonged, monotonous *wick-wick-wick-wick-wick-wick*, etc., or, if you please, *quick-quick*, heard far over and through the dry leaves. But how that single sound peoples and enriches all the woods and fields! They are no longer the same woods and fields that they were. This note really *quickens* what was dead. It seems to put a life into withered grass and leaves and bare twigs, and henceforth the days shall not be as they have been . . .

H.D.T.

March 18, 1853

How eagerly the birds of passage penetrate the northern ice, watching for a crack by which to enter! Forthwith the swift ducks will be seen winging their way along the rivers and up the coast. They watch the weather more sedulously than the teamster. All nature is thus forward to move with the revolution of the seasons. Now for some days the birds have been ready by myriads, a flight or two south, to invade our latitudes and, with this mild and serener weather, resume their flight.

H.D.T.

March 19, 1909

The Red-shouldered Hawks are back in their old haunts at Holden's Hill. As I approached the nest in the tall chestnut, in which they reared a brood of young last year and one in 1907, the male flew from a branch within a few yards of the nest. He was joined by the female, who came from the trees beyond, when both birds soared about over the woods, keeping at a distance but screaming almost incessantly. I know of no *wilder* sound than that of their loud, ringing voices. There were no chalkings or pellets under the nest. It looked rather more trim and shapely than when I left here last autumn but I am not sure that it has been really changed in this way.

W.B.

March 21, 1858

Standing by the mud-hole in the swamp, I hear the pleasant phebe note of the chickadee. It is, methinks, the most of a wilderness note of any yet. It is peculiarly interesting that this, which is one of our winter birds also, should have a note with which to welcome the spring.

H.D.T.

March 25, 1858 P.M.

To bank of Great Meadows by Peter's. Cold northwest wind as yesterday and before. . .

Going across A. Clark's field behind Garfield's, I see many fox-colored sparrows flitting past in a straggling manner into the birch and pitch pine woods on the left, and hear a sweet warble there from time to time. They are busily scratching like hens amid the dry leaves of that wood (not swampy), from time to time the rearmost moving forward, one or two at a time, while a few are perched here and there on the lower branches of a birch or other tree; and I hear a very clear and sweet whistling strain, commonly half-finished, from one every two or three minutes.

H.D.T.

March 28, 1858

From Wheeler's ploughed field on the top of Fair Haven Hill, I look toward Fair Haven Pond, now quite smooth. There is not a duck nor a gull to be seen on it. I can hardly believe that it was so alive with them yesterday. Apparently they improve this warm and pleasant day, with little or no wind, to continue their journey northward. The strong and cold northwest wind of about a week past has probably detained them. Knowing that the meadows and ponds were swarming with ducks yesterday, you go forth this particularly pleasant and still day to see them at your leisure, but find that they are all gone.

H.D.T.

March 29, 1981
Sudbury River Valley: 65 degrees, s.w. 10-20, cloudy a.m. and sun p.m.

There was a significant Snow Goose flight through the Valley today. Dick Forster had 600+ birds over Round Hill at 10:00 a.m., we had a small group (18 birds) at Nine Acre Corner at 11:30, and I saw 140 over the house in one flock at 1:00 p.m.

Dick and I saw two Turkey Vultures at Round Hill.

Wood Frogs and Spring Peepers were calling this a.m.

R.K.W.

March 31, 1895

The month came in "like a lamb" and is going out "like a lion." Although the sky was cloudless and the sun deliciously warm at noon, the ground was frozen hard and the meadows skimmed with ice this morning and all day long the North wind rages across the brown, lifeless fields and roared through the naked, shivering woods. It is true that the Song Sparrows sang merrily through the forenoon and I saw a Phoebe in the early morning but during most of the day the aspect of the country chilled and depressed me. The snow banks have lost their winter purity and freshness and the bare fields and wooded slopes look bleached and dreary enough. A little before sunset, however, the wind lulled to a moderate breeze and to my great delight Red-winged Blackbirds appeared from I know not where and, perched on the tops of the isolated maples and elms along the river, made the air ring with their *conq-quer-ees*.

W.B.

The Spring Migration

Spring is a time of contrasts in the Valley. Each year seems to provide some quirk—the season is advanced or the season is retarded, the floods are early or the floods are late. There are ice-storms in May and mid-summer days in April.

Perhaps these irregularities are the cause of our impatience. Our personal calendars are disrupted as events refuse to follow too measured a path. Perhaps it is the length of the season itself. The migration commences in late February and continues through mid-June. Somewhere in between we search for Spring.

In April we are impatient for the warbler waves of May. By May we fret over the leaves—too many to see the warblers! These are long days for the naturalist; the sun rises early. We rush about trying to catch a glimpse of everything and often end up wondering if we were in the right place at all. In the Valley we hear about a wondrous bird on Plum Island or an incredible wave at Mt. Auburn.

But Spring is also a time of fulfillment. The silence of winter is broken and it is indeed "the time of the singing of birds." One by one the summer residents return and the migrants sweep through. Early on come the ducks, the blackbirds and the hawks. Then the grosbeaks and the orioles, the cat-birds and the thrashers, the wrens and the thrushes, the vireos and the warblers—all fulfilling their promise. There is a bounty to be enjoyed and we are rewarded by both the expected and the unexpected.

April 2, 1893

Cloudless with blustering N.W. wind. A cold, raw day in exposed places, but pleasant enough on sheltered sunny slopes. The water very blue—March water.

Hoffman and I spent a quiet, uneventful night in the little log cabin at Ball's Hill. We rose this morning at daylight and found the sky perfectly clear, the air much cooler with a N.W. wind which came in puffs—forerunners of the gale that blew most of the day. Song Sparrows were singing when we stepped out of the door and a Red-wing soon joined them. Next the solemn bell-like voice of a Carolina Dove came from the Bedford shore. We scrambled up past the cabin to the top of the hill. Two Tree Sparrows were singing delightfully in the alders on the edge of the swamp and a Blue Jay giving the bell note near them. The song of a Robin came faintly from the direction of Bensen's house and that of another more distinctly from across the river...

We heard nothing more until we returned to the cabin where a Phoebe greeted us with a few brief snatches of song. Certain slight peculiarities in his voice identified him at once as the same bird which spent a month or more near the cabin last spring, but failing to secure a mate, finally left returning again for a brief visit in late summer. He had a companion this morning, a silent bird which I trust is a female although the two did not appear to be on the best of terms.

W.B.

66

April 2, 1910

About 10 A.M. we heard the wild clamor of Canada Geese coming from the far distance towards the southwest. A minute or two later we saw the birds advancing directly towards us over Great Meadow. There were two flocks, one following in the wake of the other, perhaps three hundred yards behind it. I counted eighty-five birds in the first flock and twenty-eight in the second. Rarely if ever have I seen Geese flying so very high. When directly over us, they looked no larger than Robins seen near at hand . . .

During the whole time these Geese were within hearing, they gave tongue as incessantly as a pack of hounds following a hot scent. Their sonorous voices seemed to dominate all other sounds and to fill the whole air with thrilling music more suggestive of this precise season than any other I know.

W.B.

April 6, 1891

Monday, the 6th of April, found me, with a friend who lives close to nature's heart, floating down the current of Musketaquid. We launched a light Rushton boat at the feet of the Minute-Man, and were swept past him, by the battleground, in the tide and through the eddies which Thoreau knew so well and has made immortal . . .

Beyond the bridge the river lost itself in flooded meadows. To one familiar with its rightful banks, a bunch of willows, an elm and a maple or two told the secret of its course. But to me it seemed that we were entering a beautiful lake which promised to grow wider and fairer the longer we sailed upon it. Comfortable farmhouses stood upon the higher ground and looked down at the unruly stream. Perhaps they recalled the days before the Lowell dams, when the river was a friend and not a tyrant to their fair intervales. Along the sheltered furrows in the ploughed fields and against the cold side of stone walls ribbons of white snow lay in hiding from the sun. Even in the streets of Concord we have seen good-sized drifts, and piles under roof angles. The storm of the Friday previous, which along the coast brought rain, had turned to snow here, while further inland many inches of snow had fallen, blocking roads and breaking wires. The west wind blowing across this wintry stretch of country came to us well whetted . . .

Gliding across a placid bay in the meadow we came to a wooded shore where a noble oak had just been slain. We landed, and kneeling by its stump counted the year rings. At first it had grown slowly, its young life trembling in the balance; then it gained strength, and the rings were broader and more firmly marked; sometimes narrower ones suggested years of drought; then as our count rose to a hundred, the rings grew closer and closer, as though life passed by very fast in those years. In all, the oak must have lived one hundred and twenty-five years, and have heard the echo of those musket shots which marked the dawn of Independence, the sunrise guns of American Freedom. My friend looked very grave when he saw that this tree was gone. It had been a landmark, not only on the shore of Musketaquid, but on the shore of his life, of which a precious part had been spent on this river of flooded meadows. Above the oak rose a bold headland crowned with plume like pines. It was Ball's Hill, which Thoreau called "the St. Ann's of

Concord.'' We sought the top and looked down upon the fair picture below us. Great Meadows, the ''broad moccasin print,'' was one rippling lake, dotted with islands or single trees. The river, from the stone arch bridge, just passed, down to Carlisle bridge with its wooden piers, had merged its life in this blue archipelago. The distant tower of Bedford church recalled my melting walk of a month ago, when over the snowdrifts the sun of March had nearly burned my eyes out and quite scorched the skin from my lips and cheeks. Early spring in Massachusetts is a crab-like thing, but it has its charms. In a ploughed field behind the bluff, we found fox tracks, and under a lofty pine, pellets of mouse hair, which some owl (or crow perhaps) had cast from its mouth undigested.

F.B.

April 7, 1899

Came upon three Bluebirds in Holden's pasture, a female sitting on a rock and two males dancing and fluttering about her with widespread tails and half-opened wings, warbling in a deliciously soft undertone, each evidently striving to outdo the other in the display of his beautiful plumage and exquisite voice, but neither showing the least ill temper. It was indeed a pretty picture with its setting of bleached grass and a line of wasting snow-drifts against the old stone wall that formed the background. A Flicker was shouting in an oak and six male Red-wings perched in an apple-tree not far away.

W.B.

April 7, 1982

Yesterday, last night, and today we have had to put up with another blast of winter! A Northeaster blew up the coast with the ''biggest'' April storm in a century. In Concord we received a foot of snow with some drifts to three feet. The snow ended at midnight last night and it has been blowing hard ever since. All this made for an active feeder today—species included:

White-breasted Nuthatch	3	Cardinal	1
Tufted Titmouse	3+	Common Grackle	12
Purple Finch	8	Red-winged Blackbird	5
American Goldfinch	5	Starling	5
Fox Sparrow	4	Blue Jay	1
Song Sparrow	12+	Common Crow	1
Dark-eyed Junco	16+		

R.K.W.

April 9, 1853

On a pitch (pine) on side of J. Hosmer's river hill, a pine warbler, by ventriloquism sounding farther off than it was, which was seven or eight feet, hopping and flitting from twig to twig, apparently picking the small flies at and about the base of the needles at the extremities of the twigs. Saw two afterward on the walls by roadside.

H.D.T.

April 9, 1907

The north-easter which began yesterday morning increased in violence through last night and to-day. It rained hard all this forenoon and snowed all the afternoon. Now, at nightfall, the snow lies *six inches deep* on the level, in open places, and loads the branches of the trees almost to breaking, in the woods. I had not thought to see so wintry a landscape again this spring as met my eye wherever I went late this afternoon. The beauty of the snow-burdened pines, hemlocks and birches equalled anything that I have ever seen before, even at Bethel. This, however, was only in sheltered places; elsewhere the raging northeast wind tore the snow from even the pines before it could collect there in any quantity. The birches along the river-bank were bent over the water in arches of surpassing grace and the delicate tracery of their snow-laden twigs was truly exquisite. The river appeared to be open only over its channel, for on the flooded meadows the water was everywhere covered with a dingy white slush which looked very like snow ice. In the more sheltered woods so much of the snow lodged in the tops and on the branches of the trees that the ground was nowhere very deeply covered and under the pines and hemlocks it was nearly or quite bare. This gave the birds a chance to get at the earth without much trouble and wherever it offered Fox Sparrows, Juncos and Robins were availing themselves of it.

W.B.

April 13, 1965
Sudbury Valley

Pied-billed Grebe	5	Great Black-backed Gull	1
Canada Goose	50	Herring Gull	
Mallard		Yellow-shafted Flicker	3
Black Duck		Hairy Woodpecker	1
Pintail	1	Downy Woodpecker	1
Green-winged Teal	2	Eastern Phoebe	14
Blue-winged Teal	5	Tree Swallow	700
American Widgeon	6	Bank Swallow	1
Wood Duck	50	Barn Swallow	1
Ring-necked Duck	61	Blue Jay	
Greater Scaup	2	Common Crow	
Ruddy Duck	2	Black-capped Chickadee	
Hooded Merganser	2	White-breasted Nuthatch	
Common Merganser	20	Starling	
Osprey	2	Rusty Blackbird	100
Sparrow Hawk	3	Savannah Sparrow	7
Ring-necked Pheasant	20	Song Sparrow	
American Coot	1		

R.A.F.

April 14, 1856
See from my window a fish hawk flying high west of the house, cutting off the bend between Willow Bay and the meadow, in front of the house, between one vernal lake and another. He suddenly wheels and, straightening out his long, narrow wings, makes one circle high above the last meadow, as if he had caught a glimpse of a fish beneath, and then continues his course down the river.

H.D.T.

April 14, 1934

Remarkable weather all week. Two violent northeast gales, with sleet and snow (first storm), just missing disastrous blizzard. 3+ inches of rain, floods far exceeding those of spring thaw in mid-March. Mean temperature—70 degrees for the month to date, never above 40 degrees entire week.

1. Pied-billed Grebe   1
2. Herring Gull   1
3. Amer. Merganser–Fresh Pond
4. Mallard   1 male
5. Black Duck   20 + 3
6. Wood Duck   pair
7. Golden-eye – Nash Pond
8. Greater Snow Goose, flock of 69—flying north low at 5.30 p.m. We had just reached the open field on edge of meadows beyond the deep pine woods in Wayland, when I saw a big string of geese coming in far to the south. Supposing they were Canadas give glasses to my little son. Edith uses her own and exclaims "these geese are snow white with black wings". So they were. Fly directly over our heads in wide half-moon formation, and give characteristic high pitched nasal honk and swerve slightly as they see us in open field. Every bird adult and could see pink bills. When well to the north of us, the line suddenly glowed dead white against the gray clouds, and honking as they flew, they disappeared into the distance, a beautiful and unforgettable sight in New England. They could not have been more than 100 yds. above us.
9. Marsh Hawk   1 gray male
10. Cowbird   1
11. Tree Swallow   50+ & 20
12. Robin, sev. large migrating flocks

L.G.

April 18, 1854

Scared up snipes on the meadow's edge, which go off with their strange zig-zag, crazy flight and a distressed sound,—*craik craik* or *cr-r-ack cr-r-rack*. One booms now at 3 P.M. They circle round and round, and zig-zag high over the meadow, and finally alight again, descending abruptly from that height.

H.D.T.

April 23, 1855

See a frog hawk beating the bushes regularly. What a peculiarly formed wing! It should be called the kite. Its wings are very narrow and pointed, and its form in front is a remarkable curve, and its body is not heavy and buzzard-like. It occasionally hovers over some parts of the meadow or hedge and circles back over it, only rising enough from time to time to clear the trees and fences.

H.D.T.

April 23, 1952

Sudbury Valley, 9.30 - 1.00; F. Elkins, C. Wellman, R.J. Eaton. Very hot, in high 60's last night, overcast and very windy. A. Morgan, Bill

Drury and R. Stackpole out early and made a killing! Go back in p.m. with Russ Mason and Ruth Emery. In all 34 species + 3.

1. Pied-billed Grebe   2
2. Great Blue Heron   2
3. <u>Cattle</u> <u>Egret</u> (*Ardeola i. ibis*). Discovered among cattle on Irwin Farm, in full breeding & fresh plumage; very shy and wild; <u>immediately</u> collected. Same kind as introduced in British Guiana. In M.C.Z.
4. Bittern   2
5. Canada Goose   2 feral
6. Golden-eye   1 male, 2 female
7. Bufflehead   2
8. Broad-winged Hawk   2
9. Marsh Hawk   1 male
10. Sparrow Hawk   3
11. <u>Glossy</u> <u>Ibis</u>, Hurd's Pond; first record in 102 years!
12. Herring Gull   8
13. Least Flycatcher   1, arrival 4/18
14. Bank Swallow   18, arrival 4/20
15. <u>Rough-winged</u> <u>Swallow</u>   2 in p.m., not in a.m.
16. Barn Swallow   4
17. White-br. Nuthatch   1
18. Ruby-cr. Kinglet   1 + 1 garden
19. Pipit   4
20. <u>Yellow</u> <u>Warbler</u>   1 - record date!
21. Myrtle Warbler   8
22. N. Water-thrush   1
23. Rusty Blackbird   1
24. Eve. Grosbeak   8
25. Purple Finch   2
26. Towhee   2
27. Chipping Sparrow   10+
28. <u>Upland</u> <u>Plover</u>   1

L.G.

April 26, 1981

Between 11:15 and 2:00 today the following hawks passed over the house:

37 Broadwings
7 Red-tails
2 Sharp-shins
1 Osprey
2 Kestrels

R.K.W.

May 1, 1852

I hear the first towhee finch. He say *to-wee, to-wee,* and another, much farther off than I supposed when I went in search of him, says *whip your ch-r-r-r-r-r,* with a metallic ring.

H.D.T.

May 3, 1852

Hear the first brown thrasher,—two of them . . . . They drown all the rest. He says *cherruwit, cherruwit*; *go ahead, go ahead*; *give it to him, give it to him*; etc., etc., etc.

H.D.T.

May 3, 1892

To Fairhaven, starting at 9.30 in my Rob Roy and sailing practically the entire distance. It was a great bird day; the country was simply swarming with migrants and there was much song at all hours.

As I left the house a Bobolink flew overhead, singing joyously. A Yellow Warbler and Cat Bird were singing by the river. Near the Cattle-fair Building I saw a King-bird. Brown Thrashers and Towhees numerous on Fairhaven Hill and in full song.

The woods and fields about Martha's Point were alive with migrating birds, chiefly Yellow-rumped and Yellow Palm Warblers. The latter were actually more numerous than they have been at any time previously. Heard a Parula and saw a fine male Rose-breasted Grosbeak. A Partridge drumming. Field Sparrows numerous. Got some common hornbeams and took lunch on the point.

Then sailed back to Nine Acre Bridge and went in to the Ledum Swamp where I pulled up a few plants of Labrador Tea and Laurel and a great many young Spruces.

W.B.

May 3, 1953

In the afternoon, Bill and Mary Drury and I, with our respective kayaks, drove to Southboro and paddled up-stream to the pond at the very source of the Sudbury River. A very tough pull . . .

Just before the pond (the stream) goes through dense underbrush with many dead cedars . . .

The pond itself of course is completely surrounded by an impenetrable marsh grown up to heavy, high (shrubs)—Leatherleaf and Shadbushes in full bloom today. The great majority of cedars are dead—evidently lumbered and burned. However, it is growing back to cedars, with many small ones . . . to 20 feet high . . .

Of considerable interest is a large grove (100+ trees) of Larches on the n.w. corner of the pond.

We explored the only navigable stream that feeds into the pond and were able to follow it three-quarters of a mile or so. Scrubby trees, few cedars—impenetrable to all practical intents and purposes. Big flocks of myrtles (warblers), 1 yellow (warbler), a Ruby-crowned Kinglet, and a Virginia Rail.

The pond itself shows a great deal of muskrat activity about the edges (and is) littered with mussel shells—dozens of the biggest ones I've ever seen.

There were several good sized patches of sphagnum moss. Bill Drury said we might just as well have been in Quebec—the marsh is typical of that area. Perfect habitat for nesting White-throats, Ruby-crowned Kinglets, and Rusty Blackbirds.

By far the most interesting birds were a pair of Green-winged Teal. As we first entered the pond a female flew in and started feeding busily along one edge. A male Green-wing flushed out of the brushy swamp, then circled around us in a very nervous fashion—looking us over carefully.

Beautiful adult Marsh Hawk doing courtship flight—somersaults high in the air, over and over again . . .

A.H.M.

1850

In all my rambles I have seen no landscape which can make me forget Fair Haven. I still sit on its Cliff in a new spring day, and look over the awakening woods and the river, and hear the new birds sing, with the same delight as ever. It is as sweet a mystery to me as ever what this world is. Fair Haven Lake in the south, with its pine-covered island and its meadows, the hickories putting out fresh young yellowish leaves, and the oaks light-grayish ones, while the oven-bird thrums his sawyer-like strain, and the chewink rustles through the dry leaves or repeats his jingle on a tree-top, and the wood thrush, the genius of the wood, whistles for the first time his clear and thrilling strain—it sounds as it did the first time I heard it. The sight of these budding woods intoxicates me,—this diet drink.

H.D.T.

May 9, 1959

Drive with Allen Morgan to Sudbury Valley via old route through Belmont and Lincoln. Visit every old locality in the Sudbury Valley and mourn to see how many of them are destroyed. Stay out to lunch and drive to Hoar's Dam Concord. Much surprised at the scarcity of May birds, and as usual the amateurs have been fooled by recording every species (and) taking no account of numbers. Allen and I agree that we have never done worse in the Valley on May 9. In all 72 species . . .

L.G.

May 12, 1853

This, too, is the era of the bobolink, now, when apple trees are ready to burst into bloom.

H.D.T.

May 13, 1948

(Thurs.) Out to Sudbury Valley (7:00 a.m.)—9:00; in woods around Hurd's Pond, Wayland, until 12:30. Mostly raining, sometimes hard, 8:00 a.m. on; wind light s.e. - n.e.

Greatest flight of warblers I ever saw in the Sudbury Valley!; birds remarkably active, but little or no song from transients; very difficult hard slogging! Pick up remarkable list of 84 species!

13. Black & White Warbler   25 + 1
14. Golden-winged W.   12, sev. females
15. Nashville W.   10
16. Parula W.   10
17. Magnolia W.   10
18. Black-thr. Blue W.   3

19. Myrtle W. <u>250</u> +
20. Black-thr. Green W.   15
21. Chestnut-sided W.   <u>25</u> +
22. <u>Cerulean Warbler</u> 1 female adult—bluish above, pure white below type found on 3 different occasions.
23. Yellow Palm W.   2
24. Water-thrush 2
25. <u>Hooded Warbler</u>   1 female in heart of maple swamp.
26. <u>Wilson's Warbler</u>   1
27. Canada Warbler   12
28. Redstart   20

L.G.

May 14, 1853

Suddenly there start up from the riverside at the entrance of Fair Haven Pond, scared by our sail, two great blue herons,—slate-colored rather,—slowly flapping and undulating, their projecting breastbones very visible,—or is it possibly their neck bent back?—their legs stuck out straight behind. Getting higher by their flight, they straight come back to reconnoiter us . . .

H.D.T.

May 16, 1900

Clear with light s.w. wind falling calm before sunset. 54-73 degrees, a <u>perfect</u> May day.

Today must surely mark the high-water level of the extraordinary migration of May 1900. I do not think that I have ever before seen so many small birds in one day in the Concord woods. They have been so evenly distributed that it really makes not the slightest difference where one looked for them. As the eye ranged through the trees and undergrowth it was constantly arrested by the fluttering of wings or the flashing reds, yellows, blacks and grays of the innumerable warblers that were busily engaged in gleaning for food among the branches . . .

W.B.

May 17, 1912

It is my custom when sleeping in the cabin to open a little window by the side of my bed when I first awake to enjoy the early morning singing without the trouble of rising at an inconvenient hour. When I did so at 5.30 this morning, my ears were at once greeted by an unfamiliar song, very loud and incisive and evidently coming from near at hand. Scarce more than half awake, I listened to it for ten minutes or more without getting any clue as to the identity of its author. It seemed most like the song of a Swamp Sparrow, but was louder and the notes were firmer and less run together.

At length I arose, dressed hurriedly, and then looked out towards the river through the partly opened door of the cabin. Almost at once a flash of bright yellow caught my eye. The next instant a male Prothonotary Warbler hopped out on a leafless branch over the path directly in front of the cabin and sang and sang in full voice within ten yards of me. Shortly after this, he flew to a birch stump and closely inspected several crevices and two discolored dark spots that looked like holes, as if he were in search of a nesting-place.

Gilbert came out and disturbed him a little later when he flew up the hillside and flitted about in the tops of some oaks, singing a few times. We followed, but lost him on the crest of the hill. Fifteen minutes after this I heard his loud song coming from the flooded thicket of maples, willows and button bushes across the river opposite Birch Gate. I went there in a canoe after breakfast (about 7.30) and found him still in full song and flitting about among the bushes. Presently a Wilson's Black-cap attacked and chased him about when he fled to the line of large maples a little further up the river. Then I saw him creeping about and clinging to their trunks just above the water. Dexter and I looked for him there and elsewhere along the river, but in vain, from 1 to 2 P.M. I tried again just before sunset, but without avail . . .

W.B.

May 18, 1860

The night-warbler is a powerful singer for so small a bird. It launches into the air above the forest, or over some hollow or open space in the woods, and challenges the attention of the woods by its rapid and impetuous warble, and then drops down swiftly into the tree-tops like a performer withdrawing behind the scenes, and he is very lucky who detects where it alights.

H.D.T.

May 19, 1856

Hear and see a yellow-throated vireo, which methinks I have heard before. Going and coming, he is in the top of the same swamp white oak and singing indolently, *ullia-eelya*, and sometimes varied to *eelyee*.

H.D.T.

May 23, 1854

Saw in Dakin's land, near the road, at the bend of the river, fifty-nine bank swallows' holes in a small upright bank within a space of twenty by one and a half feet (in the middle), part above and part below the sand-line. This would give over a hundred birds to this bank. They continually circling about over the meadow and river in front, often in pairs, one pursuing the other, and filling the air with their twittering.

H.D.T.

May 28, 1906

With few exceptions, the finest singers among our local birds are at their best, musically, for only a very short period—seldom, indeed, exceeding a week and sometimes not more than three or four days. This is true of the Robin, Wood Thrush, Bluebird, Catbird, Thrasher, Grosbeak, Bobolink, and Vesper and Field Sparrow. Many of the second-class performers, such as the Song Sparrow, Towhee, Tanager, and all the Vireos, sing equally well for several weeks in succession. Already the best of the spring singing is over. The Bluebirds have been wholly silent for weeks; the Thrashers, Grosbeaks, Bobolinks, Vesper Sparrows, and Field Sparrows have nearly ceased the rapturous singing of a week or two ago. The Cat-birds are still in nearly full song. The Wood Thrushes have become almost wholly silent. Strange to say, I have heard only one Veery sing this spring although the birds are as numerous here as usual and I am constantly in or near their haunts.

W.B.

The Nesting Season

In one sense, the nesting season is the most important time in the annual cycle of birdlife. As the birds move onto their nesting grounds, a complex array of conditions and events will determine whether or not the season is a successful one. When the circumstances are right the birds define territory, pair, mate, build a nest, lay eggs and raise young. The continuation of the species is assured.

For the naturalist, this is a time to take a longer and more in-depth look at the lives of our summer residents. Events seem less rushed than during the migrations. We can watch in detail the marvelous behaviors that will lead to each re-creation. In fact, we can become familiar with specific birds—the pair of cuckoos in the abandoned orchard or the house wren family in the fence post. There will be tragedies—the raided nest and the abandoned chick, but there will be many more successes.

Although a majority of the nesting activity in our area occurs between mid-May and mid-July, in actuality the season extends from late February, when the Great Horned Owls begin incubating eggs, until late August when many goldfinches are still raising young. While some of our nesting species are permanent residents, many more are here only briefly and spend a majority of their year in southern North America, Central America or South America. The nesting season provides an opportunity to enjoy and learn about a wonderful variety of bird species.

June 2, 1945

Saturday afternoon and evening. Went out to do the Wayland area.

Mr. Griscom drove Margaret Argue, Maurice and me and when we arrived there we met Frances Burnett, Martin Karplus and Cora Wellman . . . It rained hard most of the time. Mr. Griscom's car went into a ditch (the whole rear end) but we all pushed and finally got it out. We had dinner at the Swedish Coffee Shop. Very good. Then we drove all through the Sudbury Valley and listened for night calls of the birds. We heard 2 American Bitterns, a Least Bittern, Virginia Rails, both Yellow-billed (3) and Black-billed Cuckoos (9), 3 Screech Owls, 2 Barred Owls, 1 Common Nighthawk, Long-billed Marsh Wrens and 2 Short-billed Marsh Wrens, Wood Thrush and Veery, a half-hearted Ovenbird, a plaintive Field Sparrow and several Swamp Sparrows.

This was my first night-birding and we all enjoyed it very much. We ended our trip at the Griscom home in Cambridge and had a hot toddy, cocoa, soup and crackers. The Argues lived in Boston on Boylston Street and we stayed overnight with them as there wasn't any public transportation to Wollaston at the hour of 3:30 A.M.

R.P.E.

June 4, 1955

Wayland—Wash Brook marsh with Bill Drury, Rick Miller, and Don Kennedy trying to band Marsh Wrens.

Several Gallinules, a Yellow-throated Vireo singing in Heard's Pond woods (well seen), and a female Orchard Oriole on nest at Sears'.

The grand prize was a Sora's nest with three eggs—adult well seen, gave both the "whinny" and single female call note . . . also a grunting note.

Several Virginia Rails calling and an American Bittern's nest. A Great Blue Heron and two Green Herons flew over.

No Sharp-tailed Sparrows!

A.H.M.

June 5, 1979

I went back to Dakin Road (Sudbury) to watch the Bobolinks that were in the field on Sunday. There are at least two pairs and I watched them courting for about thirty minutes. Although I am not sure where the act begins or finishes, at one point the male and the female were approximately one hundred yards apart and perched at the top of trees. The female "begins" (by) flying rather rapidly past the perched male. He soon gives chase and often pulls to within one foot of her as the pace quickens. The pair goes into a steep climb with the female in the lead. As they start down, the male pulls out and flies over the open meadow, wings fluttering, legs dragging, and all the while calling his variable song. Soon both birds are on their separate perches again . . .

R.K.W.

June 9, 1857

In the sprout-land beyond the red huckleberry, an indigo-bird, which *chips* about me as if it had a nest there. This is a splendid and marked bird, high-colored as is the tanager, looking strange in this latitude. Glowing indigo. It flits from top of one bush to another, chirping as if anxious. Wilson says it sings, not like most other birds in the morning and evening chiefly, but also in the middle of the day. In this I notice it is like the tanager, the other fiery-plumaged bird. They seem to love the heat. It probably had its nest in one of those bushes.

H.D.T.

June 11, 1851

The whip-poor-will suggests how wide asunder are the woods and the town. Its note is very rarely heard by those who live on the street, and then it is thought to be of ill omen. Only the dwellers of the outskirts of the village hear it occasionally. It sometimes comes into their yards. But go into the woods on a warm night at this season, and it is the prevailing sound. I hear now five or six at once . . .

H.D.T.

June 11, 1898

At intervals through the forenoon, as I was at work near the cabin, I heard the *ki-ki-ki-ki, ki-kèer* of the mysterious "Kicker" coming from near the middle of the Great Meadow. Soon after sunset the bird began again and sang steadily up to the time I went to bed. He had apparently come a little nearer, although as I walked along the river path to Bensen's Landing I could with difficulty catch the first "chur" or *keer* of his song. What was my surprise, therefore, to find that as I continued on my walk and turned my back to the river, I carried the sound of the *ki, ki* far inland without seeming to lose much of its strength. I actually heard it with reasonable distinctness when I reached Davis's Hill, although this point is nearly half-a-mile distant from Bensen's Landing, with a pine-covered range of hills between . . .

W.B.

June 13, 1851

I heard partridges drumming to-night as late as 9 o'clock. What singularly space penetrating and filling sound! Why am I never nearer to its source?

H.D.T.

June 14, 1851

As I proceed along the back road I hear the lark still singing in the meadow, and the bobolink, and the gold robin on the elms, and the swallows twittering about the barns. A small bird chasing a crow high in the air, who is going home at night. All nature is in an expectant attitude. Before Goodwin's house, at the opening of the Sudbury road, the swallows are diving at a tortoise-shell cat, who curvets and frisks rather awkwardly, as if she did not know whether to be scared or not. And now, having proceeded a little way down this road, the sun having buried himself in the low cloud in the west and hung out his crimson curtains, I hear, while sitting by the wall, the sound of the stakedriver at a distance,—like that made by a man pumping in a neighboring farm-yard, watering his cattle, or like chopping wood before his door on a frosty morning, and I can imagine like driving a stake in a meadow. The pumper . . .

H.D.T.

June 14, 1859

The rose-breasted grosbeak is common now in the Flint's Pond woods. It is not at all shy, and our richest singer, perhaps, after the wood thrush. The rhythm is very like that of the tanager, but the strain is perfectly clear and sweet. One sits on the bare dead twig of a chestnut, high over the road, at Gourgas Wood, and over my head, and sings clear and loud at regular intervals,—the strain about ten or fifteen seconds long, rising and swelling to the end, with various modulations. Another, singing in emulation, regularly answers it, alternating with it, from a distance, at least a quarter of a mile off. It sings thus long at a time, and I leave it singing there, regardless of me.

H.D.T.

June 16, 1853

Coming down the river, heard opposite the new houses, where I stopped to pluck the tall grass, a sound as of young blackbirds amid the button-bushes. After a long while gazing, standing on the roots of the button-bushes, I detected a couple of meadow or mud hens (*Rallus virginianus*) gliding about under the button-bushes over the mud and through the shallow water, and uttering a squeaking or squawking note, as if they had a nest there or young. Bodies about the size of a robin; short tail; wings and tail white edged; bill about one and a half inches long, orange beneath in one bird; brown deepening into black spots above; turtle-dove color on breasts and beneath; ashy about eyes and cheeks. Seemed not willing to fly, and for a long time unwilling to pass me, because it must come near to keep under the button-bushes.

H.D.T.

June 16, 1886

Clear and cold with strong S.W. wind.

Starting at about ten o'clock I drove to Wayland and stabling my horse, took a boat on the river, and went in search of Marsh Wrens. For a space of half-a-mile or more they were rather numerous in the tall blue joint grass along the river bank; but I was disappointed in the colony nevertheless for I did not hear or see over twenty males in all, and could find no eggs, although they were certainly breeding.

Besides Marsh Wrens there were numerous Redwings and almost equally numerous Rails. It was useless to try to flush the latter for the grass was higher than my head; but every few minutes I heard their cries in various directions. The majority were Rallus virginianus. In fact I heard only one Carolina Rail.

In a bed of especially rank blue joint, I flushed a male Least Bittern. It rose several rods off and flew as many more in the sluggish Rail-like way which causes it to resemble a Rail much more than a Heron.

On the river I also heard a few Swamp Sparrows, and at about 3 P.M. a Bittern began "borring" and kept it up for an hour or more at intervals.

The road to Wayland is generally wild and little settled. I saw and heard many birds both going and returning; but nothing of much interest except Henslow's Sparrows, of which I heard no less than six different males on the way home . . .

W.B.

June 17, 1952

Wayland: with Dr. (H.E.) Maynard and Henry Parker—on the river in the canoe. Pelham Island Bridge to Harry Rice's farm. Two-thirds of the way up Wash Brook.

Wash Brook Marsh covered with film of DDT spray and thousands of dead fingerling pickerel. Also many horn-pout, a few sun-fish, and several small bass. A few fish up to 6-7 inches long. So many in places that the smell was terrific . . .

A.H.M.

June 17, 1978

Rifle Range trail this a.m.—of interest: ovenbird and black and white warbler singing (no sight of either bird). I also walked down to the Ruffed Grouse's drumming log in the Red Maple swamp.

Mattison's woods off Williams Road produced a pair of towhees scolding and singing. Also a black-billed cuckoo that I watched for a full ten minutes in the old orchard. The bird repeatedly uttered a low, rattling cluck as apparently I was too close to fledged young or a nest.

This p.m. I went back over to the Mattison Farm along the field edge (and) watched a female yellow warbler feeding fledged young. The young bird had no tail feathers but was able to fly several feet at a time. It was mostly brownish with some yellow on the rump. The adults were very agitated at my presence and the female came within three feet of my head chipping constantly. I also found an indigo bunting's nest in

briars and grass on the north side of the pond. The nest consisted mainly of coarse straw and was eighteen inches above the ground. It held
four newly hatched chicks and while I was at the nest, both parents
were close by . . .

I was unable to locate the whip-poor-will that has been present for the
past four days. On the north side of our hill I did find a wood pewee nest
on the horizontal limb of an oak tree. The male was singing near the nest
and at one point I watched him go to the nest and "swivel" around
several times as if shaping the structure . . .

R.K.W.

June 21, 1892

Sitting in my canoe writing these lines in the shade, the sun having sunk
behind the tops of the pines to the West. Great sulphurous white clouds
floating in a pale blue sky. The foliage of the white maples along the
river and the edges of the meadow tossing in the wind, looking thin and
dishevelled and showing the whitish under surfaces of the leaves. About
the canoe the water is covered thickly with the floating leaves of the
pond lily, floating heart, Marsilea and the long-leaved Polygonum. Further inshore rise the erect stems of Pontederia, each bearing at its top the
single large, lance-shaped, oily green leaf. They form a fine belt of green
above the margin of the placid stream. Still further in, marking the
beginning of the real land, are young maples, willows, alders and birches
overrun with grape-vines and green briars with here and there a tuft of
cinnamon ferns and one large cluster of wild roses in full bloom. Behind
and above this lower wall of diversified but generally tender green
foliage rise the somber pines and tall old oaks for which the hill is
famous.

A Pine Warbler is singing in the pines, a Veery, Cat-bird, Chestnut-
sided Warbler and Maryland Yellow-throat in the thickets near the
water. From across the river come the rich *gurgle-eea* or *per-dle-ea* of
the Red-wing and further off rises the tinkling melody of the Bobolink.
Now I hear a Robin singing and next a Grosbeak. A Wood Pewee gives
a low, sad *pee-e-e* among the pines. Now a Black-billed Cuckoo in the
extreme distance and a Song Sparrow near at hand. The fine bass voice
of the Bull Frog rolls out over the water from his reedy covert at frequent intervals, and the Green Frog answers with a *tung, tung* on his
own tight harp strings . . .

W.B.

June 21, 1898

Without question, the Wilson's Thrushes furnish the finest as well as the
most copious music of any of the birds which breed in this immediate
region. As twilight was falling this evening they made the woods fairly
ring with their clear, flute-like voices. They are almost as numerous in
the pine woods on the tops and sides of the hills as in the swamps. There
is less inequality and variability in the songs of different individuals than
is the case with the Hermit and Wood Thrushes, but yet there are some
birds whose voices are finer and clearer and whose notes are more varied
and intricate than those of the common run.

I do not remember to have noted before that the Wilson's Thrush, like
so many other birds, has favorite singing perches to which it resorts day

after day. This, at least, is true of a bird which is breeding somewhere near the east end of Ball's Hill and which sings every evening in the large red oak on the edge of Holden's Meadow, sitting invariably not only on the same branch but actually on *the same twig* and always facing towards the northwest.

W.B.

June 27, 1852

I meet the partridge with her brood in the woods, a perfect little hen. She spreads her tail into a fan and beats the ground with her wings fearlessly within a few feet of me, to attract my attention while her young disperse; but they keep up a faint, wiry kind of peep, which betrays them, while she mews and squeaks as if giving them directions.

H.D.T.

July 3, 1860

Looked for the marsh hawk's nest (of June 16th) in the Great Meadows. It was in the very midst of the sweet-gale (which is three feet high), occupying an opening only a foot or two across. We had much difficulty in finding it again, but at last nearly stumbled on to a young hawk. There was one as big as my fist, resting on the bare, flat nest in the sun, with a great head, staring eyes, and open gaping or panting mouth, yet mere down, grayish-white down, as yet; but I detected another which had crawled a foot one side amid the bushes for shade or safety, more than half as large again, with small feathers and a yet more angry, hawk-like look. How naturally anger sits on the young hawk's head! It was 3:30 P.M., and the old birds were gone and saw us not. Meanwhile their callow young lie panting under the sweet-gale and rose bushes in the swamp, waiting for their parents to fetch them food.

H.D.T.

July 16, 1949

Sudbury Valley—alone by canoe starting from the old Stone Bridge at 7:30 a.m.

Least Bittern: just below the Route 20 bridge I flushed a bird from the water's edge. It dropped into the rushes . . . so I landed to see if I could find a nest. I flushed the original bird again and searched briefly for a nest but without success. However, as I turned around to return to the canoe, there within three feet of me was a young bittern "frozen" in the rushes.

The bird was fully fledged and in beautiful plumage—just a trace of down on the top of the head.

I evidently surprised the bird in the act of turning around, because one foot was facing forward while the other was twisted around and facing backward . . .

About fifty yards downstream I flushed another bird from the water's edge—all three birds appeared to be young of the year, very brightly plumaged (and) probably just out of the nest . . .

A.H.M.

Late Summer Wanderings and the Fall Migration

Like all the seasons of the birding year, the fall migration overlaps both the end of the earlier (nesting) cycle and the beginning of the later (winter) cycle. Even before the goldfinches begin to nest, shorebirds returning from their Arctic nesting grounds are seen in the Valley. While ducklings are still in tow and marsh wrens are feeding young, the first post-breeding wanderers appear on the meadows. This is a protracted season stretching from July through November.

The fall migration is perhaps the most rewarding time of the birding year. Just the normal movement of herons, waterfowl, raptors, shorebirds and songbirds provides a rich diversity for the attentive observer. Add to this the surprising list of vagrants and you have a season with almost unlimited possibilities.

This is indeed a time of plenty. Bird numbers are at yearly highs and many species join in large flocks to migrate and to feed. At staging areas like Great Meadows, there is often both quantity and diversity. From August through October there is a continuous procession of birds into and out of our area.

There are days in the fall when the light is soft and the birds wonderous. The naturalist knows that he is in the right place, and for the moment, all is right with the world.

July, 1979

I brought an old scythe, well sharpened, to the corridor of grass. I had not swung a scythe since I was a boy, but in the midst of the wild meadow, it all came back, and for a time I saw the ranks of the high grasses falling beneath my regular sweeps. As I stood leaning on my scythe, looking at the fallen grass, looking at the dragonflies that hovered and darted and alighted around me, looking at the drifting clouds overhead, my eyes seeing what in this very place perhaps other eyes had seen in another age, it was as though three centuries had not passed.

E.W.T.

(The next four entries are Allen Morgan's account of the 1948 heron invasion.)

July 24, 1948

Wayland over the weekend. In a letter to me last weekend L. G. reported 54 egrets in the Valley. Cloudy 'til about 10 a.m. then a beautiful day.

Met the Argues and Emerys in their car and we went around together in the a.m. All herons between Sherman's Bridge and Stone Bridge, i.e., opposite Rice's.

Great Blue Heron	7 (probably more)
American Egret	37 maximum exact count
Little Blue Heron	49 maximum exact count
Green Heron	3

Snowy Egret	1 well seen in flight
Black-crowned Night Heron	85 (estimate)
Yellow-crowned Night Heron	1 immature well seen

What a day!! Spent the afternoon in the Chamberlain's canoe . . . Proceeding carefully upstream I tried to get an exact count but ended up with a total of only 86 . . . One half hour later, after picking up Virginia Armstrong and Stanwood Ball, Jr. and Sr., in the canoe in the middle of the marsh, we counted 109 white herons in the air at once. There were only two adult Little Blue Herons.

More egrets and little blues than I ever saw in Florida or the Carolinas. Absolutely phenomenal invasion.

July 31, 1948

Home over the weekend to Wayland. Out in the morning around Wayland and up to the Marlboro Sewage Beds. Hot and hazy—muggy—s.w. wind.

Great Blue Heron	6
American Egret	63
Little Blue Heron	52 (exact count), ±20
Green Heron	3
Black-crowned Night Heron	25 +
Yellow-crowned Night Heron	1 immature

My counts of white herons are accurate. The count of little blues was made by wading . . . I counted 51 in one area and estimated that there were at least 20 more scattered over the marsh. One little blue at sewage beds.

At dusk the herons took off and flew to (a) roosting spot in the direction of Concord.

August 7, 1948

Wayland—beautiful day—wind n.w., clear with scattered clouds in the afternoon, temperature 58 degrees at 7 a.m.

First thing in the morning I took an exact census of the Pelham Island Road Route . . .

Then to Rice's to look at herons . . . I waded out into the marsh and got a snowy!

Canoe from Heard's Pond to the Chamberlain's (Sherman's Bridge) . . . started at 1:45, arrived at Chamberlain's about 6:00 p.m. . . . several stops to wade, one to talk to Mr. Griscom, Mr. Cottrell, a Mrs. Parker, and another gentleman who were wading in the great marshes between Stone and Sherman bridges counting white herons.

After supper out to try and find where the herons are roosting. Met Davis Crompton and Mr. Crouse and went on with them in their car.

Located the Little Blue Heron roost in some big oaks . . . counted 151 little blues and 2 American Egrets—only 1 adult little blue.

Beautiful sight. No sign of American Egret roost but they were flying further east toward Concord center . . .

August 8, 1948

Up at 5 a.m. and to the top of Round Hill just w. of Sherman's Bridge by 5:25. At 5:30 the first flock of little blues left the roost and flew right past me (s.w.) to the marsh. One hundred and ten estimated in first flock, then in quick succession flocks of 24, 2 and 30 at 5:35, 19 right after them, then the last 4 stragglers at 5:45—total of 189!!!

Crossing Sherman's Bridge at about 6:20 a flock of 33 American Egrets going upriver.

Beautiful day—50 degrees at 6:30, clear . . .

A.H.M.

August 2, 1856

A green bittern comes, noiselessly flapping, with stealthy and inquisitive looking to this side the stream and then that, thirty feet above the water. This antediluvian bird, creature of the night, is a fit emblem of a dead stream like this Musketicook. This especially is a bird of the river. There is a sympathy between its sluggish flight and the sluggish flow of the stream . . .

H.D.T.

August 2, 1978

Met Dick Forster at the sewer beds at noon. There was a good variety of shorebirds on hand including: 1 Stilt Sandpiper, 2 Short-billed Dowitchers, 4 Least Sandpipers, 5 Solitary Sandpipers, 7 Pectoral Sandpipers, 7 Killdeer, 17 Lesser Yellowlegs, and 28 Semipalmated Sandpipers.

We walked around the north pool at Great Meadows and counted 1 Great Egret, 4 Great Blue Herons, a Gallinule with at least 2 young, 1 Greater Yellowlegs, 6 Semipalmated Plovers and numerous Woodies.

R.K.W.

August 19, 1858

We scare up a stake-driver several times. The blue heron has within a week reappeared in our meadows, and the stake-driver begins to be seen more oftener, and as early as the 5th I noticed young summer ducks about; the same of hawks, owls, etc. This occurs as soon as the young birds can take care of themselves, and some appear to be very early on the return southward, with the very earliest prospect of fall. Such birds are not only more abundant but, methinks, more at leisure now, having reared their family, and perhaps they are less shy. Yes, bitterns are more frequently seen now to lift themselves from amid the pontederia or flags, and take their sluggish flight to a new resting place . . .

H.D.T.

August 25, 1982

At Great Meadows this a.m. in rain. A single Whimbrel (last record for the Valley was in September of 1902). I picked it up over the south pool and watched it moving north, across the dike and on to the north end of the north pool. It called several times and receiving no response (and finding no place to alight) moved on . . .

R.K.W.

September 7, 1892

A few minutes after the sun had set this evening, while I was standing at my landing watching the gorgeous coloring of the clouds in the west, a Night-hawk suddenly appeared nearly overhead, coming from behind me. Turning quickly I perceived no less than thirteen others, all flying in the same direction (towards the west). The flock, for such it evidently was, spread over the whole width (150 yards) of the river and its numbers kept at approximately even distances from one another and flew with a steadiness and directness very unusual to these erratic creatures, although the temptation to turn aside to seize some tempting insect prize was not always resisted and once one chased another back and forth, pursuer and pursued doubling and twisting like startled Snipe. One bird uttered several times a flat, squeaky *paap*. Evidently these Night-hawks were migrating and following the course of the river. I watched until dark but they did not come back as feeding birds would surely have done. They were followed after a brief interval by a smaller flock of nine individuals.

W.B.

September 9, 1906

Brilliantly clear and delightfully warm with light, dry west wind.

A bird wave of unusual magnitude rolled down from the north last night. It is interesting that it should have come during the warmest night of a warm, stormless week and that the birds should have all pushed on after but a single day of rest. That they did this seems to me nearly certain, for the air was evidently filled with them from shortly after dark this evening until about 9:30 P.M. After that, their chirping became less and less frequent and when I went to bed at 11 P.M. it had almost totally ceased. Mr. Forbush, who slept in the open air, tells me that he woke at 2 A.M. and listened for some time without hearing a single call. The bulk of the flight lasted only about two hours, or from 7.30 to 9.30 P.M.

During the day, the woods and thickets were alive with warblers most of which were Black-polls. Of these there were about 25 at Ball's Hill and not less than fifty in the Birch Field. In the latter place H. W. Henshaw and I found among the Black-polls an Orange Crowned Warbler, a Bay-breast, 3 or 4 Black-throated Greens, and a Redstart. At Ball's Hill I noted a Nashville Warbler, a Connecticut Warbler and several Redstarts . . .

W.B.

September 14, 1859.

They are catching pigeons nowadays. Coombs has a stand west of Nut Meadow, and he says that he has just shot fourteen hawks there, which were after the pigeons.

H.D.T.

September 14, 1938

Wayland and Sudbury Meadows; 5.30—sunset; Cottrells and J. R. Ideal conditions as at Wenham Swamp; walk way out over meadows; many remarkable Shore-bird records locally in past month.

1. Mallard 20
2. Black Duck 700
3. Baldpate 1
4. Green-winged Teal 50
5. Blue-winged Teal 100
6. Pintail 20
7. Wood Duck 1
8. Bittern 5
9. Great Blue Heron 1
10. Egret 2
11. Little Blue Heron 9
12. Green Heron 3
13. Night Heron 6
14. Snipe
15. Pectoral Sandpiper 6
16. Semipalmated Sandpiper 25
17. Lesser Yellowlegs 50+ (Solitary Sandpiper 5)
18. Greater Yellowlegs 10
19. Killdeer 1
20. Marsh Hawk 1

R. J. Eaton has 400 Blue-winged Teal at Great Meadows, Concord; Least Bittern in both places; Knot, Stilt Sandpiper and Golden Plover (28) last Friday among special birds.

L.G.

September 21, 1952

Wayland—landbirding right around the house. Not as many warblers as yesterday but quality of course much better. One flock came through the backyard (and) had all the fancy birds.

Towhees, several Tanagers, Catbirds, etc. but nothing special in the way of landbirds except for 5-6 Olive-backed Thrushes.

Warblers

Black and White	1	Cape May	1
Nashville	1	Blackpoll	30
Parula	8-10	Prairie	1
Magnolia	1	Orange-crowned - my first ever	
Tennessee	1	in S.V.	1
Myrtle	15	Ovenbird	1
Black-throated Green	2	Yellowthroat	3
Blackburnian	3	Redstart	2

Several Juncos and a Red-breasted Nuthatch calling from the grove of Norway Spruces next door.

A terrific day—the olive-backs around most of the day, bobolinks and bluebirds overhead constantly.

A.H.M.

Fall

The loon comes in the fall to sail and bathe in the pond, making the woods ring with its wild laughter in the early morning, at rumor of whose arrival all Concord sportsmen are on the alert, in gigs, on foot, two by two, three by three, with patent rifles, patches, conical balls, spy-glass or open hole over the barrel . . .

H.D.T.

October 1, 1982
Fairhaven Cliffs at mid-day (12:40-1:50).

Two enjoyable scenes of hawks—a Sharp-shinned Hawk came around the cliffs from the N.W., went into a wing tuck position and dove to the river bottom! Another pair of birds turned out to be an American Kestrel and a Sharp-shinned Hawk—the Sharpie chased the Kestrel along the tree tops and there was much evasive tumbling and veering as the birds moved quickly through . . .

At the Great Meadows later in the afternoon . . . a Peregrine Falcon. Martha McClellan picked up the bird just over the cattails at the northern end. Moving across the pool it remained low, beating steadily and powerfully in a slightly rolling flight. Surprisingly, the falcon did not seem to startle the ducks directly below it, although at one point it swooped down within two feet of several widgeon. The bird crossed the dike about 20-30 feet above us and continued steadily south across the pool and up over the tree-line towards the sewer beds.

R.K.W.

1916
The south-bound flight of Blue Jays coming from further north was exceptionally heavy this year. Beginning about the middle of September, if not somewhat earlier, it reached its maximum height between the 20th and 25th of the month, when, for three or four days in succession, the loud-voiced birds were so abundant and widespread that one could not go anywhere without having them almost constantly in sight and hearing. During this period they especially frequented our deciduous woods through which they roamed ceaselessly in small, scattered flocks, seeking food which must have been rather scarce for most of the trees had suffered too severely from the attacks of gyspy moth and other larvae to mature fruit of any kind. There was, however, a single large scarlet oak, growing in an open field, which having been protected by spraying bore a plentiful crop of acorns and on these the Jays feasted as long as they lasted, holding them underfoot while hammering them with their beaks to remove the outer shell and thronging the tree at all hours of the day. I saw them thus engaged for the last time on October 6. During the remainder of that month it was unusual to note more than two or three daily and almost none remained after November 1.

W.B.

October 4, 1879
A clear, soft, mellow autumn day of the very rarest type. For the past week the weather has been continuously warm and, at times, almost sultry, but this morning there was that crisp, sparkling quality in the air that is peculiar to autumn . . .

The woods were simply glorious. They may now be said to be at the height of their autumnal coloring. The deep wine-color of the oaks, the pure gold of the hickories, the olive-purple or rich salmon of the ash trees, mingling with the countless shades of green, scarlet and crimson of many other species made up a whole of wonderful beauty. But few leaves have as yet fallen, tho' the first rain-storm will nearly strip the earlier trees, as their foliage is fully ripened . . . .

It is in the broad woodlands that one may see October to the best advantage. There is a ripe golden quality there that I miss in the open places where the grass is still as green as in midsummer. The dropping of acorns and chestnuts is an ever-present sound there and the squirrels are all busy with their annual harvest. Their chatter, chuckling, and rustle keep perfect accord with the screaming of the Blue Jays and the ceaseless whisper of the falling leaves.

W.B.

October 5, 1851

I hear the red-wing blackbirds by the riverside again, as if it were a new spring. They appear to have come to bid farewell . . .

H.D.T.

October 8, 1892

There was a Great Blue Heron on the river this morning, a noble bird but in the young plumage. I started him first from Wild Rice Island and drove him before me to the Holt where he doubled back. Once he alighted on the top of the bank where the ground was hard and smooth and the grass short. Over this he moved with slow, stately steps towards the water's edge, occasionally stopping and stretching up his long neck to look at me. He reminded me of a Sandhill Crane which he resembled not only in motions but in his nearly uniform bluish ashy coloring— between the blue of the river and sky, as Thoreau says. Poor bird! I hope that a shot which I heard at this bend an hour later did not end his career but I saw nothing of him when I paddled homeward this evening. There is a skeleton of one of these Herons under the pines on Davis's Hill—shot there by some camper, I suppose, and left to rot where it fell! It is indeed sad to think that the few large birds which still visit this river are so mercilessly pursued and wantonly slain. This fine creature, for instance, one evening adding life and interest to the meadows by its picturesque form and imposing flight, the next a heap of carrion and dishevelled feathers under the pines where it met its fate!

W.B.

October 10, 1851

The air this morning is full of bluebirds, and again it is spring . . .

As I stood amid the witch-hazels near Flint's Pond, a flock of a dozen chickadees came flitting and singing about me with great ado—a most cheering and enlivening sound,—with incessant *day-day-day* and a fine wiry strain betweenwhiles, flitting ever nearer and nearer and nearer, inquisitively, till the boldest was within five feet of me; then suddenly, their curiosity satiated, they flit by degrees further away and disappear, and I hear with regret their retreating *day-day-days*.

H.D.T.

October 17, 1894

At about 2 P.M. . . .as I was dining in the cabin with some friends, we heard the call of a Greater Yellow-leg repeated several times in quick succession and evidently very near. Rushing out, I saw the bird coming directly towards me from the opposite side of the river, flying low and, as it struck me, rather feebly. Greatly to my surprise it plunged directly into the belt of bushes (alders, cornels, willows, etc.) which borders the shore in front and a little to the east of the cabin. I now for the first time saw that it was pursued by a Duck Hawk which must have been twenty or thirty yards behind the Yellow-leg when the latter reached the shore and which, on losing sight of its quarry, bounded straight upward to a height of forty feet or more and then poised for several seconds, beating its wings rapidly and incessantly, bending its head downward like a hovering Sparrow Hawk or Kingfisher as it closely scanned the thicket beneath. I had a fine view of it—it was within thirty yards or less—and made it out to be a young male. Presently it saw me and, turning, flew off towards the southwest over Great Meadow . . .

W.B.

October 18, 1981

At Nine Acre Corner this a.m. (7:15-9:30) to do a Sparrow Survey.

Results:

Savannah Sparrow	52	Lincoln's Sparrow	2
Dark-eyed Junco	19	Swamp Sparrow	23
White-crowned Sparrow	3	Song Sparrow	28
White-throated Sparrow	10		

Also several Ruby-crowned Kinglets and Bobolinks.

R.K.W.

October 19, 1856

The fall, now and for some weeks, is the time for flocks of sparrows of various kinds flitting from bush to bush and tree to tree.

H.D.T.

October 27, 1891

Concord—Cloudy with light rain during most of the morning. After-noon gloomy with high N.W. wind and falling temperature.

Spent the forenoon and part of this afternoon in the house writing. At 4 P.M. started down river in the Buttrick's boat. The pickerel weed and other semi-aquatic vegetation has been killed by the late frosts and the river now has a forlorn aspect which was heightened, this afternoon, by the almost total absence of bird life. I saw only a few Tree Sparrow in the bushes along the stream and heard nothing but the occasional scream of a distant Jay or the cawing of a Crow.

On reaching Hunt's Pond I landed on the south bank of the river and entered the Great Meadows. Four Marsh Hawks were beating about at one time, in fact for several minutes they kept close together and ap-peared to be hunting in company. Three of them were old males, the fourth a brown bird, apparently a female. I squatted in the grass for a moment and when one of the males came within hearing, squeaked like a mouse. The bird at once turned and came directly towards me, flying very swiftly just above the grass, and in a perfectly straight line. He was within sixty or seventy yards when he discovered either me or my dog and sheered off. Perhaps I moved my head a little. At all events the bird, beyond question, discovered at the last moment that something was wrong. I suppose these Marsh Hawks were northern birds migrating together. They remained in the meadow until it was too dark to see them, however.

The middle of the meadow proved to be in excellent condition for Snipe but I could start none although I went over the ground, with the help of the dog, rather thoroughly. There were more Titlarks than I remember to have ever seen here before—over one hundred certainly. They were scattered about and rose singly and in small parties collecting into one great flock and whirling about for many minutes before alighting . . .

W.B.

The Winter Season

Ludlow Griscom noted that the winter season is a "variable proposition in New England." This is particularly true in the Valley. From mid-November through late February, there are times when the barren landscape appears devoid of all birdlife. A trip through the Valley in late January may produce nothing more than a flock of crows, a few ducks, a sparrow or two and perhaps a Red-tailed Hawk. On the other hand, the winter scene is normally not so bleak. There can be a surprising diversity of bird species. In flight years, nuthatches, shrikes, grosbeaks, crossbills, redpolls and siskins may complement the more usual winter populations. The increase in bird feeding over the past quarter century has also served to enhance the local winter birdlife. With the advent of the season's first snows, many species begin to concentrate around feeding stations and other natural food sources. Stragglers and vagrants also play a part in the winter season. While the occasional wood duck, heron, oriole or towhee may linger, it is the expectation of a rarer visitor—a Varied Thrush, a Bohemian Waxwing, or even a Hawk Owl, that keeps our hopes alive.

Although the winter season often seems to overstay its welcome, it also provides some unmatched moments. At times the snow-covered land sparkles in the crisp, bright light and furnishes the perfect setting for brightly colored birds.

November 1, 1855

This is the aspect under which the Musketaquid might be represented at this season: a long, smooth lake, reflecting the bare willows and buttonbushes, the stubble, and the wool-grass on its tussock, a muskrat-cabin or two conspicuous on its margin amid the unsightly tops of pontederia, and a bittern disappearing on undulating wing around a bend.

H.D.T.

November 4, 1902

The country is now almost completely drained of its summer resident birds and early and mid-autumn migrants. The last Bluebirds, Robins and Rusty Blackbirds departed nearly a week ago and the Titlarks have nearly all gone. I saw a stray Chippy on the 2nd and heard a Yellow-rump to-day. Chickadees, Kinglets, Creepers, Crows, Jays, Goldfinches, and Partridges with an occasional Downy or Hairy Woodpecker or Flicker are now about the only birds I am likely to find in these woods during a morning's tramp. I saw the first Tree Sparrow to-day. The Juncos have nearly all gone . . .

W.B.

November 11, 1952

Sudbury Valley—Heard's Pond and Broad Meadow.

First day of the duck hunting season. Four autos at the south end of Heard's—ten hunters in the marsh. As far as we could tell they had killed only four birds—2 blacks and 2 woods.

At Stone Bridge were 14 cars—Broad Meadows crawling with hunters afoot and in boats. We talked to only a few and saw 11 dead Blacks, 2 Pintails, 3 Green-winged Teal, 2 Wood Ducks, and 1 Mallard.

A.H.M.

November 20, 1857

The hardy tree sparrow has taken the place of the chipping and song sparrow, so much like the former that most do not know it is another. His faint lisping chip will keep our spirits up till another spring.

H.D.T.

November 21, 1896

Despite the depressing and very disagreeable weather I saw some interesting birds and one that was actually new to me. I took it to be a Gray Gyrfalcon. It was of about the size and general coloring of an immature female Gos-hawk but it had the long, sharp-pointed Falcon wings and it flapped them as a Duck Hawk does with a continuous, rapid, vibrating movement. My experience with this bird was as follows:

I was paddling past the Buttricks' on my way down river at about 8:30 A.M. when I noticed three tame Pigeons flying high in air towards Mr. Derby's barn, coming from the direction of the town. Just as they were passing over the Buttricks' house, the Falcon appeared about one hundred yards off and coming directly towards them. They turned back at once, at the same time separating. The Falcon chose a white bird (the other two were blue) and pursued it hotly.

The Pigeon made scarce one hundred yards before it was overtaken but it had been rising the while and when its pursuer came up he was a yard or more under it. Wheeling with easy grace and bounding upward twenty feet or more with a single effort of his powerful wings he got well above his prey and shot towards it down a steep incline. "Poor bird, your fate is sealed!" I said to myself as, with the field glass pressed to my eyes, I gazed breathelessly, watching the Falcon's belly with the full expectation of seeing him extend his legs to seize his victim. To my surprise, he did not show so much as the tips of his talons but, on overtaking the Pigeon, he seemed to strike it with his breast, half upsetting it and sending it a yard or more downward before it could recover its equilibrium. Then, setting his wings, he scaled off swiftly towards the Estabrook woods—the direction whence he had first come—leaving the Pigeon to pursue its way unmolested, at a lower level, to its home in the Derby barn.

W.B.

December 2, 1981

Cold gray day. Walked at Meadows from Borden entrance. Thin layer of ice over all with an occasional open place. Great Blue Heron hunched at edge of one of Borden's (ponds).   Watched a Canada Goose trying to get up onto ice—but each attempt only broke the ice—finally it found a firmer place and scrambled up—wagged wings and honked.

At the upper pool—central area somewhat ice free so a pond within a pond was formed. V's of geese were coming in, groups of 25-30, from the east, but some from across the river. The open water was more and more crowded—also occupied by mallards, coot, a few blacks (and) several shovelers. The coot were often scrambling, in the water or on the ice, wings going up almost vertically over their back. The geese had to land on the ice since there was no room in the water. Feet out, tail down and used as a brake, as they scraped along the ice. They could come to a full stop in a foot or two. Much vocalizing, shifting of places and the smaller ducks seeming to fit themselves in the "cracks". About 20 minutes later it was much quieter—many were asleep and there was far less swimming around. The whole congregation must have fit in a 30 x 50 yard area . . .

E.B.P.

December 12, 1858

P.M.—Upriver on ice to Fair Haven Hill.

Crossing the fields west of our Texas house, I see an immense flock of snow buntings, I think the largest that I ever saw. There must be a thousand or two at least. There is but three inches, at most, of crusted and dry frozen snow, and they are running amid the weeds which rise above it.

H.D.T.

December 14, 1982

John Hines called last night to say that there was a Snowy Owl at Great Meadows. He had flushed it out of the marsh and it had flown onto the ice of the south pool and remained there at least until sunset. I went to the Meadows three times today but did not see the owl.

On my third trip, at sunset, the wind had died down and it was a joy to be on the frozen meadows. The straw yellow of the grasses and reeds, the soft white of the snow, and the lavender-pink of the clouds all gained intensity in the crisp, sparkling air . . .

R.K.W.

December 19, 1854

Off Clamshell I heard and saw a large flock of *Fringilla linaria* over the meadow . . . Suddenly they turn aside in their flight and dash across the river to a large white birch fifteen rods off, which plainly they had distinguished so far. I afterward saw many more in the Potter swamp up the river. They were commonly brown or dusky above, streaked with yellowish white or ash, and more or less white or ash beneath. Most had a crimson crown or frontlet, and a few a crimson neck and breast, very handsome. Some with a bright-crimson crown and clear-white breasts. I suspect that these were young males. They keep up an incessant twittering, varied from time to time with some mewing notes, and occasionally, for some unknown reason, they will all suddenly dash away with that universal loud note (twitter) like a bag of nuts. They are busily clustered in the tops of the birches, picking the seeds out of the catkins, and sustain themselves in all kinds of attitudes, sometimes head downwards, while about this. Common as they are now, and were winter before last, I saw none last winter.

H.D.T.

December 20, 1958

Allen Morgan kindly takes me and Edith out to Concord, Massachusetts, and shows me <u>Hawk Owl</u> 1. Here for a week on corner of Lowell Road and the next side street. It has been living near a lumber yard where it gets plenty of mice and is obviously well fed. It was seen today by a large crowd of birders and photographed in color with movies. Its long tail was broken and frayed and when it flew it reminded me of a Sharp-shinned Hawk always flying very low, and rising to a conspicuous perch. It has been seen to catch mice several times. Last seen in Concord in 1907. And last reported in the States in 1927. I now believe that I have glimpsed it twice in Essex Co. but I'm glad I waited for a really good view.

L.G.

December 24, 1851

Saw some pine grosbeaks, magnificent winter birds, among the weeds and on the apple trees; like large catbirds at a distance, but, nearer at hand, some of them, when they flit by, are seen to have gorgeous heads, breasts, and rumps (?), with red or crimson reflections, more beautiful than a steady bright red would be. The note I heard, a rather faint and innocent whistle of two bars.

H.D.T.

December 30, 1891

I rowed up to Bird's Nest Island and back without seeing a living thing save a fine Gray Squirrel which was in the old hemlocks. He passed rapidly from one tree to the next, running out over the branches and leaping from one to another, finally climbing the main trunk of a large tree and concealing himself among the foliage.

On returning to the Buttricks' and just as I was stepping out of the canoe at the landing, I happened to look up and at once perceived a Shrike—a large, brown bird—sitting on the top of a bean pole on the hill-side above. His attitude was easy, yet erect, and he did not move in the least for several seconds. Then, after a flirt of the tail, he took wing and crossed the river in long, graceful undulations finally passing out of sight beyond Honeysuckle Island. The Shrike is perhaps as characteristic a feature of our winter landscape as is any other bird, not even excepting the Snow Bunting. There is a certain easy nonchalance in his bearing which assures one of the bird's hardiness and indifference to cold or hunger.

W.B.

January 7, 1851

The snow is sixteen inches deep at least, but it is a mild and genial afternoon, as if it were the beginning of a January thaw. Take away the snow and it would not be winter but like many days in the fall. The birds acknowledge the difference in the air; the jays are more noisy, and the chickadees are oftener heard.

H.D.T.

January 12, 1979

15 degrees, clear, no snow cover—full moon.

At 3:30 P.M. I drove over to the Pantry Brook area behind Round Hill where a Short-eared Owl was reported on the Concord Christmas Count. The river is frozen and two dogs were using it as a pathway. A

Northern Shrike was in the treetops beside the river. I saw 2 Downy Woodpeckers and I believe I heard a Flicker. There were a few Tree Sparrows about and a flock of 15 Canada Geese flew overhead.

This area is a beautiful one. The marsh still and golden, the bare deciduous trees dark and sinewy, and clusters of pines providing more solid shapes and color . . .

A White-throated Sparrow was in the yard today.

R.K.W.

January 14, 1953
Heavy thaw Jan. 11-16.

P.M. Sudbury Valley tour with A. Cottrell, 3:00 - 4:30, mild.

1. Black Duck   1
2. Golden-eye   15
3. Mourning Dove   7
4. Hairy Woodpecker   1
5. Downy Woodpecker   7
6. Blue Jay   several
7. Crow   40
8. Starling   10
9. House Sparrow
10. Meadowlark   17
11. Redwinged Blackbird   1
12. Junco   10
13. Tree Sparrow   200 + 1 + 4 + 1
14. Song Sparrow   1
    Red-shouldered Hawk   1 adult (Cottrell)

Bald Eagle, Goshawk and Swamp Sparrow reported (in) next two days!

L.G.

January 15, 1978

On Sunday, Ken Hamilton and I decided to spend a leisurely morning birding from our homes in Framingham to Great Meadows National Wildlife Refuge in Concord. Due to the general paucity of land birds this Winter our expectations were low. Ken arrived at my house and announced that he had seen 32 pine grosbeaks at his home. At our first stop along the Sudbury River in Framingham we observed a rosy male pine grosbeak in a maple tree. At our next stop on the river a flock of 43 pine grosbeaks alighted in the top of two large white pines. Yet another stop along the river produced a lone pine grosbeak calling overhead. Our next stop along the river was on the Framingham-Wayland line at a location known locally as Stone Bridge. Our initial count here was about 45 individuals but the group was continually being augmented by birds seemingly coming out of the sky and by others moving through the treetops. The primary food crop of these birds was ash seeds and by the time we left the flock had swelled to a total of 85 birds.

Our route roughly paralleled the Wayland-Sudbury line finally arriving at Concord Center and then on to Great Meadows. Group counts along the route were 3, 18 and 55 individuals. By now it was becoming evident that inordinate numbers of pine grosbeaks were present. While watching 4 soras at the sewer outlet we noted 9 pine grosbeaks and several white-winged crossbills flying overhead. On Old Bedford Road in Concord we noted 23 pine grosbeaks feeding on spruce cones and ash seeds.

Our last flock of pine grosbeaks was seen on Route 20 in Wayland where the Sudbury River crosses under the road. This group, numbering 120 individuals, fed predominantly on ash seeds . . .

I called Dick Walton in Concord to advise him of the numbers of pine grosbeaks present. In several hours of searching Concord and Sudbury he counted 179 pine grosbeaks, making the combined count for the morning a total of 569 individuals. Counts of this magnitude aren't often recorded in Massachusetts. Epic flights have occurred in the winters of 1892-93, 1930-31, 1951-52, and 1961-62 . . .

R.A.F.

January 17, 1982

Today we did the first Sudbury River Valley Winter Raptor Census. Ken Hamilton, Dick Forster, Don and Lillian Stokes, and Fid and I did the field work. We covered the area of the Sudbury River Valley floodplain between the Massachusetts Turnpike and Route 225 in Carlisle. The weather was brutal— -1 to +5 degrees with N.W. winds at 20 m.p.h.

Results: Red-tailed Hawk   17
        Rough-legged Hawk   1
        American Kestrel   4

R.K.W.

January 22, 1950

Wayland—Snowing hard in the morning (2-3 inches), stopping by noon but still overcast, 26 degrees. From Saxonville to Stone Bridge in the morning—river open but marshes and Heard's Pond frozen. In the afternoon for an hour at the Chamberlain's (Sherman Bridge) . . .

List:

Pied-billed Grebe	1	Crow	50
Black Duck	5	Chickadee	10
Red-tailed Hawk	1 adult	White-breasted Nuthatch	1
Pheasant	1	Carolina Wren	1
Herring Gull	1	Starling	9
Mourning Dove	6	Junco	11
Hairy Woodpecker	1	Tree Sparrow	50
Downy Woodpecker	2	Song Sparrow	2
Blue Jay	15		

Carolina Wren has been coming to the Chamberlain's feeder for the past two months . . . a beautiful bird eating peanut hearts and suet.

A.H.M.

PART III—THE CHECKLIST

The goals of the checklist are:

    I To indicate the present status of the various bird species in our area.

    II To indicate the relative abundance of each species.

    III To define periods of general occurrence.

    IV To provide examples of typical as well as atypical records.

    V To provide remarks of historical or biological interest.

I   The classifications and criteria for the status are as follows:

    A. Permanent Residents - Species that are present throughout the year - not necessarily the same individuals (e.g. Song Sparrow).

    B. Summer Residents - Species that nest in our area (e.g. Brown Thrasher).

    C. Winter Residents - Species whose normal winter range includes the Sudbury River Valley but do not breed there (e.g. American Tree Sparrow).

    D. Winter Visitor (often with Irregular) - Species that occur in winter but do so irregularly and are not to be expected annually (e.g. Common Redpoll).

    E. Migrant - Species whose normal migration route or post-breeding dispersal area includes the Sudbury River Valley (e.g. Rusty Blackbird and Song Sparrow).

    F. Vagrant - Species not normally found in the Sudbury River Valley, and whose habitat preferences and migration patterns make them unlikely visitors (e.g. Red-breasted Merganser).

II   The terms of relative abundance are defined according to the frequency with which an observer may expect to encounter each species. These characterizations assume that the appropriate season and habitat are taken into consideration. A familiarity with the habitat requirements of the various species and the locales of the Valley will help the observer (see Appendix A). For example - American Wigeon is abundant in fall at Great Meadows while at the same time it would be relatively uncommon elsewhere in the Valley. On the other hand, Blackpoll Warbler, during its fall migration period in our area, can be relatively abundant throughout the woodlands of the Valley.

When used in reference to breeding status, these terms indicate relative abundance only.

    A. Abundant - should be seen on 90% of the field trips.

    B. Common - should be seen on 75% of the field trips.

    C. Fairly Common - should be noted on 50% of the field trips.

D. Uncommon - should be expected on less than 25% of the field trips.

E. Markedly Uncommon - will probably be recorded each season but will be missed by many observers.

F. Rare - may not be recorded each year.

G. Very Rare - an active observer may not record these species during a decade of field work.

III Periods of general occurrence indicate when a species may be expected in our area. They are guidelines by which to measure normal and/or unexpected observations.

IV Records cited include dates, observers, number of birds reported, and locations (see below for explanation of location-symbol abbreviations). The date format is month/day(s)/year. The day category may include a range and in some cases uses "thru" - meaning throughout the month. The observer's name is given in parentheses. The boldface numerals indicate the number of birds reported. A lower case "b" means that the bird(s) was banded. In describing the occurrence of certain species, I have used the "From . . . to . . ." format. This presents the earliest and latest seasonal records for the relevant species. Records given without any location symbol refer to sightings published as "SV" (Sudbury Valley) or to combined sightings from more than one place in the Valley.

Unless otherwise stated, field records cited are ones which are usual with regards to date and number. I have also included some minimum and maximum as well as early and late data for comparative purposes.

The records cover the period between 1949 (following the publication of Ludlow Griscom's *The Birds of Concord*) and October 1, 1984. A majority of records are taken from the following sources:

1949-1960	*Records of New England Birds*
1961-1963	Reporting Slips*
1964-1968	*Records of New England Birds*
1969-1972	Reporting Slips
1973-1984	*Bird Observer of Eastern Massachusetts*
1960-1983	Concord Christmas Count published in *American Birds,* formerly *Audubon Field Notes*

*During the years 1961-1963 and 1969-1972 there was no "official" publication of local field notes comparable to the *Records of New England Birds* or *Bird Observer of Eastern Massachusetts*. There are, however, reporting slips for these periods. These represent the observations of many field workers throughout the state and are compiled by month and species. Normally, an editorial group would review this data and select certain reports for publication. For the years when no publication was undertaken, the researcher must review all the slips and select those pertinent to his area of study. These reporting slips are stored at the Massachusetts Audubon Society in Lincoln.

In most cases the records are of observations made in either Concord, Sudbury or Wayland. The Concord Christmas Count, however, includes part or all of sixteen different towns. As such, this exceeds the boundaries of the Sudbury River Valley. Data cited from this source is meant to provide a general indication of the early winter status for the relevant species (see Appendix B). I have also used some unpublished data from various observers who have done field work in the Valley.

V   The remarks section is used to provide historical, biological and environmental information pertinent to some of the species. A list of the sources and references which are footnoted follows the species accounts.

The following list of abbreviations are used throughout the species accounts.

ad.	adult bird
b	indicates bird(s) was banded
BBC	Brookline Bird Club
C	Concord
CCC	Concord Christmas Count
Cl	Carlisle
et al.	indicates a multi-observer record where a reporter or leader is listed but not the other observers (e.g. Smith *et al.)*
GM	Great Meadows (only that portion of the wildlife refuge west of Monsen Road in Concord)
HP	Heard's Pond (Wayland)
imm.	immature bird
L	Lincoln
NAC	Nine Acre Corner (Concord)
RH	Round Hill (Sudbury)
S	Sudbury
SSBC	South Shore Bird Club
TBOC	*The Birds of Concord* - Griscom (1949)
vo	various observers
W	Wayland
*	indicates an introduced species when preceding species name

Red-throated Loon - *Gavia stellata*

Status: A very rare migrant.

Records: 4/15/56 (Wellman) **1** GM
11/9/77 (Walton) **2** GM
11/16/79 (Forster) **1** HP
12/20/74 (N. Clayton) **1** C

Remarks: Ludlow Griscom published one record in *The Birds of Concord (TBOC)*—11/11/1858.

Common Loon - *Gavia immer*

Status: A markedly uncommon migrant.

Occurrence: Although some migrants are on the move by the end of March, a majority of spring records for the Valley occur in the latter half of April and the first half of May—4/19/81 (Forster) **2** W.

Fall migrants are recorded most often in September—maxima: 9/28/64 (J. Baird) **5** S. There is one November record—11/22/64 (Mazzarese) **4** GM.

Remarks: Nineteenth century records indicate that this species sometimes tarried on local ponds. Most present-day records are of migrants in flight, although inclement weather will occasionally cause birds to put down.

Pied-billed Grebe - *Podilymbus podiceps*

Status: An uncommon migrant.

Occurrence: This grebe species moves into the Valley in March when sightings of one to three birds are normal. Spring migrants are usually present through May—maxima: 3/29/55 (Stackpole) **8**.

In fall, small groups (3 to 7 birds) congregate at Great Meadows during September and October—maxima: 10/11/65 (Eldred) **11** GM. Most individuals leave before late November.

On at least two occasions (1954-1955 and 1955-1956) Pied-billed Grebe have overwintered in the Valley.

Remarks: Formerly a summer resident and common migrant, the last confirmed nesting for this species was in 1963. Griscom estimated that there were six nesting pairs in Wayland and Sudbury between 1932 and 1940.

Horned Grebe - *Podiceps auritus*

Status: A rare migrant.

Occurrence: This grebe departs from its coastal wintering grounds in late March and April and is seen in the Valley when spring rains retard its flight to the Canadian interior. Birds in both winter plumage—3/21/82 (Hines) **1** C and breeding plumage occur—maxima: 4/24/66 (Leverett) **4** GM.

The fall flight has resulted in three October records in our area—maxima: 10/9/57 (Stackpole) **3** W.

Remarks: Griscom published four records. There have been thirteen published records since 1949: eight in spring, three in fall, and two in winter.

Red-necked Grebe - *Podiceps grisegena*

Status: A very rare migrant.

Records: The last record for the Valley was in March of 1939. See *TBOC* for three spring, one fall and two mid-winter records.

Leach's Storm-Petrel - *Oceanodroma leucorhoa*

Status: A vagrant.

Records: None in the last eighty years. See *TBOC* for two fall hurricane-related records.

Northern Gannet - *Sula bassanus*†

Status: A vagrant.

Records: 10/6/64 (Garrey) **1** GM
10/16/80 (Holland) **1** GM

†formerly Gannet

Great Cormorant - *Phalacrocorax carbo*

Status: A vagrant.

Records: 2/1/56 (Gleason) **1**
10/9/83 (Walton) **1** GM

Remarks: This cormorant species is increasing along our coast in winter. Records from just outside the Valley (Cambridge Resevoir) and inland in general are being reported with increasing frequency. (1)

Double-crested Cormorant - *Phalacrocorax auritus*

Status: A fairly common migrant.

Occurrence: Since 1949, all spring records for this species have occurred during April and the first half of May—maxima: 4/21/80 (Forster) **180** W.

Most fall migrants are observed between mid-September and mid-October—maxima: 10/3/54 (Morgan) **150** W.

Remarks: Although single birds occasionally alight, this species is normally observed overhead in flocks of ten to fifty birds.

The Double-crested Cormorant has experienced a population boom in the last decade and will, no doubt, become an even more common migrant over our area. (1)

American Bittern - *Botaurus lentiginosus*

Status: An uncommon migrant and summer resident.

Occurrence: Resident birds move into our area in early April—rarely in March. The "pumping" of the American Bittern can be heard along the river marshes through June, particularly at Great Meadows and Wash Brook—5/14/60 (Seamans) **5** C.

Because of this species' secretive nature and habitat preference, breeding is difficult to confirm. Individuals are, however, seen regularly throughout the summer months—maxima: 7/16/49 (Morgan) **13**.

This species is frequently recorded at Great Meadows throughout September. A few fall migrants remain through October and into November during mild years.

A straggler was recorded on the 1979 Concord Christmas Count (CCC)—12/29/79 (Walton) **1** GM. (2)

Remarks: Morgan's count cited here has not been matched in the last several decades. There may well have been a decline of this species locally over this period.

Least Bittern - *Ixobrychus exilis*

Stauts: A markedly uncommon summer resident.

Occurrence: Although there are two late April records, the normal arrival time of residents is mid-May—5/23/82 (Walton) **2** W.

This species is even more secretive than the American Bittern but males can sometimes be heard "cooing" at Wash Brook and Great Meadows marshes through June. Nesting begins in the latter half of May. Forster observed a female carrying nesting material at Wash Brook on 5/19/79.

Post-breeding birds are observed from July through August with some individuals lingering into September. There are two October records—lastest: 10/30/49 (Wellman) **1** GM.

Remarks: Griscom estimated that three pairs were nesting in the Heard's Pond area in 1945. There are probably no more than three pairs in the entire Valley at the present time. (2)

Great Blue Heron - *Ardea herodias*

Status: An uncommon spring and common fall migrant with a few individuals remaining into winter.

Occurrence: The first spring migrants arrive in late March—3/27/55 (Mason) **3**. A majority of spring records are in April—4/3/82 (Walton) **4** C. By mid-May most migrants have passed through.

Post-breeding groups appear by mid-July and reach a peak in late August or September—maxima: August/September 1978 (v.o.) **25** GM.

It is not unusual for individuals to remain into November and a few stragglers have overwintered in this area.

Remarks: The increased protection afforded this species (once a favorite target of indiscriminate hunters) has resulted in a dramatic increase in the numbers of Great Blue Herons nesting in Massachusetts. While no rookeries have yet been found in the Valley, there is an established colony in Westboro.

Griscom noted an increase in this species in the period between 1930 and 1948. This trend has continued and records of Great Blue Heron in our area, particularly in the fall, reflect this change.

Great Egret - *Casmerodius albus*

Status: A markedly uncommon migrant.

Occurrence: A majority of spring records occur in the April to May period—maxima: 4/21/76 (Walton) **9** GM.

Sightings of post-breeding individuals at such places as Great Meadows, Nine Acre Corner and Heard's Pond occur in July and August—7/19/80 (Stymeist) **2** GM. There are two reports of birds remaining into September.

Remarks: In July of 1948 there was a general irruption of the southern herons into New England. This species reached maximum numbers in the Valley in early August when over one hundred birds were recorded by Griscom and Morgan. (2, 3)

Snowy Egret - *Egretta thula*

Status: A rare spring and uncommon fall migrant.

Occurrence: The three spring records for the Valley are between mid-April and late May—5/30/78 (Forster) **1** NAC.

In late summer and early fall most sightings are of one or two individuals, usually immatures, that are part of the post-breeding movement—7/26/80 (BBC) **2** GM.

Remarks: This heron was extremely rare in Massachusetts before the 1948 flight. The first record for the Valley occurred that year—7/21/48 (Elkins, Griscom, Wellman) **1** ad. S.

Little Blue Heron - *Egretta caerulea*

Status: A rare migrant.

Occurrence: There are four spring records: one in April—4/15/82 (Hines) **1** W and three in the latter part of May—5/19/83 (Walton) **1** GM.

Most present-day records are of single birds observed during their post-breeding movements in July and August—7/3/76 (Forster) **1** GM. There are two records of birds remaining into early September.

Remarks: This species was well represented in the 1948 heron flight. Morgan counted 189 birds leaving the roost near Round Hill on August 8, 1948.

At the present time this species is truly rare in the Valley. Observers should exercise care in identifying immatures of this species because of the difficulties in distinguishing these from immature Snowy Egrets. (2,3)

Cattle Egret - *Bubulcus ibis*

Status: A rare migrant.

Occurrence: The occurrence of this species in the Valley has an interesting history. The first specimen of Cattle Egret for North America was collected in Wayland on April 23, 1952 by Drury, Morgan and Stackpole. Six years then elapsed without any Valley records for Cattle Egret.

Between 1959 and 1968 this species was recorded in seven out of ten years and always in late April or early May—maxima: 5/1/62 (Ernst) **17** W. Two spring records of single birds occurred in 1983—both in May—5/19/83 (Bertrand) **1** C.

In 1977, 1979, and 1980 three late fall records occurred—all between early October and late November—10/16/80 (Forster) **1** W.

Remarks: The late fall records cited above most likely indicate reverse migration. (2,4)

Green-backed Heron - *Butorides striatus*†

Status: An uncommon spring migrant and summer resident; common at times in late summer.

Occurrence: The spring movement of this heron into our area occurs during the latter half of April and throughout May—5/6/53 (Morgan) **1** W.

Residents begin nesting in the latter half of May and continue through June. Local family groups are observed in July—7/13/81 (Hines) **6** W.

Towards the end of July numbers begin to build as summer residents are joined by a few migrants at the larger marshes. The movement southward begins to peak in early September and most birds have moved out by mid-October. Seamans recorded an exceptionally large count at a relatively late date—maxima: 10/5/56 (Seamans) **23** C.

A remarkable record for this species was the 1979 CCC sighting—12/29/79 (Forster) **1** S. This bird was still present in the new year—1/1/80. (2)

†formerly Green Heron

Black-crowned Night-Heron - *Nycticorax nycticorax*†

Status: A rare spring migrant and common mid-summer wanderer and fall migrant.

Occurrence: Although spring migrants were regularly reported in the early 1950s—3/29/50 (deWindt) **3** S, there have been only four spring reports since 1967—5/27/82 (Hines) **1** W.

All present-day records are of post-breeding wanderers or non-breeding birds. Both adult and immature birds appear along the river and at Great Meadows during the first part of July—7/15/78 (Walton) **4** GM. Numbers build through the first half of September—maxima: 8/10/74 (Merriman) **42** GM. A few stragglers remain into October—latest: 10/16/57 (Sommers) **1** GM.

Remarks: The author finds no convincing proof that this species has nested in the Valley in the last fifty years. Reports of birds in May and June probably represent non-breeding subadults. (2)

†formerly Black-crowned Night Heron

Yellow-crowned Night-Heron - *Nycticorax violaceus*†

Status: A vagrant.

Records: Only seven records for the Valley since 1949. From 4/17/54 (Wiggin) **1** S to 8/16/60 (King) **1** GM; the most recent—5/26/83 (Barton) **1** GM.

Remarks: Three birds of this species accompanied the 1948 heron flight. (2,3)

†formerly Yellow-crowned Night Heron

Glossy Ibis - *Plegadis falcinellus*

Status: A rare migrant.

Occurrence: Griscom refers to a Glossy Ibis shot in 1850 and presented to the Boston Society of Natural History. The next record for the Valley was in 1952—4/23/52 (Morgan, Drury, Stackpole) **1** W. Since that time there have been twenty records.

A majority of the records have been from late April to early June—maxima: 4/29/81 (Heil) **9** C.

There are three records for August and September—maxima: August, 1975 (v.o.) **7** GM.

Remarks: The first nesting record for Massachusetts was in 1974. By the late 1970s close to one hundred and fifty pairs were breeding in the state. As the Glossy Ibis has increased its status as a summer resident along the coast, the number of local sightings has increased. (2)

Tundra Swan - *Cygnus columbianus*†

Status: A vagrant.

Records: 4/3/63 (Holden) **3** C
11/9-30/59 (Holderby) **1** GM

Remarks: These are the only two records for the Valley. Most records for this species in Massachusetts occur between November and January. Spring records are unusual.

† formerly Whistling Swan

*Mute Swan - *Cygnus olor*

Status: A rare wanderer into our area.

Records: Recorded in seven of the past twenty years—from April to December; the most recent: 5/6/83 (Gregory) **1** W. Between 1973 and 1975 a single bird and then a pair took up residence at Great Meadows. Nesting did not occur as the pair was relocated by refuge personnel.

Remarks: This European species was introduced in the Long Island, New York area in the nineteenth century. Feral birds have gradually extended their range to include the Atlantic coastal region from New Jersey to s.e. Massachusetts. (5)

Greater White-fronted Goose - *Anser albifrons*

Status: A vagrant.

Records: 3/9/57 (Coolidge, Wiggin) **3** HP

Remarks: Because of the popularity of waterfowl, every vagrant waterfowl that turns up is the subject of debate. The pessimists feel that the burden of proof that the bird(s) is indeed wild, and not an escapee, lies with the optimists who tend to regard every exotic record as a "legitimate" wild bird. In the present instance, the date of the record cited here is consistent with the beginning of the spring migration of this species from its Mexican and Gulf Coast wintering grounds to breeding territories in Alaska. (6)

Snow Goose - *Chen caerulescens*

Status: An uncommon migrant.

Occurrence: Of the twenty-one spring records for the Valley, all but two occur between mid-March and mid-April—maxima: 3/29/81 (Forster, Walton) **817** S&C.

A majority of fall reports occur between October and early December—maxima: 10/9/83 (Hines) **82** W.

Remarks: As a migrant, this species is probably more common than the record indicates (38 reports in the Valley since 1949). Although a few individuals put down in agricultural areas, like the one at Nine Acre Corner, the bulk of migrants pass overhead unnoticed.

Brant - *Branta bernicla*

Status: A vagrant.

Records: 5/29/50 (Morgan) **1** W
10/19/66 (Bart) **19** GM
10/25/50 (Morgan) **1** W

Remarks: This species is a regular migrant and winter resident on the coast of Massachusetts. With the exception of annual sightings of migrants passing over the Connecticut River Valley, it is rarely seen inland.

Canada Goose - *Branta canadensis*

Status: A small resident population, a common spring and abundant fall migrant, and a variable wintering population.

Occurrence: Spring migrants move in and out between early March and late April—3/28/65 (Mazzarese) **232** HP.

Some local pairs have young by the second week of May.

By mid-August the fall build-up begins and may continue through October—10/14/74 (Hinds) **900** GM.

The Canada Goose population in our area may be abundant through November and even into December if ponds and rivers remain open. A major freeze is necessary to move this reluctant migrant farther south. A small population always seems to find some open water along the rivers and with the slightest thaw more birds move into our area from the southern perimeter.

Remarks: Valley records for this species become much more numerous after 1960 and indicate a growing population in the last quarter century. Most resident birds are probably the offspring of feral geese whose ancestors were kept by local citizens as live decoy groups. (7)

Wood Duck - *Aix sponsa*

Status: A common migrant and summer resident.

Occurrence: The first spring migrants arrive in early March with the flight continuing through mid-April—3/21/82 (Hines) **19** W.

Resident females are incubating eggs as early as April and ducklings are reported from late May through June.

Local groups begin to congregate at places like Great Meadows by the latter part of July. These are joined by migrants and peak numbers occur in late September or October—9/17/81 (Gove) **150** GM; 10/22/83 (Forster) **90** HP.

By mid-November most birds have departed although stragglers are sometimes reported throughout the winter.

Remarks: The Valley is noted for its Wood Duck population. This is due, in part, to the nesting box program of the Massachusetts Division of Fisheries and Wildlife. Begun in the late 1940s, this program supplements scarce natural nesting cavities with nesting boxes. An indication of the success of this program is the 1982 nesting data. Over 275 preflight young were banded in the Concord-Carlisle area. Successful nesting occurred in approximately 85% of the 124 nesting boxes. (pers. comm. H.W. Heusmann) (8)

Green-winged Teal - *Anas crecca*

Status: A common spring and abundant fall migrant; an irregular and local summer resident.

Occurrence: In spring the first migrants appear in early March with numbers building into the first half of April—3/18/79 (Roberts) **15** W; n.axima: 4/13/52 (Morgan) **100**.

A few scattered pairs nest irregularly along the river meadows and have been observed with young towards the end of June.

Local birds and a few migrants begin moving into staging areas like Great Meadows during September. These groups are eventually joined by an influx of migrants and peak numbers are reached in October or early November—10/14/74 (Hinds) **250** GM.

Of the two teal species in our area, this is the hardier one; stragglers are reported to December but rarely later.

Remarks: The first Massachusetts' nesting record for Green-winged Teal occurred in the Valley—6/28/40 (Morgan) female and young W.

American Black Duck - *Anas rubripes*†

Status: A common spring and fall migrant; an uncommon summer resident.

Occurrence: The black duck is one of the earliest spring migrants. In mild winters a few birds will arrive by late February. During March and early April the migration continues—3/4/53 (Morgan) **100**.

Residents are nesting by late April or early May and family groups are observed in June.

Local groups begin to congregate by late July and are joined by migrants in the staging areas during August and September. The black duck is a hardy species and many birds remain in our area through October and November—11/7/82 (Walton) **59** GM.

A few individuals will overwinter in mild years.

Remarks: There is concern over the future of this species. The black duck, a favorite of sportsmen and the most representative "wild duck" of New England and the Northeast, is threatened Its population has been declining for a number of years—apparently a result of habitat loss, competition with Mallards and over-hunting. Interestingly enough, the competition with Mallards is not solely exclusionary but often involves hybridization as is attested to by the many hybrids noted in our area. (9)

†formerly Black Duck

Mallard - *Anas platyrhynchos*

Status: Permanent resident with several different populations involved: a permanent resident group, a local population that remains in our area most of the year but disperses to other areas during prolonged freezes, and a smaller migrant population.

Occurrence: Local numbers show a definite increase during March and April—4/3/82 (Walton) **29** C.

Resident birds nest during April and May.

Fall concentrations which include local residents and migrants build at staging areas from August through October—10/14/74 (Hinds) **200** GM.

A resident population is usually present throughout the winter around farm ponds, agricultural drainage ditches and melt spots along the rivers.

Remarks: The Mallard is the "wild duck" of the Midwestern and Western states. Many eastern birds are feral and it is normally impossible to distinguish the wild and the "escaped" populations.

Northern Pintail - *Anas acuta†*

Status: A fairly common spring and fall migrant.

Occurrence: This species is an early migrant arriving rarely in late February—2/26/82 (Hines) **2** W, and more generally in early March—maxima: 3/11/79 (Forster) **42** C. The spring flight has usually gone through by mid-April.

The first southbound migrants normally arrive around mid-September and numbers build through October and early November—maxima: 10/27/74 (Alden) **30** C. Since 1949, there have been seven reports of pintails in December.

Remarks: Although nesting was suspected by Griscom in 1948 there have been no substantiating records.

†formerly Pintail

Blue-winged Teal - *Anas discors*

Status: A fairly common spring and common fall migrant; an uncommon and local summer resident.

Occurrence: The first spring migrants arrive during the latter half of March and the flight continues through April—maxima: 4/8/62 (Sweet) **100** C; 4/19/67 (Petersen) **17** GM.

Suspected nesting pairs are observed in cattail and tussock marsh areas in June.

Fall migrants join local groups at staging areas beginning in August and numbers build through September—9/17/81 (Gove) **60** GM; maxima: 9/25/55 (Stackpole, Morgan) **600**. Most Blue-winged Teal have left our area by mid-October.

There are ten November records. One Blue-winged Teal was recorded on the CCC in 1974. Another straggler was recorded in January—1/12/78 (Walton) **1** GM.

Northern Shoveler - *Anas clypeata*

Status: An uncommon spring and fairly common fall migrant.

Occurrence: Of twenty-two spring records, six occur in March —earliest: 3/6/51 (Wellman) **1** W, sixteen in April—4/12/75 (Cassie) **4** GM, and two in May.

Fall migrants occur most often from late September to mid-November—maxima: 11/4/78 (Gove) **26** GM. There are four reports for December and no January records.

Remarks: Both Griscom and Bailey* mention the Concord area as a good location to find this species. Records for the past ten years indicate that the local occurrence of Northern Shoveler is increasing.

*Wallace Bailey - author of *Birds in Massachusetts: When and Where to Find Them* (1955)

Gadwall - *Anas strepera*

Status: An uncommon spring and a fairly common fall migrant; an irregular and local summer resident.

Occurrence: Spring migrants generally occur during the latter half of March and throughout April—3/24/79 (O. Komar) **14** GM.

Nesting Gadwall and adults with broods were observed in 1965. However, there have been no recent confirmed nestings.

Fall groups are regularly recorded from late September through late November—11/22/78 (Walton) **55** GM. There are several December and January records.

Remarks: Gadwall were introduced to the ponds just south of Great Meadows (Monsen Road Unit) by R. Borden in August of 1957 (27 young) and again in April of 1965 (50 birds). Seven pairs from the 1965 release nested on Borden's ponds and produced six broods with a total of forty-three ducklings. (10)

Prior to Borden's releases in 1957 and 1965, Gadwall were markedly uncommon in the Valley (*TBOC*); it is tempting to relate the increase of Gadwall in the fall to those releases.

Eurasian Wigeon - *Anas penelope*†

Status: A vagrant.

Records: 3/20/82 (Walton) to 4/19/82 (Hines) **1** W.
4/2/55 (Stackpole, Morgan) **1** W
10/5/74 (Claflin) **1** GM
10/30/71 (Seron) **1** GM
10/30/72 (Seamans) **1** GM

Remarks: Most reports of this European visitor are from coastal locations. Thus, the number of records for the Valley is notable.

† formerly European Wigeon

American Wigeon - *Anas americana*

Status: A fairly common spring and abundant fall migrant.

Occurrence: The first spring migrants arrive around mid-March —3/13/76 (Forster) **12** S, and the flight continues through April -rarely into May—maxima: 4/5/64 (Seamans) **30** GM.

The fall movement begins in mid-September and numbers build through October when this species is abundant at Great Meadows—maxima: 10/12/58 (Forster) **1250** GM; 10/28/81 (Hines) **295** GM.

December stragglers have been recorded at least ten times and in one instance a large flock was still present at a late date—12/2/70 (Forster) **275** GM. The CCC provides a January record—1/2/83 (Hines) **1** W.

Canvasback - *Aythya valisineria*

Status: A rare migrant.

Occurrence: Nine spring records from mid-March to the latter part of April—3/30/82 (Hines) **2** HP; maxima: 4/2/68 (Garrey) **6** NAC.

Five fall records in late October. In 1955, a high count was made in November—maxima: 11/17/55 (Garrey, Stackpole) **22**, and three birds lingered into the latter half of December.

Remarks: The October through December period of 1955 was a remarkable one for the occurrence of diving ducks in the Valley. The relatively high water level of the rivers (brought on in part by Hurricane Diane in late August) resulted in the following species being present during all or part of that season: Canvasback, Redhead, Ring-necked Duck, Lesser Scaup, Oldsquaw, Common Goldeneye, Bufflehead and Ruddy Duck.

All the diving ducks are generally more prevalent in spring when the river meadows are flooded by seasonal rains and snow melt. In fall there are relatively few locations where water levels are suitable for the diving ducks.

Redhead - *Aythya americana*

Status: A rare migrant.

Occurrence: Of the seven spring records since 1949, all occur during March and April—4/4/77 (McClellan) **1** W.

Sixteen fall records for the October through December period—9/24 thru 10/19/83 (Gove) **1** GM; maxima: 10/25/65 (Foley) **25** GM.

Remarks: Griscom mentions two spring and four fall records between 1936 and 1948.

Ring-necked Duck - *Aythya collaris*

Status: A common to abundant spring and markedly uncommon fall migrant.

Occurrence: During the spring migration, a few birds may be observed in late February and a few in early May. The bulk of the migrants are recorded in March and April with peak numbers occurring in the first half of April—maxima: 4/9/78 (Forster) **336**.

Although there have been several reports of Ring-necked Ducks lingering into the summer months, there is only one confirmed nesting record for our area—May 1951 (Chandler) GM, ad., nest and eggs.

Fall birds were reported fairly regularly between 1952 and 1968. Since that time, however, there have been less than six October to November records—10/17/81 (Sommers) **3** GM.

Remarks: In the springtime the majority of Ring-necked Ducks are seen on the flooded river meadows. Fall birds are most often encountered on ponds or at the Great Meadows impoundments.

Greater Scaup - *Aythya marila*

Status: A rare migrant.

Records: 3/24/82 (Hines) **3** HP
4/12,16/82 (Forster) **4,4** HP (different)
4/13/65 (Forster) **2** W
4/19/65 (Kearney) **2** C
4/21/66 (Rhome) **1** GM˙
12/28/80 (Alden) **1** C

Lesser Scaup - *Aythya affinis*

Status: A rare migrant.

Occurrence: The records since 1949 become progressively fewer and farther apart with only eight reports in the last two decades.

Although there were regular spring reports in March and April of 1955 and 1956—maxima: 4/22/56 (Stackpole) **11,** there have been only eight spring reports since that time.

There are sixteen fall and early winter records since 1949—maxima: 11/12/54 (Stackpole) **27.**

Remarks: Conventional wisdom has held that inland scaup are Lesser Scaup with Greater Scaup occurring in coastal situations. Unfortunately, as with most generalizations, there are exceptions. Because of the difficulty in distinguishing the two scaup species, the exact status of each remains somewhat unclear.

Harlequin Duck - *Histrionicus histrionicus*

Status: A vagrant.

Records: 2/14-24/57 (Gleason) **1**

Remarks: This individual was observed near the dam at Saxonville on the Sudbury River. Although somewhat outside the area traditionally covered by the naturalists working in the Valley, this record is of historical interest - being the only inland record for Harlequin Duck in the state.

Oldsquaw - *Clangula hyemalis*

Status: A vagrant.

Records: 4/16/83 (Hines) **1** HP
5/2-10/57 (Stackpole) **1** HP
10/18/71 (Hecht) **1** GM
11/18/55 (Stackpole) **1**

Remarks: Griscom published one record in *TBOC*—10/29/38.

Black Scoter - *Melanitta nigra*

Status: A very rare migrant.

Records: 10/5/79 (Forster) **1** W
10/18/67 (Garrey) **7** GM
10/20/77 (Forster) **1** W

Remarks: Of the three scoter species, this is the one most likely to be encountered during the fall migration in the Sudbury River Valley. Inclement weather is invariably a factor in causing this bird to alight.

Surf Scoter - *Melanitta perspicillata*

Status: A vagrant.

Records: None in the last eighty years. Griscom published three records in *TBOC*, the last—10/14/04.

White-winged Scoter - *Melanitta fusca*

Status: A vagrant.

Records: 10/21/77 (Forster) **1** HP

Common Goldeneye - *Bucephala clangula*

Status: A fairly common spring and rare fall migrant.

Occurrence: During the 1950s and 1960s spring birds, in March and early April, were common and large groups were occasionally reported—3/15/53 (Freeland) **70**. The spring occurrence of this species in the last decade is limited to sightings of relatively smaller groups—maxima: 3/31/83 (Walton) **35**.

There have been ten records during the October through December period since 1949 and half of these occurred during the unusual 1955 season (see Canvasback account)—maxima: 12/2/55 (Stackpole) **70**.

Remarks: Griscom felt that the increase of this species, between 1930 and 1948, was due to the decline in hunting. The records indicate that this relative abundance continued through the mid-1950s. Thereafter, there is a decline of this species in our area.

Barrow's Goldeneye - *Bucephala islandica*

Status: A very rare spring migrant.

Records: 2/4-12/55 (Stackpole, Drurys, Morgan) **2** W
3/25/59 (Garrey) **1** W
3/26/56 (Stackpole) **1** W
3/27 to 4/1/83 (Gove, Nielson, Walton) **1** GM

Remarks: The 1955, 1956, and 1983 records coincide with relatively large flocks of Common Goldeneye in the Valley.

Bufflehead - *Bucephala albeola*

Status: A fairly common spring and uncommon fall migrant.

Occurrence: The first spring migrants arrive in early March -rarely in February. Although the majority of migrants are observed in March—maxima: 3/31/83 (Walton) **19** GM, there are several April and one May record.

The Bufflehead is a late fall migrant. Most Buffleheads seen in the Valley during this season are noted between early October and mid-December —11/7/64 (Forster) **7** GM.

Hooded Merganser - *Lophodytes cucullatus*

Status: A fairly common spring and uncommon fall migrant; sporadic nesting history.

Occurrence: The bulk of spring migrants are seen between the first of March and mid-April—maxima: 3/14/82 (Walton) **18**.

Nesting occurs in April and May. The first nesting record for Hooded Merganser in the Valley was in 1947. A Wood Duck box at Great Meadows was the nest site. Since that time, there have been similar records of this species nesting in our area: 1950-1952, 1963-1966, and 1974-1975. At the present time, no regular pattern of nesting has been established. (11)

Fall migrants are recorded from late September through the first half of December—10/19/76 (Hamilton) **7** W. Stragglers are present, rarely, on the rivers in December.

Common Merganser - *Mergus merganser*

Status: A common spring and rare fall migrant.

Occurrence: This merganser appears in late February if the ice is out—2/21/81 (Morrier) **55** W. Migrants are seen throughout March and into the first half of April—maxima: 3/14/80 (Forster) **91** W.

A late fall migrant, most records for this species in the Valley occur during November and December—12/2/70 (Forster) **26** HP.

Red-breasted Merganser - *Mergus serrator*

Status: A vagrant.

Records: 5/11/82 (Forster) **7** HP
12/30/62 (R. Corey) **1** C
1/8/56 (Seamans) **2** C

Remarks: Although this species is often an abundant migrant and winter resident along the coast, it is normally rare inland. Griscom mentions only six records in *TBOC*.

Ruddy Duck - *Oxyura jamaicensis*

Status: A rare spring and uncommon fall migrant.

Occurrence: Of the ten spring records since 1949, eight are in April and report one to four birds.

Fall migrants are recorded from late September into the first half of November—10/28/81 (Hines) **5** HP. An unusually high count was made in 1956—maxima: 11/16/56 (Seamans) **75** GM.

Remarks: There are few suitable ponds in the Valley to attract Ruddy Duck migrants. As a result, groups seen locally are usually few in number and quick to move on.

Turkey Vulture - *Cathartes aura*

Status: An uncommon spring and rare fall migrant.

Occurrence: Most spring records generally occur between the first of March and mid-May with a majority of reports in April—maxima: 4/15/82 (Ryan) **5** S; latest: 6/3/84 (Hines) **2** S.

There are only three fall records—from 9/20/59 (Verrill) **2** W to 10/7/83 (Williams) **1** GM.

Remarks: The Turkey Vulture is being reported with increasing frequency as it extends its range into the Northeastern states. Local records of migrants reflect this change.

It is interesting to note that three of the four records in *TBOC* are of fall sightings.

Osprey - *Pandion haliaetus*

Status: A fairly common migrant.

Occurrence: The bulk of spring migrants pass through in April—maxima: 4/15/82 (Forster) **6**. A few late March and early May birds are reported.

The fall movement is prolonged with sightings generally from late August to early November—maxima: 9/17/82 (Walton) **7**; latest: 12/3/83 (Walton) **1** GM.

Remarks: In 1952 Ospreys built a nest at Heard's Pond in Wayland. One adult was reportedly shot off the nest. Another nesting attempt was made on a transmission tower above Wash Brook. This nest was dismantled by the utility company and nest prevention structures were added to the towers. (pers. comm. A. Morgan)

In the 1950s and 1960s there was a general decline of Ospreys in the Northeast. This was attributed to the widespread use of DDT and related pesticides. With the banning of these compounds, Osprey populations in New England began to show some increase in the 1970s. (12)

American Swallow-tailed Kite - *Elanoides forficatus*†

Status: A vagrant.

Records: 5/30/84 (Stowe) **1** C.

†formerly Swallowed-tailed Kite

Bald Eagle - *Haliaeetus leucocephalus*

Status: A rare migrant and winter visitor.

Occurrence: Approximately half of all the Bald Eagle sightings in the Valley since 1949 have occurred in March—maxima: 3/2-3/81 (L. Taylor) **3** GM.

Additional records occur in every month.

Mid-winter sightings of wandering immature eagles have been reported five times—12/29/83 (Forster) **1** HP.

Remarks: The Great Meadows impoundments have proved to be the best site to see the spring birds. These sightings coincide with ice melt and the availability of winter-killed fish.

Northern Harrier - *Circus cyaneus*†

Status: An uncommon migrant.

Occurrence: Late February birds are unusual. Most spring migrants pass through during late March and April—4/11/82 (Morrier) **2** W. A few birds are recorded in May.

Most fall sightings occur between early September and mid-November—maxima: 11/10/59 (Gardler) **11** C. In recent years more than two birds per day is unusual.

Remarks: From Thoreau's time down to Griscom's era the Northern Harrier was a common migrant and nested regularly in the Concord area. There has been no confirmed nesting of this species for over a quarter century. The last June records were in 1955.

†formerly Marsh Hawk

Sharp-shinned Hawk - *Accipiter striatus*

Status: An uncommon spring and common fall migrant; a markedly uncommon winter visitor.

Occurrence: Spring migrants are reported in late March and April. Sightings usually involve single birds on the move.

During the September and October fall flight Sharp-shinned Hawks are seen singly or in small groups of two to five birds—maxima: 9/18/81 (Roberts) 33 GM.

Stragglers are reported in November. Occasionally, individual birds will over-winter, at times in association with flocks of feeder birds or in years when winter finches are present in abundance.

Remarks: Griscom commented in *TBOC* that "this hawk is always present in winters of great Redpoll flights, and virtually unrecorded in birdless winters." Data from the Concord Christmas Count indicate that there may now be a few wintering Sharp-shinned Hawks around even in non-flight (Redpoll) years. A sharp increase in bird feeding over the past two decades has probably contributed to increased winter occurrence.

Cooper's Hawk - *Accipiter cooperii*

Status: A rare migrant and winter visitor.

Occurrence: Spring birds are most often reported between mid-March and late April. Reports are almost always of single birds.

A majority of fall sightings are between mid-September and late November—10/31/81 (Gove) 1 GM.

A Cooper's Hawk is reported, on average, one out of two winters.

Remarks: Griscom's estimate of ten birds per spring seems high judged by the experience of present-day observers, but may reflect the scarcity of this species in the past twenty-five years.

Northern Goshawk - *Accipiter gentilis*†

Status: A rare migrant and winter visitor; probably a local and sporadic summer resident.

Occurrence: The records for the fall occurrence of this species since 1949 are few and far between. Eight reports are published for the period between late August and the end of October; the most recent—10/6/83 (Gove) **1 GM.**

Winter visitors, usually immature birds, occur in December, January and February. The goshawk has been reported on seventeen of twenty-four CCC.

Almost all spring records (eighteen in thirty years) are confined to the month of March.

A scattering of summer records (5) indicates irregular nesting—7/6/78 (Petersen) **1 GM.**

Remarks: Although the Northern Goshawk is definitely not an avian feature of the Valley (see *TBOC* p. 197), there are at least two known nesting sites for this species on the perimeter of the Valley.

†formerly Goshawk

Red-shouldered Hawk - *Buteo lineatus*

Status: A rare migrant.

Occurrence: Presently, it is unusual to record more than one or two birds during the mid-March through April spring flight—maxima since 1960, 4/11/82 (Forster) **4 RH.** Since 1970, there have been seven years when no Red-shouldered Hawks were reported. Thirty years ago this was a common spring migrant—3/19/54 (Wellman) **52.**

A common summer resident until the mid-1950s, absent for twenty-five years, one or two pairs observed in the general area in the last five years.

The fall migration has never materialized in our area and it is probable that the Valley is considerably east of the Red-shoulder's normal fall route.

Remarks: This was the common nesting buteo into the 1950s (Griscom estimated 25 breeding pairs in 1949). The rapid decline in the local population that occurred in the late 1950s was undoubtedly related to the use of "hard" (DDT) pesticides so prevalent at that time. In the last few years there has been a slight increase in migrants and at least one pair of Red-shouldered Hawks has nested close by (Carlisle 1982).

Broad-winged Hawk - *Buteo platypterus*

Status: A fairly common spring migrant, common at times in the fall; an uncommon summer resident.

Occurrence: The spring flight begins in mid-April and peaks towards the end of the month—maxima: 4/26/81 (Walton) **37 C.**

Local summer residents are on territory from May through July.

The majority of fall migrants pass through during September. Normal fall counts range between twenty-five and fifty birds on good days—maxima: 9/16/84 (Walton) **717** NAC.

Remarks: Typical nesting habitat for this species is the drier upland sections of the Valley in mature mixed or deciduous woodlands.

Swainson's Hawk - *Buteo swainsoni*

Status: A vagrant.

Records: 4/8-9/1893 (Brewster) **1**
9/12/1876 (Allen) **1** collected

Red-tailed Hawk - *Buteo jamaicensis*

Status: A permanent resident and uncommon migrant.

Occurrence: Migrants are occasionally reported from the beginning of March to mid-April and from mid-September through October.

Resident birds are a familiar sight, throughout the year, on perches along the tree-lines bordering the cultivated fields and river meadows. Courtship flights are observed as early as late February. Adults are often feeding young by late May.

A winter census of raptors in the Valley yielded the following totals for Red-tailed Hawk: 1/17/82 (Walton *et al.*) **17**; 2/28/82, **30**; 1/23/83, **14**; 2/27/83, **23**.

Remarks: In Thoreau's time the Red-tailed Hawk was the common buteo of the Valley. By the late 1880s the local population had been greatly reduced. In 1888, according to Brewster, this species was superseded by the Red-shouldered Hawk. Since 1960 the Red-tailed Hawk has experienced a dramatic rise in population in our area and is once again the common resident hawk of the Valley.

Christmas Count data at five year intervals indicates this trend: 1960, **2**; 1965, **5**; 1970, **15**; 1975, **34**; 1980, **91**.

This species, once commonly referred to as "Hen Hawk", may have suffered more from persecution than any other raptor. Stricter law enforcement and a generally more enlightened public have served to successfully remedy this situation.

Rough-legged Hawk - *Buteo lagopus*

Status: An irregular winter visitor.

Occurrence: Although recorded between October and mid-April, Rough-legs seldom appear in our area until November or December. In flight years, typically one to three birds will move onto territories in close proximity to the river meadows where, once found, they can be relocated with regularity—maxima: 2/13/65 (Forster, Petersen) **15**.

Golden Eagle - *Aquila chrysaetos*

Status: A very rare migrant.

Records: 4/15/55 (Elkins, Claflin) **1**
4/19/62 (Elkins, Claflin) **1**
10/30/80 (Floyd, Roberts) **1** GM

Remarks: Griscom published one record—1/22/47 (Griscom, Mason) **1**.

American Kestrel - *Falco sparverius*

Status: An uncommon permanent resident; a fairly common migrant.

Occurrence: In spring, migrants are observed between mid-March and the end of April.

Nesting begins during the month of May.

The peak of the fall flight occurs during the latter half of September—maxima: 9/25/65 (J. Baird) **22** RH.

The winter resident population is variable with counts of one to eight birds along the river-bottom land.

Remarks: Between the 1880s and the 1920s this species was a rare migrant, unrecorded in many years (see *TBOC* p.207).

Merlin - *Falco columbarius*

Status: A markedly uncommon migrant.

Occurrence: Most spring records occur during April—4/11/76 (Roberts) **1** C; maxima: 4/23/83 (Walton) **2** C.

The majority of fall reports occur between mid-September and mid-October—maxima: 9/25/65 (J. Baird) **2** RH.

Remarks: This falcon goes unrecorded one out of every three years. In years when the water level is low at the Great Meadows impoundments in late summer and fall, and shorebirds are numerous, a Merlin may linger in the area for several days.

Peregrine Falcon - *Falco peregrinus*

Status: A rare migrant.

Occurrence: Thirteen spring records occur between mid-March and mid-April—4/9/74 (Sprong) **1** C.

The sixteen fall reports are in September and October—maxima: 10/4/80 (Gove) **2** GM.

Remarks: The eastern race (*F. p. anatum*) of this species was extirpated during the era of widespread use of chlorinated hydrocarbons (e.g. DDT). The banning of these compounds in the United States and Canada in the late 1960s and a Peregrine reintroduction program have helped to alter an extremely pessimistic picture.

In the fall of 1982, record high numbers of this falcon were reported at several traditional observation posts along the east coast. Locally, there seems to be an increase in Peregrine sightings which may reflect positive changes. (13,14)

Gyrfalcon - *Falco rusticolus*

Status: A very rare winter visitor.

Records: 11/21/1896 (Brewster) **1**
11/11/43 (Armstrong) **1**

*Ring-necked Pheasant - *Phasianus colchicus*

Status: A common permanent resident.

Remarks: Pheasants were first introduced to Massachusetts in 1894. For many years the state Department of Fisheries and Game conducted a stocking program for the benefit of hunters. Locally, this program was discontinued in the 1950s and present-day populations of pheasants in the Valley are self-sustaining groups.

Ruffed Grouse - *Bonasa umbellus*

Status: An uncommon permanent resident.

Occurrence: Found in the upland forests or wooded swamps of the Valley, where the males can be heard drumming and the females with their broods can be seen in woodland habitats such as Estabrook Woods.

In the late winter season grouse may be seen in poplar and apple trees where they feed on the buds. CCC minima: 1977, **2**; maxima: 1966, **52**.

Remarks: For an explanation and description of the cyclic nature of Ruffed Grouse see Griscom's *TBOC*. (15)

Wild Turkey - *Meleagris gallopavo*

Status: Long extirpated from our area; recently reintroduced to western Massachusetts.

Remarks: See Part I, Ch. 5. (16)

Northern Bobwhite-*Colinus virginianus*†

Status: Indigenous population extirpated; a few individuals recorded from time to time; scattered nesting records.

Occurrence: The call of the bobwhite is sometimes heard in spring and early summer on the edges of upland fields. It has been seen on eight of twenty-four CCC—maxima: 1969, **18**; most recent nesting record—9/24/83 (Walton) **1** adult and **3** young S.

Remarks: The original, indigenous population was strong at the end of the last century. During the first part of the present century, this species' popularity among hunters and other sportsmen resulted in many pen-reared quail being stocked for hunting as well as released for field trials. Nevertheless, the bobwhite population declined rapidly—partly as the result of increased hunting pressure and possibly because the newly introduced bobwhite populations were ill-suited to endure our New England winters. The ongoing loss of farmlands and the severe reduction of old-field and second growth habitat has deterred any possible re-establishment of a Northern Bobwhite population. (17)

†formerly Bobwhite

Yellow Rail-*Coturnicops noveboracensis*

Status: Of historical interest as it was once taken fairly regularly by hunters on the river meadows during migration. Although there has been little evidence, direct or indirect, of the occurrence of this species in the last fifty years, it is possible that the Yellow Rail still moves through our area in small numbers.

Remarks: Griscom described this species as "by no means uncommon". Unfortunately, part of his supporting evidence was based on a vocalization that is now attributed to the Virginia and possibly other rails. (18,19)

King Rail - *Rallus elegans*

Status: A rare and irregular summer resident.

Occurrence: Since 1949, the King Rail has been recorded on the average of once every three years. Residents arrive between mid-April and the end of May—4/21-23/77 (Walton) **1** C.

A family group was observed in early August—8/9/65 (Kings) **1** ad., **1** imm. W. Another August sighting recorded two adults—8/2/75 (Horn) **2** GM.

A lingering King Rail was found in a muskrat trap in Concord on 11/21/53 by R. Borden. This bird was released from the trap (apparently unharmed), banded and photographed. The rail was found in the same trap on 12/13/53 and once again released.

Remarks: Among summer resident rails in Massachusetts, this is the species about which the least is known. Both its secretive habits and habitat preference (the dense cover of extensive cattail marshes and river meadows) make it difficult to observe. Even its status as a species is tentative, in that many researchers feel that it is conspecific with the coastal Clapper Rail. (18)

Virginia Rail - *Rallus limicola*

Status: A fairly common but irregular summer resident; fairly common at times as a fall migrant.

Occurrence: Residents arrive at the cattail marshes at Great Meadows and Wash Brook by mid-April. This species can be heard "singing" through May—5/5/76 (Davis) **6** C.

Family groups are observed in June and July—6/29/80 (Stymeist) **3** ad., **6** chicks GM.

Fall numbers build through September—9/20/80 (Stymeist) **7** GM. By mid-October most birds have departed.

It is not unusual for stragglers to linger into November. Overwintering Virginia Rails have been recorded from December through February—1/1-14/78 (Walton) **4** C.

Remarks: The occurrence of rails in winter is often an artifact of warm water seepage areas such as the one at the Concord sewer beds abutting the GM. (18)

Sora - *Porzana carolina*

Status: An uncommon and irregular summer resident; common at times as a fall migrant at Great Meadows.

Occurrence: Residents arrive at their breeding locations beginning in mid-April. Arrivals continue through May—5/16/75 (Forster) **5** W.

Adults with broods are seen in late May or June—5/31/76 (A. Clayton) adult with chicks C.

In late summer, local groups are joined by migrants and numbers peak during the second half of September—9/20/80 (Stymeist) **30+** GM. By late October most Soras have moved southward.

Although a few records exist of stragglers during the November to February period, this species is much less likely to tarry than the Virginia Rail—1/15/78 (Walton) **5** C. (18)

Purple Gallinule - *Porphyrula martinica*

Status: A vagrant.

Records: 7/31/83 (Billings) **1** ad. GM
9/7-13/80 (Barton) **1** imm. GM
9/17/81 (Prybis, Gove, Cutler) **1** ad. GM
10/24/82 (Rubenstein) **1** imm. GM

Remarks: Griscom published two records. (18)

Common Moorhen - *Gallinula chloropus*†

Status: An uncommon summer resident of the extensive cattail marshes.

Occurrence: Resident birds arrive in April and are often heard in the marshes throughout the summer—4/29/62 (Getting) **12** GM.

Adults with young are frequently seen in June and July—6/12/76 (E. Taylor) **5** ad., **7** imm. GM.

Local groups of adults and birds of the year remain through the end of September and sometimes into October—9/16/77 (Stymeist) **15** GM.

There are three November and one December records—latest: 12/2/70 (Forster) **1** GM.

Remarks: A rare summer resident in the 1940s, this species became much more prevalent in the mid-1950s. Although Brewster found it nesting as early as 1888, the creation of the Great Meadows impoundments provided the Common Moorhen with ideal habitat. (18,20)

†formerly Common Gallinule

American Coot - *Fulica americana*

Status: An uncommon to rare spring, and a fairly common fall migrant.

Occurrence: Spring records occur between mid-March and the end of April. The numbers of spring coot have always been small compared to fall counts and within the last decade spring records have decreased significantly—maxima since 1965: 4/11/76 (Roberts) **10** GM.

The first nesting record in the Valley was at Great Meadows—5/15/59 (Shaw) adult on nest. Sporadic nesting continued until 1965; thereafter there are no records of summer residents.

The fall movement occurs relatively late with peak numbers reached towards the end of October or beginning of November—10/28/74 (Weaver) **200** GM; 12/18/75 (Hines) **75** C.

Remarks: The nesting history of the American Coot in the Valley is significant in that this species is a rare nesting bird in all of Massachusetts and has been confirmed at only two other locations.

Griscom characterized the Concord Region as a poor locality for this species. Between 1949 and the late 1960s the record indicates a dramatic increase in coot—particularly as a fall migrant—maxima: 11/9/65 (Eldred) **350** GM. Since the late 1960s the situation has turned around and we seem to be in a period of general decline for the American Coot in our area. (18)

Sandhill Crane - *Grus canadensis*

Status: A vagrant.

Records: 10/9/70 (Hecht) **1** ad. GM

Black-bellied Plover - *Pluvialis squatarola*

Status: A rare migrant.

Occurrence: Only three spring records, all in May—maxima: 5/31/61 (Stackpole, Bezemer) **4** NAC.

A majority of fall records occur between mid-September and the end of October. Most sightings are of one to ten birds—maxima: 9/21/63 (Albee) **30** GM.

Remarks: Although this species is more apt to be seen in fall than in spring, it is recorded less often inland than the Lesser Golden-Plover.

Lesser Golden-Plover - *Pluvialis dominica*

Status: A markedly uncommon fall migrant.

Occurrence: Flocks of one to ten birds are seen from late August through mid-October—maxima: 9/21/75 (Stymeist) **29** GM.

Remarks: This species is most often seen or heard at Great Meadows. If the water level is low and there are exposed "flats", it will frequently put down there in fall. A few small flocks have also been recorded on the fields at Nine Acre Corner.

Semipalmated Plover - *Charadrius semipalmatus*

Status: A rare spring and uncommon fall migrant.

Occurrence: The twelve spring records are during the latter half of May and early June—5/19/82 (Walton) **2** NAC; maxima: 6/5/54 (Lewis) **20** C.

A majority of fall records occur during September and the first half of October—9/7/61 (Petersen) **2** W.

Remarks: The occurrence of this and many other migrant shorebirds in late summer and fall is subject to conditions at Great Meadows. In years of low water and exposed flats the list of shorebirds can be impressive.

Piping Plover - *Charadrius melodus*

Status: A vagrant.

Records: 7/20/75 (Forster) **1** GM.

Remarks: This is the only inland record for Massachusetts.

Killdeer - *Charadrius vociferus*

Status: A common migrant and fairly common summer resident.

Occurrence: An early migrant, Killdeer often appear in late February or early March. Peak spring numbers occur in April—4/2/74 (Forster) **27** NAC. By early May most migrants have passed through and residents are on territory.

Chicks are seen away from the nest by late May or early June.

Fall groups build from late August through October—10/18/80 (Forster) **41** C. It is not unusual for Killdeer to remain through November—11/20/77 (Forster) **15** NAC.

Rarely, stragglers are reported in December and January.

Remarks: The Killdeer requires a bare substrate upon which to nest. The fact that it regularly nests on flat, gravel-covered roofs in Concord (a less than optimal habitat) reflects the demise of agriculture in the region.

Greater Yellowlegs - *Tringa melanoleuca*

Status: An uncommon migrant.

Occurrence: Most spring birds are seen during April and the first half of May—5/2/82 (SSBC) **5**.

Although fall records exist from late July through mid-November, a majority of reports occur in October—10/9/72 (Weaver) **3** GM; maxima: 10/31/53 (Greenough) **11** GM.

Remarks: In both seasons the Greater Yellowlegs is most often reported either singly or in small groups of two to five birds.

Lesser Yellowlegs - *Tringa flavipes*

Status: A rare spring and uncommon fall migrant.

Occurrence: Ten spring records have been reported for the period between mid-April and mid-May—4/27/81 (Walton) **2** C.

The fall movement of adult Lesser Yellowlegs begins in early July with numbers usually peaking in late July or early August—maxima: 8/1/78 (Walton) **51** GM. Juvenile birds move through our area during the period from late August to mid-October—9/27/80 (SSBC) **50** GM.

Remarks: The main spring flight path of this species is northward through the Mississippi River Valley—hence the few spring records. In fall, the Lesser Yellowlegs follows an Atlantic coastal route south. Of the two yellowleg species, this is the earlier fall migrant.

Solitary Sandpiper - *Tringa solitaria*

Status: An uncommon migrant.

Occurrence: Most spring reports occur from mid-April through the end of May—maxima: 5/6/83 (Walton) **14**. By June the Solitary Sandpipers have moved on to their Canadian breeding grounds.

The fall flight begins relatively early and we may see southbound migrants in our area at the beginning of July—7/2/77 (Murphy) **1** GM. Numbers peak around the end of July or the beginning of August—8/1/59 (E. Jones) **12** C. Most birds move south of our area by the end of September although stragglers may remain well into October—latest: 10/25/82 (Walton) **1**.

Remarks: The Valley is one of the better spots in the state to see Solitary Sandpipers.

Willet - *Catoptrophorus semipalmatus*

Status: A vagrant.

Records: 5/15/64 (Sprong) **1** GM.

Remarks: Griscom published two records: 9/20/21 and 8/30/45.

Spotted Sandpiper - *Actitis macularia*

Status: An uncommon summer resident and fairly common fall migrant.

Occurrence: Although spring migrants are seldom recorded, Forster observed a flock of Spotted Sandpipers at Heard's Pond—5/18/80 (Forster) **9** HP.

Resident birds arrive at nesting areas along the rivers, sloughs and pond edges in late April and in May—5/21/61 (Seamans) **5** C. Nesting occurs in June.

From mid-July through September small groups of adults and birds of the year become fairly common—8/1/76 (A. & N. Clayton) **10** C. Occasionally, a few birds will linger into October—latest: 11/4/57 (Stackpole) **1** W.

Upland Sandpiper - *Bartramia longicauda*

Status: A rare migrant.

Occurrence: Nine spring records are published between 1951 and 1964. They include two late March records and seven records for the period between mid-April and mid-May—maxima: 4/30/56 (Wellman, Elkins) **2** NAC.

The only fall records since 1949 are: 8/10/70 (Brown) **2** GM and 9/2/77 (Forster) **1** GM.

Remarks: In 1983 and 1984 several pairs of Upland Sandpipers nested successfully at the Hanscom Field located at the junction of Concord, Bedford and Lincoln.

Whimbrel - *Numenius phaeopus*

Status: A very rare migrant.

Records: 8/25/82 (Walton) **1** GM

Remarks: Griscom published two records: 7/21/01 (Brewster) **1** and 9/20/02 (Paine) **1**.

Hudsonian Godwit - *Limosa haemastica*

Status: A very rare migrant.

Records: 9/23/84 (Walton) **1** GM
10/6-13/71 (McClellan) **1** GM
10/8/76 (Walton) **1** GM
10/12/61 (Shaw, Seamans) **1** dead C

Ruddy Turnstone - *Arenaria interpres*

Status: A very rare migrant.

Records: 8/16/75 (Forster) **1** GM
8/23/71 (Alden) **1** GM

Remarks: Although Griscom speaks of single birds each fall "with favorable conditions", this has definitely not been the case since 1949. The only records are cited above. Griscom published one "recent record"—8/30/38 (Bergstrom) **1**.

Red Knot - *Calidris canutus*

Status: A very rare migrant.

Records: None since 1938. Griscom published one record—8/8/38 (H.E. Maynard) **3** W.

Sanderling - *Calidris alba*

Status: A rare migrant.

Records: 7/29/78 (Forster) **1** GM
8/3/68 (Forster) **2** GM
9/4/84 (Forster) **1** HP
10/4/80 (Brain) **1** GM

Remarks: Griscom published two records: 9/20/10 (Brewster) **2** and early November 1898 (H.E. Maynard) **9**.

Semipalmated Sandpiper - *Calidris pusilla*

Status: A rare spring and fairly common fall migrant.

Occurrence: Of the six spring records, all but one are in May and report one to three birds.

The southbound flight generally moves through our area between mid-July and mid-September. Flocks of between five and fifty birds are usual—maxima: 7/24/75 (Forster) **300** GM. A few birds may linger into October and there is one November record—latest: 11/1/59 (Shaw) **30** C.

Remarks: A majority of the records are from Great Meadows and the Concord sewer beds.

Western Sandpiper - *Calidris mauri*

Status: A very rare fall migrant.

Records: 8/5/76 (Ferris) **1** C
8/23/59 (Gardlers) **3** C
8/28/74 (Petersen) **2** C
10/11/71 (Weaver) **2** GM

Least Sandpiper - *Calidris minutilla*

Status: A fairly common migrant.

Occurrence: Small groups of spring birds are seen in May at the sewer beds and Great Meadows as well as Nine Acre Corner—5/22/82 (Walton) **17** NAC.

Around mid-July the southbound flight of adult birds moves into our area—maxima: 7/24/75 (Forster) **300** GM. By early August the brightly marked juvenile birds begin to arrive. The flight continues into September—9/5/56 (Bolton, Jr.) **36** GM and there have been three October reports—latest: 10/18/57 (Stackpole) **1** W.

White-rumped Sandpiper - *Calidris fuscicollis*

Status: A very rare fall migrant.

Occurrence: Less than ten records since 1949. These accounts are grouped between late July and early November—maxima: 7/21/75 (J. Baird) **5** GM; latest: 11/2/57 (Stackpole) **1** W.

Baird's Sandpiper - *Calidris bairdii*

Status: A very rare fall migrant.

Occurrence: Only reported in three years since 1930: 1974, 1975, and 1980. From late July to early September—maxima: 9/2/75 (Brown) **3** GM.

Remarks: Griscom published only one record for the Valley proper—9/2/30 (H.E. Maynard) **1** collected.

Pectoral Sandpiper - *Calidris melanotos*

Status: An uncommon spring and fairly common fall migrant.

Occurrence: Reports of one to five birds during April and the first half of May occur fairly regularly—4/4/74 (Forster) **2** C. An extraordinary flight was recorded in the spring of 1981 when one count at the coast exceeded 1000 birds, and in Concord unprecedented April numbers were observed—4/27/81 (Walton) **68** C.

The fall flight occurs in our area between mid-July and early November—maxima: 8/30/55 (Morgan, Drury) **52**. Normally, during this season, groups of one to five birds are recorded.

Remarks: There has been a substantial increase in both spring and fall sightings in recent years. In the springtime, Pectoral Sandpipers can be found in the region's flooded fields. In the fall, this species is often present at Concord's sewage filter beds.

Dunlin - *Calidris alpina*

Status: A rare migrant.

Occurrence: The seven spring records occur during the mid-April through May period. Each of these is a report of a single bird and only four years are involved: 1961, 1965, 1966, and 1967.

The ten fall records occur during the latter half of September and throughout October—maxima: 10/21/59 (Stackpole) **9** W.

Remarks: Griscom noted four fall records.

Stilt Sandpiper - *Calidris himantopus*

Status: A rare fall migrant.

Occurrence: Seen in only seven years since 1949. Records are from mid-July through September. Most sightings are of one to three birds—9/11/80 (Walton) **3** GM; maxima: 9/3/55 (Morgan) **35** W.

Remarks: Although most reports come from Great Meadows and the sewer beds, Morgan's record count was made at the Wayland Golf Course following the flooding brought on by Hurricane Diane.

Buff-breasted Sandpiper - *Tryngites subruficollis*

Status: A very rare fall visitor.

Records: 9/22/59 (Gardler) **1** W

Remarks: Griscom published two September records from the Framingham sewer beds.

Ruff - *Philomachus pugnax*

Status: A vagrant.

Records: 4/12/60 (Stackpole) **1** NAC
5/23/61 (Wiggin, Claybournes) **1** NAC
7/27 to 8/5/75 (P. Buckley) **1** GM

Short-billed Dowitcher - *Limnodromus griseus*

Status: A rare migrant.

Records: Two spring records, both in May—5/17/59 (Stackpole) **2** C.

Five fall records occur from late July through September—maxima: 7/24/75 (Forster) **9** GM.

Long-billed Dowitcher - *Limnodromus scolopaceus*

Status: A rare fall migrant.

Records: This species has been reported in only four years since 1949: 1959, 1965, 1978, and 1980. Most reports have been of one to three birds between mid-September and mid-October—maxima: 9/22/59 (Gardler) **7** W.

Common Snipe - *Gallinago gallinago*

Status: A fairly common spring and uncommon fall migrant.

Occurrence: Early spring migrants move through in late March. Numbers build through April when maximum numbers are recorded around sloughs and on flooded fields—maxima: 4/9/72 (Howard) **200** RH.

The fall movement begins in mid-July and continues through October. Fall snipe are normally seen in groups of one to three birds—hardly ever in numbers comparable to spring flocks—10/19/80 (Walton) **7** GM.

Stragglers occur fairly regularly in November and there are records of over-wintering birds found around open agricultural drainage ditches and seepage areas. The Common Snipe has been recorded on sixteen of twenty-four CCC.

Remarks: Although Griscom described this species as "Formerly an abundant transient . . . particularly in fall", present-day records indicate that this species occurs in greater numbers in spring.

There have been no nesting records for at least fifty years.

American Woodcock - *Scolopax minor*

Status: An uncommon migrant and summer resident.

Occurrence: Residents arrive on their nesting territories between late February (in mild seasons) and late March—earliest: 2/24/76 (Walton) **2** C.

Family groups are observed from May through June: 5/13/82 (Walton) **1** ad., **4** chicks C.

Most often, single birds are reported in the fall—maxima: 10/28/55 (Cutler) **12** C.

Remarks: The hunting accounts from the last quarter of the nineteenth century indicate just how abundant this species once was as a fall migrant. Griscom relates how "over 1000 birds" were reported killed on 11/11/1894 around Framingham and that "hundreds (were) killed around Concord" on 10/15/1876.

Present-day pressure on local woodcock populations stems mainly from the natural succession of old-field to shrub communities and suburban development. Both of these factors reduce suitable habitat for this species.

Wilson's Phalarope - *Phalaropus tricolor*

Status: A rare migrant.

Occurrence: Five spring records: four in May and one in June—maxima: 5/28/79 (BBC) **3** GM.

Nine fall reports are published for the period from mid-July to late September—latest: 9/27/80 (Petersen) **1** GM.

Remarks: This is the most likely species of phalarope to be seen in the Valley. Most fall phalarope reports come from Great Meadows.

Red-necked Phalarope - *Phalaropus lobatus*†

Status: A very rare fall migrant.

Occurrence: Nine fall records have been reported from the period between early August and mid-October—maxima: 8/3-23/75 (Merriman) **2** GM.

†formerly Northern Phalarope

Red Phalarope - *Phalaropus fulicaria*

Status: A very rare fall migrant.

Records: 9/22/77 (Ferris) **1** GM
9/27/80 (Petersen) **1** GM
10/9/78 (N. Clayton) **1** C

Remarks: This is the least likely species of phalarope to be seen inland.

Bonaparte's Gull - *Larus philadelphia*

Status: A rare migrant.

Occurrence: Four spring reports—maxima: 4/15/74 (Robinson) **2** GM.

Four reports between mid-July and late September—the most recent 9/17/83 (Walton) **1** imm. GM.

Ring-billed Gull - *Larus delawarensis*

Status: An uncommon migrant; in winter an uncommon visitor from the coast.

Occurrence: Spring migrants occur between mid-March and the end of May—5/22/82 (Walton) **12** NAC.

Fall birds returning to coastal wintering grounds are reported from mid-September through November—maxima: 9/17/78 (Cassie) **25** C.

During the winter months, one or two gulls of this species are seen sporadically—often in the company of Herring and Great Black-backed Gulls around land-fills.

Remarks: This species has undergone a dramatic population increase throughout its range in the last twenty years. Its regular occurrence in the Valley reflects this change as it was unrecorded before 1949.

Herring Gull - *Larus argentatus*

Status: An abundant migrant and winter visitor, occasionally seen in summer.

Occurrence: Spring migrants are observed overhead and on the flooded meadows between March and mid-May—4/18/59 (Seamans) **400** C.

Occasional birds wander inland from their coastal nesting grounds during June and July.

By late August, migrants are moving through our area towards coastal wintering grounds.

During much of the year, but especially during the winter months, mixed flocks of gulls, including this species, make daily round-trips from the coast to visit the local land-fills and inland bodies of water.

Remarks: The Herring Gull is one of the avian success stories of this century. In 1925 there were less than one hundred pairs nesting on our coast and E.H. Forbush wrote with concern, "It is improbable that the Herring Gull can long maintain itself anywhere on the coast of southern New England." Since that time, aided by conservationists, dumps and its own resourcefulness, this gull's population has boomed. In excess of 25,000 pairs nested on the coast of Massachusetts in the late 1970s. In 1981, 3300 Herring Gulls were reported on the CCC. (21)

Iceland Gull - *Larus glaucoides*

Status: A rare winter visitor.

Occurrence: Most records occur between January and April. The first reports of this species in the Valley were in 1957—2/9-19/57 (Armstrong) **3** C. Thereafter, one or two birds per winter was usual.

Remarks: Both this species and the Glaucous Gull are to be looked for in the mixed flocks of Herring and Great Black-backed Gulls around land-fills or resting on the ice cover of rivers and ponds.

Glaucous Gull - *Larus hyperboreus*

Status: A rare winter visitor.

Occurrence: A majority of the twenty records for the Valley occur between January and April—earliest: 11/16/80 (Morrier) **1** W; latest: 5/19/79 (Shaw) **1** C.

Remarks: Of the two "white-winged" gulls that visit the Valley in winter, this species is reported less frequently. Stackpole recorded the first one for the Valley on 3/11/47.

Great Black-backed Gull - *Larus marinus*

Status: A common winter visitor—seen occasionally on migration; immature birds sometimes recorded in summer.

Occurrence: The great majority of reports of this species are made between November and April when the mixed flocks of visiting winter gulls are in our area—1/16/83 (Walton) **85** NAC.

Remarks: Until the mid-1950s this was an uncommon species in the Valley at all seasons. The population increase since that time is indicated by the CCC data: 1960, **1**: 1970, **152**; 1980, **208**. A record high for the count was reported in 1981 when **1100** Great Black-backed Gulls were noted.

Caspian Tern - *Sterna caspia*

Status: A very rare migrant.

Records: 4/23/72 (Howard) to 4/26/72 (Hecht) **1** GM
4/24/66 (Leverett) **1** GM
4/26/84 (Roberts) **1** GM
8/31/54 (Morgan) **2** L

Common Tern - *Sterna hirundo*

Status: A vagrant.

Records: 5/21/80 (Forster) **1** W
8/31/54 (Stackpole) **200** Hurricane Carol W

Remarks: Griscom published several records associated with spring and fall coastal storms.

Arctic Tern - *Sterna paradisaea*

Status: A very rare migrant?

Records: 5/20/79 (Forster) **16** HP

Remarks: This exceptional record occurred during a period of heavy fog and prolonged easterly winds. It is not known whether the disorientation occurred to a flock migrating north along the coast or to one engaged in overland migration to their high arctic nesting grounds. (22)

Least Tern - *Sterna antillarum*

Status: A vagrant.

Records: 9/1/54 (Borden) **1** C

Black Tern - *Chlidonias niger*

Status: An uncommon migrant.

Occurrence: Spring migrants are reported, mainly from Great Meadows and Heard's Pond, during the May to mid-June period—maxima: 5/12/56 (Morgan) **16**.

Fall reports occur during the mid-July to early September period. These reports are usually of single birds, rarely two or three—latest: 9/6/71 (Albee) **1** GM.

Remarks: This is the most likely species of tern to occur in our area and passes through annually in small numbers.

Dovekie - *Alle alle*

Status: A vagrant during late fall and winter storms.

Records: 11/3/62 (Gifford) **1** C
12/7/62 (Finley, Richardson) **1, 1** C, W

Remarks: Inland records are associated with severe coastal storms that occur during the period of Dovekie migration and may result in great numbers of this species being "blown" inland. Because the Dovekie cannot take off from land, grounded individuals will perish if not assisted to water. (23)

Thick-billed Murre - *Uria lomvia*

Status: A vagrant.

Records: 1/2/77 (Walton) **1** C
3/7/62 (*fide* C. Smith) **1** W

*Rock Dove - *Columba livia*

Status: Abundant permanent resident around town centers and agricultural areas.

Remarks: Although its origins are obscure, it seems probable that the "pigeon" was brought to North America by the colonists as a domestic species. Escaped birds soon began to form feral populations that have been augmented by additional escapees (or releases). These birds have thrived around urban centers and farms which provide feeding, roosting and nesting sites.

Mourning Dove - *Zenaida macroura*

Status: A common permanent resident, abundant at times in the fall.

Occurrence: Resident birds begin "singing" (cooing) in February and may begin nesting in March. Although this population is joined by some migrants, it is normally difficult to distinguish the two groups.

In fall, large flocks of Mourning Doves are seen in the agricultural fields. Most migrants have moved southward by the end of October.

Winter residents are regular visitors at feeding stations.

Remarks: The Mourning Dove has steadily increased its population in our area over the last fifty years. Within the last three decades its status has changed from a summer resident to a permanent resident. Concord Christmas Count data indicate the increase in size of the wintering population: 1960, **79**; 1965, **341**; 1970, **987**; 1975, **876**; 1980, **1422**. Migrant populations are subject to some hunting pressure in that this wide-spread gamebird is hunted in thirty-three states. (24)

Passenger Pigeon - *Ectopistes migratorius*

Status: Extinct.

Remarks: Last record: Summer 1886 - See Part I, Ch. 5.

Black-billed Cuckoo - *Coccyzus erythropthalmus*

Status: An uncommon summer resident.

Occurrence: The first migrants arrive around mid-May—5/14/59 (Wiggin) **1** W; and the migration continues into June.

Nesting occurs in June and July—6/27/81 (Hines) **1** ad. **3** imm. W.

In fall the majority of birds have moved southward by the end of September.

Remarks: The variable nature of the cuckoo populations (both Black-billed and Yellow-billed) has been noted by many observers. Conventional wisdom associates this with the availability of hairy caterpillars upon which they feed.

Yellow-billed Cuckoo - *Coccyzus americanus*

Status: An uncommon to rare summer resident.

Occurrence: This migrant arrives in mid-May, usually after the Black-billed Cuckoo—5/26/82 (Walton) **3**.

Nesting occurs towards the end of May and throughout June—6/13/81 (Forster) **4** W.

Most migrants have passed through our area by the end of September although a few October records exist—10/11/81 (Walton) **1** C.

Remarks: Ordinarily, this species is less common than the Black-billed Cuckoo. The recent wave of Gypsy Moths in our area has been accompanied by a noticeable increase in Yellow-billed Cuckoo—thus lending support to the "caterpillar connection".

Common Barn-Owl - *Tyto alba*†

Status: A very rare visitor.

Records: Only six records since 1949. Two barn-owls were in the Concord area in the summer of 1959—6/30/59 to 9/2/59 (Gardler); the most recent: 4/30/84 (*fide* Walton) **1** C.

Remarks: During the present century there has been some extension of the range of this owl to the milder southeast coastal area of the state. Massachusetts remains, however, at the northern edge of the Common Barn-Owl's range. As such, it is a rare species throughout the state save for a few traditional nesting sites.

†formerly Barn Owl

Eastern Screech-Owl - *Otus asio*†

Status: A fairly common permanent resident.

Occurrence: This species is more often heard than seen. The screech-owl's descending tremolo may be heard around residential areas with mature woodlands, orchards and river flood plains. Nesting occurs in April and May and family groups are sometimes observed during the summer—7/7/78 (Walton, Forster) **2** ad., **3** imm. C.

Remarks: Although this species is seldom seen, the results of Christmas Count censusing in recent years lends credence to the supposition that this may be our most common nesting raptor—1981: **18**, 1982: **21**, 1983: **22**. (CCC).

†formerly Screech Owl

Great Horned Owl - *Bubo virginianus*

Status: An uncommon permanent resident.

Occurrence: Like the previous species, this bird is more often heard than seen. The hooting is noted at dawn or dusk often on the edge of extensive woodlands. Nesting occurs in March and fledged young are often out of the nest by late April or May—4/24/76 (Hinds) **1** ad., **1** imm. C.

Remarks: The increase in woodland acreage and a maturing forest during the past 80 to 100 years have provided substantial habitat for this species. The Great Horned Owl's relatively large territorial requirements do, however, limit the numbers of pairs in our area.

Snowy Owl - *Nyctea scandiaca*

Status: A rare winter visitor.

Occurrence: Most records (6 out of 9) since 1949 occur between November and January—12/13/82 (Hines) **1** GM. Although Griscom mentions one winter (1945-1946) in which five Snowy Owls were present, all records since 1949 are of single birds—latest: 4/17/61 (Bennett) **1**.

Remarks: This bird is much more apt to be encountered at the coast than at inland locations.

Northern Hawk-Owl - *Surnia ulula*†

Status: A winter vagrant.

Records: 11/28/58 to 1/20/59 (Holden, Coreys, Mott) **1** C

Remarks: This bird was originally discovered by Holly Holden. Although reported to a knowledgeable ornithologist, the report was not taken seriously. Subsequently it was rediscovered—12/19/58 (Coreys) and the rush was on to Concord. The hawk-owl was enjoyed by many —including Ludlow Griscom. The bird was found dead on 1/20/59 by Mott.

†formerly Hawk Owl

Barred Owl - *Strix varia*

Status: An irregular visitor; possibly nesting.

Occurrence: Scattered reports throughout the year of one or two birds—no reports in some years.

Remarks: Although it is probable that this species nests in our area, there has been no confirmed breeding in the Valley proper in recent decades.

Great Gray Owl - *Strix nebulosa*

Status: A very rare winter visitor.

Records: 2/25/79 to 3/19/79 (Malcolm) **1** C

Remarks: The flight of Great Gray Owls in the winter of 1979 was unprecedented in the Northeast. At least eighteen different individuals were recorded in Massachusetts and many made their way to the larger river valleys. Two birds were recorded in this general area.

Long-eared Owl - *Asio otus*

Status: A very rare visitor.

Occurrence: A majority of records occur between November and mid-March. The most reliable sites are known winter roosts where this species congregates during the day—12/17/65 (Tandy) **5** W.

Remarks: Although Griscom speculated that this might prove to be the second most common nesting owl species in our area, there has been no confirming field data for this theory.

Short-eared Owl - *Asio flammeus*

Status: A rare winter visitor.

Records: Ten records, a majority of which fall between November and February. The most recent—12/25/81 (Bertrand) **1** C.

Boreal Owl - *Aegolius funereus*

Status: A winter vagrant.

Records: Griscom describes the 1922-1923 winter flight at which time C.J. Maynard located 5 or 6 birds in Lincoln, Wayland and Sudbury. No subsequent records.

Northern Saw-whet Owl - *Aegolius acadicus*†

Status: An uncommon to rare migrant and winter visitor.

Occurrence: One October record, seven reports between November and February, one April record—4/5/53 (White) **1** W, and one report in July.

Remarks: Like many nocturnal species, precise information on the exact status of the Northern Saw-whet Owl is difficult to obtain. This diminutive owl may be more common than the record indicates.

†formerly Saw-whet Owl

Common Nighthawk - *Chordeiles minor*

Status: A fairly common spring and common fall migrant.

Occurrence: The spring migration generally occurs in our area during the latter part of May and early June. Most often in spring, reports are of one to four birds—5/20/81 (McClellan) **1** GM. A remarkable flight was noted in 1983—5/31/83 (Walton) **106** C.

The fall migration is unusually predictable and peaks during the last week of August and the first week in September—8/24-27/82 (Walton) **88** S. Flocks of three to twenty birds are typical at this time.

Remarks: Consistent field work during the peak of the fall migration would, no doubt, yield higher totals for this species.

Whip-poor-will - *Caprimulgus vociferus*

Status: A rare summer resident.

Occurrence: Summer residents generally arrive during May and early June. There is no noticeable fall movement through our area.

Remarks: This species was a common summer resident in Thoreau's time. As the woodland acreage declined, so did this species. It has never returned to our area in its former numbers—despite the regrowth of the forests.

Chimney Swift - *Chaetura pelagica*

Status: A common migrant and fairly common summer resident.

Occurrence: Although some April birds are reported—earliest: 4/17/82 (Forster) **1** RH, spring migrants usually peak in the latter part of May—5/31/82 (Porter) **25** GM.

Nesting occurs in May and June.

Large concentrations of swifts are sometimes observed over meadows and agricultural fields from late August through September—maxima: 9/20/74 (E. Taylor) **500 + C**. Most have passed well to the south of our area by October—latest: 10/18/77 (Walton) **1** GM.

Ruby-throated Hummingbird - *Archilochus colubris*

Status: A rare spring and uncommon fall migrant.

Occurrence: The few (8) spring records are during the first three weeks of May—5/1/54 (Stackpole) **1** W.

Most fall migrants are noted towards the end of August and beginning of September—maxima: 9/6/65 (BBC) **6** GM.

Remarks: The relatively late blooming Jewelweed (*Impatiens capensis*) often attracts these migrants in fall.

Belted Kingfisher - *Ceryle alcyon*

Status: An uncommon summer resident.

Occurrence: The first migrants are normally seen in our area in late March or early April—3/28/53 (Morgan) **2** W.

Nesting begins in the latter half of May and continues into June. Family groups are seen by July—7/18/82 (Walton) **6**.

Kingfishers regularly remain in our area through September —maxima: 9/10/53 (Morgan) **10**, with one or two stragglers usually reported into the winter months—1/23/83 (Hines) **1** C.

Red-headed Woodpecker - *Melanerpes erythrocephalus*

Status: A vagrant.

Occurrence: Approximately fifteen records since 1949. On two occasions individuals have overwintered—12/25/62 to 4/15/63 (Shabeck, H. Sprong) **1** C, and 11/19/78 to 3/31/79 (Anderson, Walton) **1** C.

Migrant Red-headed Woodpeckers are occasionally seen in October.

Red-bellied Woodpecker - *Melanerpes carolinus*

Status: A vagrant.

Records: Single birds reported on three Concord Christmas Counts: 1968, 1979, and 1983. The 1983 bird, a male, was initially recorded in the fall—9/11/83 (Harte) **1** Cl., and was joined in the spring by a female—4/14/84 (Harte) **2** Cl. Nesting is suspected but not confirmed.

Yellow-bellied Sapsucker - *Sphyrapicus varius*

Status: A rare migrant.

Occurrence: Less than ten spring records—all in the second half of April—4/21/61 (Young) **1** C.

The most likely time to find this species in our area is during the last ten days of September and the first week of October—10/1-5/81 (Hines) **3** W. There are two November records—the latest: 11/2/75 (Parker) **1** W.

Downy Woodpecker - *Picoides pubescens*

Status: A common permanent resident.

Occurrence: This species is the common resident woodpecker of the Valley. It favors wooded areas but often visits suburban neighborhoods.

Nesting occurs in May and throughout June.

In the fall and early winter the Downy can sometimes be found foraging on cornstalks that have been left in agricultural areas.

Hairy Woodpecker - *Picoides villosus*

Status: An uncommon permanent resident.

Occurrence: Similar in appearance and habits to the Downy, this woodpecker is associated more with the larger wooded tracts. The Hairy Woodpecker is encountered less frequently than its smaller relative and seems to maintain a population that is approximately one-third that of the Downy. See CCC data.

Black-backed Woodpecker - *Picoides arcticus*†

Status: A vagrant.

Records: This northern species has been recorded four times since 1949.

        1/1/72 to 3/8/72 (Leahy, Alden, Brown) **1** C
        5/9/59 (Alden, Seamans) **1** C
        5/21/61 (Shaw) **1** C
        10/22/74 (Gintoli) **1** GM

†formerly Black-backed Three-toed Woodpecker

Northern Flicker - *Colaptes auratus*†

Status: A common summer resident and migrant.

Occurrence: The vanguard of spring arrivals may be expected shortly after mid-March—3/20/54 (Morgan) **1** W. Numbers build through April—4/12/64 (Baird) **30** S.

Nesting occurs in May and June.

Local family groups are recorded during July and are later joined by an increasing number of migrants. By mid- to late September migrant flickers become fairly numerous—9/26/65 (Baird) **31** S. Most of these birds move south of our area by mid-October.

Single, overwintering birds are not unusual. The Northern Flicker has been recorded, in small numbers, on twenty-one out of twenty-four Concord Christmas Counts since 1960—maxima: 1983, **14**.

†formerly Common Flicker

Pileated Woodpecker - *Dryocopus pileatus*

Status: A markedly uncommon permanent resident.

Occurrence: Sporadic reports occur in all seasons. Although pairs have been observed in spring, and undoubtedly nest in our area, I can find no confirmed nesting record for the Valley proper.

Remarks: This species maintains a large territory and thus a relatively small population resides in our area.

Olive-sided Flycatcher - *Contopus borealis*

Status: A very rare migrant.

Occurrence: Only eight records since 1949. Four spring records from 5/22/55 (Stackpole) **1** W to 6/7/83 (Carter) **1** C.

Four fall records occur between mid-August and mid-September—maxima: 9/12/64 (Kearney) **2** C.

Eastern Wood-Pewee - *Contopus virens*†

Status: An uncommon summer resident.

Occurrence: The spring movement into our area occurs during the latter half of May—maxima: 5/24/53 (Freelands) **15 W.**

Residents begin nesting in June and territorial males are vocal through much of the summer.

A few migrants are noted in late August and September.

†formerly Eastern Wood Pewee

Yellow-bellied Flycatcher - *Empidonax flaviventris*

Status: A rare migrant.

Occurrence: Less than fifteen records since 1949. Only three spring reports—all in May—5/14/57 (Seamans) **1 C.**

All but one fall record occurred between late August and the end of September—9/1/78 (Walton) **1 GM.** One October record—10/3/66 (J. Baird) **1 b. RH.**

Alder Flycatcher - *Empidonax alnorum*

Status: A rare summer resident.

Occurrence: The scant spring records occur between mid-May and mid-June—6/3/76 (Hines) **2 W.**

Nest building by Alder Flycatchers has been observed only once—6/11/83 (Walton) **2 W.**

Because this species is identifiable in the field solely by voice, non-vocal fall migrants pass unrecorded.

Remarks: Until 1973 this species and the Willow Flycatcher were considered to be conspecific. Perhaps future field workers will locate additional nesting pairs.

Willow Flycatcher - *Empidonax trailii*

Status: A common summer resident.

Occurrence: This relatively late spring migrant arrives towards the end of May and the first part of June—5/30/81 (A. & N. Clayton) **4 GM.**

Nesting birds are common along the river meadows during June and July—6/13/81 (Forster) **14 W.**

By early August this species stops singing and field identification becomes moot.

Least Flycatcher - *Empidonax minimus*

Status: A markedly uncommon spring migrant and rare summer resident.

Occurrence: The record of the past two decades is sparse. Single birds are occasionally noted throughout May and into early June—5/28/81 (Forster) **1** W.

The first nesting record in nearly two decades—7/6/84 (Hines) **2** ad., **2** fledged young W.

Remarks: This species was a common migrant and nesting species into the early 1950s—5/7/53 (Griscom) **35** S. Although a small population of summer residents existed as late as the mid-1960s—6/22/65 (Kearney) **4** W, the local population of this flycatcher was rapidly decreasing. In 1951 the towns of Concord, Sudbury and Wayland had 452 acres of orchard—a preferred nesting habitat of the Least Flycatcher. The McConnell-Cobb study (see Part I, Ch. 8) indicates that by 1971 orchard lands had shrunk to a mere 4 acres total for the three towns. These changes may have played a significant part in the decline of the Least Flycatcher in our area.

Eastern Phoebe - *Sayornis phoebe*

Status: A common summer resident.

Occurrence: The first migrants usually arrive during the latter half of March—3/20/74 (Emery) **1** W. A general arrival occurs in early April—maxima: 4/8/56 (Drury) **35-40** W.

Nesting takes place from mid-April through early August.

The fall movement is most noticeable from mid-September through early October—9/25/54 (Fowler) **12** C. Stragglers are reported in late October—10/25/52 (Talbot) **1,1**, S,W.

Eastern Phoebe has been recorded once on the CCC—1/1/68, **1**.

Great Crested Flycatcher - *Myiarchus crinitus*

Status: An uncommon summer resident.

Occurrence: Migrants can be expected during the first part of May—5/2/54 (Morgan) **1** S; maxima: 5/18/68 (Seamans *et al.*) **25** C.

Nesting begins in the latter part of May and continues throughout June.

The fall movement is rarely noticed with only occasional reports of birds after June—7/11/82 (Walton) **1** W.

Western Kingbird - *Tyrannus verticalis*

Status: A fall vagrant.

Records: Six records since 1949. All but one between mid-September and the end of October—9/27/57 (Stackpole) **1** W; latest: 12/9/58 (Mrs. W. Shaw) **1** C. No records since 1966.

Eastern Kingbird - *Tyrannus tyrannus*

Status: A common summer resident.

Occurrence: A general arrival occurs during the first part of May—5/15/65 (Seamans *et al.*) **15** GM.

Nesting begins in mid-May and continues throughout June.

Towards the end of July and throughout August small groups congregate for the journey southward—8/25/81 (Hines) **10** W.

A few birds are observed in September and there is one October record: 10/27/58 (Armstrongs) **1** S.

Scissor-tailed Flycatcher - *Tyrannus forficatus*

Status: A vagrant.

Records: 6/12-16/59 (Benjamin, Morgan) **1** W.

Horned Lark - *Eremophila alpestris*

Status: An uncommon migrant and irregular winter visitor.

Occurrence: Spring migrants are occasionally seen from late February through April—3/21/68 (Sprong) **43** C.

Fall birds have been noted between mid-October and the end of November—11/7/65 (Coreys) **30** C.

At the present time this species is most often recorded as a winter visitor on agricultural fields in our area—1/7/78 (Walton) **84** C.

Remarks: Griscom described the two distinct populations that constitute the majority of records: 1. Northern Horned Lark (*alpestris*) —identified by their *yellow* eyebrow and described by Griscom as a "regular transient . . . occasional late winter flocks"; 2. Prairie Horned Lark (*praticola*)—identified by their *white* eyebrow (a few individuals of this population were summer residents in Concord as late as 1949). See *TBOC* for further discussion as well as the description of another race of Horned Lark (*hoyti*).

Purple Martin - *Progne subis*

Status: A rare spring migrant.

Occurrence: Between 1949 and 1966 spring birds were reported almost annually during the period from mid-April to the end of May—maxima: 4/25/54 (Wellman) **3** W. Thereafter, in many years there are no records. In 1983 a single bird was noted—5/15/83 (Walton) **1** C. In 1984, following a period of continuous rain, an unusually high count was made—6/2/84 (Hines) **10** W.

Remarks: This species was once a common summer resident in our area. This population was extirpated by the unusually cold weather and heavy rains in June of 1903. There are still a few enclaves of summer resident martins in Massachusetts but they have failed to recolonize our area. Although the return of this species to the Valley would be desirable, Purple Martins are not a panacea for the mosquito problem.

Tree Swallow - *Tachycineta bicolor*

Status: An abundant migrant and common summer resident.

Occurrence: Spring migrants are recorded from mid-March through mid-May—4/7/79 (Gove) **350** GM. Counts of over 1000 birds have been made on several occasions.

Nesting occurs during May and June.

Although the fall flight is a prolonged one and transients are observed between mid-July and late September, large flocks of migrants are most often recorded between mid-August and mid-September—maxima: 8/18/59 (Freeland) **1300** GM. Stragglers are noted in October—rarely in November—latest: 11/7/82 (Walton) **1** GM.

Northern Rough-winged Swallow - *Stelgidopteryx serripennis*†

Status: An uncommon spring migrant and summer resident.

Occurrence: Although early migrants are recorded in the first half of April—4/13/80 (Forster) **4** W, most spring records occur during the latter half of the month and into early May—5/7/65 (Coreys) **2** C.

Nesting occurs in May and June.

This species leaves our area by early August—latest: 8/21/49 (Morgan) **2**.

†formerly Rough-winged Swallow

Bank Swallow - *Riparia riparia*

Status: A common spring and uncommon fall migrant; a common but local summer resident.

Occurrence: First arrivals are recorded in early April, with the majority of migrants noted between mid-April and mid-May—4/19/80 (Forster) **50** S.

Nesting colonies are active during May and June. Summer residents move out of our area during July.

There are occasional records of fall migrants during August and September—9/11/80 (Stymeist) **15** GM. October records are rare—latest: 10/3/78 (Forster) **1** GM.

Cliff Swallow - *Hirundo pyrrhonota*

Status: An uncommon migrant.

Occurrence: Spring migrants occur from mid-April to the latter half of May—5/2/74 (Forster) **3** W.

Although the fall flight is even less pronounced than the spring one, occasional sighting of individuals or small groups of these swallows are made as they move south through our area from mid-July into September—9/11/80 (Stymeist) **1** GM; latest: 9/25/49 (Morgan) **2**.

Barn Swallow - *Hirundo rustica*

Status: An abundant migrant and a common summer resident.

Occurrence: A general arrival of Barn Swallows can be expected during the latter part of April—earliest: 3/29/76 (Evans) **1** GM. The spring movement continues into the first half of May—5/5/56 (Talbot) **40**.

Nesting occurs during the latter part of May and throughout June.

Southbound migrants are recorded, sometimes in large concentrations, between late July and mid-September—maxima: 8/21/81 (Hines) **800** W. Stragglers are reported in October. There is one extremely late record—12/6/53 (Wellman) **2** C.

Blue Jay - *Cyanocitta cristata*

Status: A permanent resident of variable status; a common summer resident, uncommon to abundant in winter, and often a common migrant.

Occurrence: Although there are always Blue Jays in our area, this species is most noticeable in winters when abundant and when migrating.

Spring flights are most often recorded in late April and early May—5/2/82 (SSBC) **200**, and fall movements between mid-September and late October—9/24/82 (Walton) **85**.

The winter status varies from uncommon, as in the 1982-1983 season, to abundant—1976 (CCC) **2054**—a record high count for the entire continent.

American Crow - *Corvus brachyrhynchos†*
Status: A common permanent resident, abundant at times as a fall migrant and winter resident.

Occurrence: Spring birds on the move are noted during the latter part of February and throughout March—3/13/52 (Searle) **150** S. Sizable flocks are sometimes noted during April and May—5/28/83 (Walton) **35** W.

Nesting occurs from late April through June.

Migrating flocks in fall are recorded throughout October and into the first half of November—maxima: 11/11/80 (Forster) **1000 +** .

Wintering flocks are an increasingly common feature of the winter landscape.

Remarks: Although Griscom characterized this species as "regular in winter in very small numbers . . . ", Morgan noted sizable flocks in the early 1950s: 1/22/50, **50**; 2/12/50 **75** W. CCC data indicate the increasing abundance of the winter population—1960, **130**, 1965, **907**; 1970, **979**; 1975, **852**; 1980, **1705**; maxima: 1981, **3048**.

†formerly Common Crow

Fish Crow - *Corvus ossifragus*

Status: A fairly common but local winter resident; possible summer resident.

Occurrence: This species is most often found, with American Crows, at the Sudbury and Wayland land-fills during the winter months—maxima: 11/20/82 (Forster) **60** W.

Individuals are regularly noted in the spring months and in 1983 a pair of Fish Crows was observed in the pines at Heard's Pond.

Remarks: Similar to the American Crow, but smaller, the Fish Crow is most easily detected by its distinctive voice. This species was first recorded in the Valley in March of 1961; the first record for the CCC was in 1977.

Black-capped Chickadee - *Parus atricapillus*

Status: A common permanent resident; abundant at times as a fall migrant.

Occurrence: A trip through the Valley will produce a half dozen to twenty or more Black-capped Chickadees in most seasons.

This species becomes somewhat less obvious during the nesting season in May and June.

Some Black-caps migrate every fall and from time to time there occurs exceptionally large movements that take place between mid-September and late October—9/25/54 (Fowler) **50** GM. (25)

Boreal Chickadee - *Parus hudsonicus*

Status: A rare migrant and winter visitor.

Records: From 10/26/63 (Coreys) **1** C to 4/28/70 (Smith) **1** W; maxima: 11/19/61 (R. Corey) **3** C.

Remarks: Spruce plantations are the preferred habitat for this winter visitor. (26)

Tufted Titmouse - *Parus bicolor*

Status: A common permanent resident.

Occurrence: Regularly observed in oak and mixed woodlands throughout the Valley—4/24/82 (Walton) **13**.

This species becomes somewhat less obvious during the nesting period in May, June and July.

During the winter months it is attracted to areas where feeding stations are maintained.

Remarks: Prior to 1957 this species was rare in Massachusetts. During the fall of 1957 there was a general invasion into our state as the Tufted Titmouse expanded its range northward. The first published record for the Valley was—1/18/58 (Hage) **2** W. Breeding was confirmed in 1962 —6/2/62 (Alden, Woodin) **2+** young C. Christmas Count data record the increase of this species: 1960, **0**; 1965, **9**; 1970, **115**; 1975, **288**; 1980, **604**; maxima: 1983, **636**. (27)

Red-breasted Nuthatch - *Sitta canadensis*

Status: A rare and irregular summer resident; an irregular winter visitor in variable numbers.

Occurrence: In flight years, birds are recorded as early as late July and into September.

The winter population is highly variable and dependent on the southward movement of this species into our area during the fall. There have been thirteen years (since 1960) when totals for this species on the Concord

Christmas Count were ten or less (unrecorded in two years); maxima: 1/2/77 (CCC) **142**.

Nesting records (usually after flight years) occur in the latter half of May and throughout June—6/1/81 (Hart) **2** ad. **4** imm. W.

White-breasted Nuthatch - *Sitta carolinensis*

Status: A common permanent resident.

Occurrence: Counts of two to six birds are fairly regular in early spring when this species becomes vocal.

Nesting begins in April and continues through June.

In winter White-breasted Nuthatches are often attracted to feeders. Christmas Count numbers indicate the sizable population: 1960, **43**; 1965, **188**; 1970, **231**; 1975, **242**; 1980, **408**; maxima: 1983, **515**.

Brown Creeper - *Certhia americana*

Status: An uncommon permanent resident.

Occurrence: The winter population is variable, as data from the CCC indicate—minima: 1960, **6**; maxima: 1973, **64**. The northward migration begins in March.

Nesting begins in late April and early May and may be overlooked by many observers—possibly because of its relatively early start.

The fall migration begins in late August and extends into November. This movement is hardly noticeable in the Valley.

Carolina Wren - *Thryothorus ludovicianus*

Status: An erratic visitor.

Occurrence: Sightings of single birds have been reported for every month except July and November; most recent: 9/4/84 (Forster) **1** HP. Almost half of the records occur during the March to May period. Nesting has not been confirmed although it remains a possibility.

Remarks: Basically a southerner, this wren's normal range lies well south of our area. However, the Carolina Wren is a permanent resident in southeastern Massachusetts where its numbers fluctuate according to the severity of the winters.

House Wren - *Troglodytes aedon*

Status: A fairly common spring migrant and summer resident; uncommon in the fall.

Occurrence: Spring arrivals are reported towards the end of April or beginning of May—maxima: 5/5/49 (Griscom) **20**.

Nesting occurs during the latter part of May and throughout June.

Occasional reports are made of migrants in September and early October—latest: 10/10/58 (Alden) **1** C.

Winter Wren - *Troglodytes troglodytes*

Status: A rare migrant and winter visitor with a sporadic nesting history.

Occurrence: Only nine spring records—all during April and the first part of May.

Nesting has been confirmed in the Estabrook Woods on several occasions—summer 1977 (Hinds) nest with young.

Reports of single birds in fall occur most often in late September and October—maxima: 9/29/75 (Hines) **2** W.

Of the twenty-four years of the Concord Christmas Count, this species has been recorded on twelve counts—maxima: 1966 and 1975, **4**.

Sedge Wren - *Cistothorus platensis*†

Status: A rare fall migrant.

Occurrence: Six spring records (May and early June) during the period 1949-1959. Since that time there have been no spring records and less than ten fall (September) records—9/6/81 (Forster) **1** GM.

Remarks: Towards the end of the nineteenth century this species was a common summer resident of the sedge meadows along the rivers. The numbers gradually declined and by 1945 Griscom knew of only one pair in the Valley (See *TBOC*).

†formerly Short-billed Marsh Wren

Marsh Wren - *Cistothorus palustris*†

Status: A common summer resident of the extensive cattail marshes.

Occurrence: A few birds are reported in late April but it is usually May before a general arrival occurs—5/15/65 (Seamans *et al.*) **6** C.

Nesting occurs from late May into July.

This species remains fairly common in its habitat throughout September—9/21/59 (Freeland) **35** GM, and individuals are regularly reported in October—10/13/75 (Hinds) **3** GM.

One or two individuals of this species have been recorded on the Christmas Count in eight out of twenty-four years.

†formerly Long-billed Marsh Wren

Golden-crowned Kinglet - *Regulus satrapa*

Status: An uncommon migrant; an irregular winter visitor.

Occurrence: A few small flocks (two to ten birds) are noted on their northward movement during April—4/11/79 (Walton) **3** C. After these birds leave, this species is absent from our area until the latter part of September or early October when southbound migrants may be observed—maxima: 9/27/52 (Taylor) **6** C.

Wintering populations are variable, as indicated by the CCC: 1965, **0**; 1973, **273**.

Ruby-crowned Kinglet - *Regulus calendula*

Status: A fairly common migrant; a few winter records.

Occurrence: Although some records exist of early April arrivals—4/4/81 (Rogers) **1** GM, most spring records are between mid-April and mid-May—5/5/56 (Talbot) **20**.

Fall reports occur most generally during September and October—10/10/81 (Walton) **2** C.

Between one and four stragglers have been reported on nine out of twenty-four Christmas Counts.

Blue-gray Gnatcatcher - *Polioptila caerulea*

Status: An uncommon spring migrant and markedly uncommon summer resident.

Occurrence: Spring migrants are most often reported between mid-April and mid-May—earliest: 4/15/74 (Hinds) **1** C.

Nesting occurs during June and has been confirmed on at least four occasions in the past four years.

Late summer sightings are rare and may be local family groups—8/23/82 (Walton) **3** S.

Remarks: This species has occurred in increasing numbers since the late 1940s with a decided increase since 1975. (28)

Eastern Bluebird - *Sialia sialis*

Status: A rare migrant and summer resident.

Occurrence: Present-day sightings of spring migrants are reduced to records of one or two birds in March or April.

The last nesting record I can find for the Valley proper was in 1974—8/2/74 (Gifford) adult and young C.

Fall records are even more sparse than spring; maxima (in the last twenty years):—10/15/80 (Benjamin) **7** W.

Remarks: Competition with House Sparrows and Tree Swallows, as well as drastically reduced habitat, has resulted in the virtual extirpation of this species which was once common. (29)

Veery - *Catharus fuscescens*

Status: An uncommon migrant and summer resident.

Occurrence: Spring arrival occurs about the first of May—5/6/54 (Wellman) **3** W.

Residents on territory can be fairly common in a few of the Valley's wet woodlands and nesting begins towards the end of May. Vocalizing birds are noted into early July—7/5/82 (Walton) **5**.

It is unusual for fall migrants to be noted on their southward journey—8/29/81 (Hines) **3** W.

Gray-cheeked Thrush - *Catharus minimus*

Status: A rare migrant.

Occurrence: This species most often goes unrecorded in spring. The best time to find it is during the latter half of May—5/18/62 (Hart) **1** W.

Records of fall migrants occur during the latter half of September and early October—maxima: 9/26-30/64 (J. Baird) **6** b RH.

Swainson's Thrush - *Catharus ustulatus*

Status: A rare spring and uncommon fall migrant.

Occurrence: Most records for spring migrants occur in the latter half of May and are restricted to sightings of one or two birds—5/31/83 (Walton) **2** RH. The spring of 1984 was a notable one for this species; numbers were well above normal—5/13/84 (Walton) **7** C.

In fall, the latter half of September proves to be the best time to see this thrush—9/19/62 (Junkin) **2** b RH. Only twice in the last thirty years have "waves" been reported—maxima: 9/25/49 (Morgan) **63**.

Hermit Thrush - *Catharus guttatus*

Status: An uncommon migrant, local summer resident and rare winter straggler.

Occurrence: This is the "early" spring thrush and is noted in our area during the month of April—maxima: 4/13/57 (BBC) **6** C.

Between three and six singing males have been noted in the Estabrook Woods during May and June and indicate probable nesting—1976, 1977 (Hinds) and 1983 (Walton).

Fall migrants are sometimes seen during the latter half of September but more often during October—10/9 and 11/66 (J. Baird) **3** b, **2** b RH.

A "late" thrush will most likely be this species and it has been recorded on half the Christmas Counts in the last twenty-four years—maxima: 1/2/77 (CCC) **5**.

Wood Thrush - *Hylocichla mustelina*

Status: A common spring and uncommon fall migrant; a fairly common summer resident.

Occurrence: A general arrival occurs during the first weeks of May—5/8/82 (Walton) **2** W; maxima: 5/13/50 (Parker *et al.*) **25**.

Singing males are often heard around wooded areas during the nesting period in the latter part of May and throughout June.

In the last weeks of August the Wood Thrush begins moving south. A few birds are recorded in September—9/21-26/68 (Howard) **5** b RH. A straggler was recorded on the CCC—12/26/71, **1**.

American Robin - *Turdus migratorius*

Status: A common migrant and summer resident; an uncommon winter resident.

Occurrence: The vanguard of spring migrants arrives by mid-March, however, it is not until the latter half of the month and the first part of April that numbers peak—maxima: 4/9/82 (Walton) **433** C, S.

Residents nest between late April and late July.

Large groups of fall migrants have been noted as early as late July—maxima: 7/28/64 (Kearney) **814** (at roost) W and as late as the latter part of October—10/18/64 (Baird) **350** S.

Wintering flocks of robins, in varying numbers, are to be expected—CCC minima: 12/30/62, **3**; maxima: 1/2/77, **229**.

Varied Thrush - *Ixoreus naevius*

Status: A vagrant.

Records: 12/25/77 to 1/8/78 (Parker) **1** C

Remarks: This western species occurs in Massachusetts mainly as a winter visitor.

Gray Catbird - *Dumetella carolinensis*

Status: A common spring migrant and summer resident; an uncommon fall migrant and rare winter straggler.

Occurrence: A general arrival occurs during the first part of May. Large counts are sometimes made as the migrants move through—5/15/65 (Seamans *et al.)* **60** C.

Nesting begins around mid-May and continues into July.

The fall flight is prolonged (mid-August to mid-October) and normally numbers are well below spring counts—9/24/82 (Walton) **7.**

This species has been recorded on nine out of twenty-four Concord Christmas Counts—maxima: 1982, **3.**

Northern Mockingbird - *Mimus polyglottos†*

Status: A common permanent resident.

Occurrence: Griscom published only four records in *TBOC*—1/1/39 (Clemensson) to 4/12/47 (Argue, Emery).

During the decade of the 1950s winter birds were seen approximately every two years. In 1962 the first confirmed nesting for the Valley was reported—7/17/62 (McWilliams) C.

Since the early 1960s the mockingbird has gradually established itself as a permanent resident in our area. An indication of the dramatic increase can be seen in the following CCC data: 1960, **0**; 1965, **4**; 1970, **24**; 1975, **139**; maxima: 1980, **314.**

Remarks: Along with the Cardinal and Tufted Titmouse, the Northern Mockingbird has increased its range northward over the past two decades. It is now commonplace and well established throughout the area. (27)

†formerly Mockingbird

Brown Thrasher - *Toxostoma rufum*

Status: An uncommon summer resident.

Occurrence: This species arrives between late April —4/22/54 (Morgan) **2** and mid-May—maxima: 5/15/65 (Seamans *et al.*) **20** C.

Nesting occurs from late May through June. Local birds are noted throughout July and into August.

A few migrants are recorded during September—9/6/65 (BBC) **3** GM.

Winter stragglers are occasionally reported as late as February. Recorded on ten Christmas Counts since 1960—maxima: 12/26/70 (CCC) **6**.

Water Pipit - *Anthus spinoletta*

Status: An uncommon to abundant migrant.

Occurrence: Spring flights occur between mid-March and mid-May. In the last twenty years the maximum count recorded for spring was: 4/11/65 (Elkins) **20** C. In the 1950s counts of thirty birds were common at this season—4/27/50 (Elkins) **30**.

The fall flight occurs between mid-September and mid-November. Numbers over the past two decades have been greater than spring tallies—maxima: 10/19/80 (Forster) **150+** C.

There are two records for late November and one for December—latest: 12/1/79 (Forster, Walton) **1** C.

Bohemian Waxwing - *Bombycilla garrulus*

Status: A rare winter visitor.

Records: 12/23/80 to 1/4/81 (Forster) **1** C
12/30/78 to 1/3/79 (Forster) **2** C
1/1/70 (Petersen) **1** C
1/23/62 (Parziale) **2** C
3/3-10/79 (Walton) **1** C
3/16/76 (Steadman) **3** W

Cedar Waxwing - *Bombycilla cedrorum*

Status: An uncommon summer resident; fairly common spring and fall migrant; an irregular winter visitor.

Occurence: Flocks of spring migrants are noted from mid-May to mid-June—maxima: 5/19/73 (E. Taylor) **100** W; 6/11/83 (Walton) **11** W.

Nesting occurs in June and throughout July.

Fall migrants are most often noted during September and October —9/20/81 (Hines) **20** W.

Wintering flocks may first appear in November and will often remain through April if there is an adequate food supply—1/7/79 (Walton) **80** C.

Northern Shrike - *Lanius excubitor*

Status: An uncommon winter visitor.

Occurrence: This shrike species may appear in the Valley in early November and remain as late as early April. During the last thirty years it has been absent in only nine years. Numbers vary from one to five individuals in any given year—maxima: 2/16/79 (Walton) **5**.

Remarks: The Valley is one of the better areas in the state to find Northern Shrike.

Loggerhead Shrike - *Lanius ludovicianus*

Status: A very rare migrant.

Occurrence: Late winter records have always been rare. The last two are 2/5/59 (Stackpole) **1** S and 1/2/77 (Kenneally, Miliotis) **1** C.

Two March and two early April reports indicate spring migrants—4/5/58 (Wiggin, Pratt) **1** S.

There are fifteen different reports of this species during the late August to late December period. All of these records are from the 1950s and early 1960s—maxima: 11/18/53 (Morgan, Wellman) **2**.

Remarks: The local occurrence of this species has declined dramatically since the early 1960s. The January 1977 sighting was the first in over a decade and none have been seen since. This population decline is taking place throughout its range and once again pesticides are believed to be the causal agent.

*European Starling - *Sturnus vulgaris*†

Status: An abundant permanent resident.

Records: 5/8/13 (Brewster) **1**—the first.
          10/24/67 (Mazzarese) 70,000 W—at roost.

Remarks: This species has enjoyed remarkable success in a mere half century.

†formerly Starling

White-eyed Vireo - *Vireo griseus*

Status: A vagrant.

Records: 4/23/77 (Hines) **1** W
5/13/50 (Griscom) **1**
5/22/60 (Jodrey, Soucy) **1** W
8/5/51 (Armstrong) **1** C
9/27/52 (Barry) **1** C

Solitary Vireo - *Vireo solitarius*

Status: An uncommon migrant and a sporadic breeder.

Occurrence: Spring records for this vireo fall between late April and early June—from 4/28/70 (Raabe) **1** GM to 6/6/76 (Clayton) **1** C. A majority of the records are during early May—maxima: 5/1/56 (Wellman) **3**.

Although the June record cited above may indicate a wandering non-breeder, the Solitary Vireo has been confirmed as a local nesting bird twice in the last ten years. R. Anthony found a Solitary Vireo on a nest in the Estabrook Woods in the summer of 1977.

Fall migrants are noted during September and October with most reports occurring in the latter half of September—maxima: 9/25/49 (Morgan) **4**.

Yellow-throated Vireo - *Vireo flavifrons*

Status: An uncommon migrant and local summer resident.

Occurrence: Twelve spring records since 1949. The spring arrival of this species occurs in the second half of May—5/20/83 (Forster) **1** W.

There are four nesting records for Yellow-throated Vireo: 1949, 1959, 1981, and 1983. Two of these resulted in successful nesting—the most recent: June 1983, **2** fledged young.

Warbling Vireo - *Vireo gilvus*

Status: A fairly common summer resident.

Occurrence: Although some summer residents arrive in early May, the general arrival of this species can be expected around mid-May—5/17/82 (Walton) **4** W.

Nesting occurs in late May and throughout June.

Southbound migrants are occasionally sighted during the latter part of August and throughout September—9/3/64 (Rhome) **2** W.

Remarks: Summer resident territories are often adjacent to rivers, streams and ponds.

Philadelphia Vireo - *Vireo philadelphicus*

Status: A rare migrant.

Records: 5/11/55 (Drury) **1** C
5/28/67 (Raabe) **1** GM

Ten fall records—all in September—maxima: 9/22/53 (Claflin) **2**.

Red-eyed Vireo - *Vireo olivaceus*

Status: A common summer resident.

Occurrence: Migrants arrive in our area in May —the vanguard being noted early in the month with numbers peaking in the latter half of May—maxima: 5/16/64 (Seamans *et al.*) **112** C.

Nesting occurs during the period from late May through mid-July. Males on territory are often heard at this time.

Towards the end of August a few southbound birds are recorded. One to three individuals per trip may be noted up to mid-September—latest: 10/26/58 (Alden) **1** C.

Blue-winged Warbler - *Vermivora pinus*

Status: An uncommon summer resident.

Occurrence: Summer residents move onto territories in the latter half of May—5/14-25/81 (Walton) **3** C. Nesting birds are noted throughout June—6/13/81 (Hines) **2** W and family groups have been reported in early July—7/2/78 (Walton) **2** ad., **1** fledgling S.

Fall migrants are sometimes noted in August and early September—latest: 9/3/81 (Hines) **1** W.

Remarks: During the past fifteen years there has been an increase in this species in upland areas adjacent to the river.

Golden-winged Warbler - *Vermivora chrysoptera*

Status: A markedly uncommon migrant.

Occurrence: Only ten spring records—all but one in May. This species is usually noted after the first week of May and all sightings are of one or two individuals—5/26/80 (Claytons) **1** GM.

There are only three fall records—from early August to early October —latest: 10/6/66 (Dalton) **1** S.

Remarks: Although Griscom noted that in his era there was no lack of suitable habitat for this species in our area, this is no longer true and accordingly there are no recent nesting records.

Tennessee Warbler - *Vermivora peregrina*

Status: A fairly common migrant.

Occurrence: The majority of spring migrants are noted in the second half of May. Normally one to five individuals are noted per trip although consistent field work may yield higher totals—5/16-23/75 (Forster) **75-100** S,W.

Most fall records are in September—maxima: 9/thru/66 (Howard) **22** b RH.

Orange-crowned Warbler - *Vermivora celata*

Status: A rare fall migrant.

Occurrence: Not more than half a dozen records since 1949. On the rare occasions that this species is found late in the year, the individual sometimes remains in and around one location. Overwintering birds apparently can survive by visiting feeding stations. The last record for the Valley was in Concord—9/28/78 (Cassie) **1.**

Remarks: Griscom published one spring record—5/13/06 (Brewster) **1.**

Nashville Warbler - *Vermivora ruficapilla*

Status: An uncommon migrant and rare summer resident.

Occurrence: Most spring migrants occur in the first half of May—5/6/56 (Bolton) **3** S.

There are probably less than ten breeding pairs in our area and I am aware of only two nesting confirmations—one in 1954 and one in 1979.

Fall migrants are noted during September and early October—maxima: 9/13-30/66 (Howard) **15** b RH.

Northern Parula - *Parula americana*

Status: An uncommon migrant.

Occurrence: Most spring records occur in late April and the first half of May.

September is the month that the majority of fall migrants are observed in our area—9/17-27/66 (Howard) **7** b RH.

Remarks: This species was a fairly common breeding bird in our area towards the end of the nineteenth century. Statewide its status as a summer resident has been greatly reduced in this century. Locally, no breeding pairs remain.

Yellow Warbler - *Dendroica petechia*

Status: A common spring migrant and summer resident.

Occurrence: A few birds appear in late April, but it is usually not until the first half of May that there will be a general arrival—5/1/82 (Walton) **15**.

Nesting occurs from late May through June at numerous sites along the river meadows.

Although a few migrants occur in September, this becomes a difficult species to find after August.

Remarks: The Yellow Warbler is one of the more common hosts of cowbird parasitism.

Chestnut-sided Warbler - *Dendroica pensylvanica*

Status: An uncommon migrant and rare summer resident.

Occurrence: Spring migrants most generally occur during the middle two weeks of May—5/20/84 (Walton) **3** C.

Nesting begins in late May and continues into June.

A few migrants are noted in the latter part of August and throughout September—10/15/80 (Ewer) **1** GM.

Remarks: Although Griscom described this as the "third most abundant woodland bird in the Region", this is definitely not the case today. There are a few scattered pairs (I know of two) nesting in our area but it takes a concerted effort to locate these. Griscom associated this species' success with the cutting and regrowth of the woodlands. Perhaps the continued maturation of our woodlands has gradually reduced suitable habitat for this species. Other factors, including the possible destruction of wintering habitat in the tropics, may be playing a part in the decline of this species.

Magnolia Warbler - *Dendroica magnolia*

Status: An uncommon migrant.

Occurrence: Most spring reports occur in the latter half of May and are records of one or two birds—5/24/83 (Walton) **2** C.

Fall migrants can be found throughout September and early October—maxima: 9/thru/66 (Howard) **19** b RH.

Remarks: The fall banding record cited above gives us an indication of the actual abundance of this species. Even an active observer would be fortunate to find this number of Magnolia Warblers in any given season.

Cape May Warbler - *Dendroica tigrina*

Status: A markedly uncommon migrant.

Occurrence: A few spring birds are recorded during the second and third weeks of May—5/13/54 (Stackpole) **2** W.

Fall reports, which are often more numerous than those in spring, occur between late August and the first half of October—maxima: 9/1/84 (Forster) **45**; 10/1-10/64 (J. Baird) **9** b RH.

Remarks: The recent increase in fall reports may be related to the outbreaks of spruce budworm in northern Maine and the Maritimes. (30)

Black-throated Blue Warbler - *Dendroica caerulescens*

Status: A markedly uncommon migrant.

Occurrence: Most spring records occur during the first half of May and report only one or two birds—5/5/56 (Talbot) **1**.

The fall flight occurs in the latter half of September and early October. The largest Valley count resulted from a bird-banding project at Round Hill—9/8-30/66 (Howard) **8** b RH.

Yellow-rumped Warbler - *Dendroica coronata*

Status: A common, at times abundant, migrant.

Occurrence: Although there are two late March reports—3/30/82 (Walton) **3** C, the majority of spring migrants pass through our area between mid-April and mid-May. At Heard's Pond woods on a good day, this species can be an abundant migrant—5/9/80 (Forster) **48** HP.

A singing Yellow-rump was noted at a late date in the spring of 1984—6/16/84 (Hines *et al.*) **1** W.

The fall movement generally occurs between mid-September and mid-October—maxima: 10/1-10/68 (Howard) **247** b RH. Most Yellow-rumped Warblers have moved south of our area by the end of October.

This warbler species often attempts to overwinter. The 1982 CCC recorded its highest total for this warbler—1/2/83, **35**.

Black-throated Green Warbler - *Dendroica virens*

Status: An uncommon migrant; an uncommon and local summer resident.

Occurrence: Spring migrants and a few summer residents are noted fairly regularly in a few of the region's mature pine wood stands. Estabrook Woods and Castle Hill are two places these birds can be found in June.

The fall flight occurs during September and early October—9/thru/66 (Howard) **12** b RH.

Remarks: Although this species was once a much more common summer resident, it has been assumed that the cutting of the old-field pine in the latter half of the nineteenth century (see Part I, Ch. 4) had a major local, negative effect on this species. Deteriorating conditions on this species' wintering grounds (Central and South American tropics) must also be considered as a possible factor in this warbler's status.

Blackburnian Warbler - *Dendroica fusca*

Status: An uncommon migrant.

Occurrence: Most spring migrants are noted during the second and third weeks of May—5/13-23/80 (Forster) **7** HP.

Fall migrants pass through our area during late August and September—9/24-29/66 (Howard) **5** b RH.

Remarks: This species was a summer resident in Brewster's era, but is no longer breeding in our area. Its habitat requirements are similar to those of the Black-throated Green Warbler and thus is probably subject to similar pressures.

Yellow-throated Warbler - *Dendroica dominica*

Status: A vagrant.

Records: 4/25/79 (Forster) **1** W

Remarks: A southern species and early spring migrant that is most likely to be encountered with flocks of Yellow-rumped Warblers.

Pine Warbler - *Dendroica pinus*

Status: An uncommon spring migrant and summer resident.

Occurrence: This warbler is a relatively early spring migrant. Individuals are noted from early April to early May—4/11/54 (Elkins) **3** C.

A female gathering nesting material was observed by Walton on 5/3/83 C. Singing males have been reported in mature pine stands in late May and June—6/21/79 (Forster) **3** W.

Fall migrants are decidedly rare.

Prairie Warbler - *Dendroica discolor*

Status: A markedly uncommon migrant and summer resident.

Occurrence: This species arrives in our area during the first half of May—5/2/65 (Corey) **2** C.

There are probably between five and ten pairs of summer residents in our area and these nest between late May and the end of June.

The majority of reports of fall migrants occur during September—9/3/56 (Seamans) **3** GM.

Remarks: The typical nesting habitat for this species in s.e. Massachusetts is Pitch Pine and Scrub Oak. Locally, disturbed areas with second growth near sandy soil are the preferred nesting habitat.

Palm Warbler - *Dendroica palmarum*

Status: A fairly common migrant.

Occurrence: In springtime, Palm Warblers are most often reported during the second half of April—4/19/82 (Turin) **12** W.

Fall migrants are most often seen in late September and early October —10/7/83 (Walton) **7** S.

Stragglers are not uncommon—the latest for our area—11/6/59 (Garrey) **1** S.

Remarks: Two races of this species are identifiable in the field: 1. Western Palm (*D. p. palmarum*) with *whitish* belly and 2. Yellow Palm (*D. p. hypochrysea*) with *yellow* belly.

Bay-breasted Warbler - *Dendroica castanea*

Status: An uncommon migrant.

Occurrence: Spring migrants are reported throughout May with the peak of the flight normally around mid-month—5/12-19/80 (Forster) **9** HP.

Fall migrants are recorded most often in September with a majority of the records during the first half of the month—9/6-28/66 (Howard) **11** b RH.

Remarks: The Bay-breasted Warbler may be another species that is profiting from the budworm outbreaks on their northern nesting territories. (30)

Blackpoll Warbler - *Dendroica striata*

Status: A fairly common spring and abundant fall migrant.

Occurrence: Spring migrants can be expected around mid-May with the flight continuing into June—5/13-28/80 (Forster) **28** W.

The fall movement occurs mainly in September and early October. Banding data from Round Hill indicate just how numerous this species can be in this season—September and October 1966 (J. Baird) **2131** b.

Cerulean Warbler - *Dendroica cerulea*

Status: A vagrant.

Records: 5/16/79 (Hayes) **1** W
5/17/64 (Preston) **1** W
5/17/81 (Forster) **1** HP

Black-and-white Warbler - *Mniotilta varia*

Status: A fairly common migrant and an uncommon summer resident.

Occurrence: Spring migrants generally arrive towards the end of April and beginning of May—5/1/54 (Morgan) **3** W.

Nesting occurs in late May and throughout June.

Fall migrants are recorded during late August and throughout September—9/thru/66 (Howard) **21** b RH.

An extremely late migrant may have been a reverse migrant—12/1/79 (Forster, Walton) **1** C.

Remarks: A maturing forest should improve local conditions for this species. It may well become a more common summer resident, providing that the forests do not become too fragmented by future development.

American Redstart - *Setophaga ruticilla*

Status: A common migrant and rare summer resident.

Occurrence: The majority of spring migrants are recorded during the last three weeks of May—5/23/80 (Forster) **8** W.

Nesting occurs in June (see Remarks).

Fall migrants are noted in late August and throughout September—maxima: 9/thru/66 (J. Baird) **21** b RH.

Remarks: It is difficult to believe that this species, which Griscom characterized as "one of the two most abundant woodland birds in eastern Massachusetts", could have declined so rapidly, but I know of only five confirmed nestings in our area within the last five years.

Prothonotary Warbler - *Protonotaria citrea*

Status: A vagrant.

Records: 5/10/81 (Walton) **1** W
6/12-17/84 (Forster) **1** W

Remarks: Griscom published three spring records as well as Brewster's 1886 August records for 2 males, a female, and a juvenile bird. See *TBOC* for details of what Brewster thought might be a nesting records.

Worm-eating Warbler - *Helmitheros vermivorus*

Status: A very rare migrant.

Records: 5/22/67 (Garrey) **1** W
9/1/59 (Gardler) **1** S

Remarks: This species is a rare and local summer resident in Weston.

Ovenbird - *Seiurus aurocapillus*

Status: A fairly common spring and markedly uncommon fall migrant; a fairly common summer resident of mature forests.

Occurrence: The period of general arrival in spring is during the first half of May. Normally two to four birds per trip will be seen or heard at this time. An exceptionally large count was made in 1950—maxima: 5/13/50 (Parker *et al.*) **50**.

Nesting occurs in June.

Fall migrants move southward through our area in September—9/thru/66 (J. Baird) **16** RH.

Northern Waterthrush - *Seiurus noveboracensis*

Status: A common migrant and an uncommon and local summer resident.

Occurrence: A majority of spring migrants are recorded during the first half of May—5/2/82 (Walton) **2**.

Singing males have been recorded in several of the Red Maple swamp areas of the Estabrook Woods and Heard's Pond throughout May and June.

Fall sightings of Northern Waterthrush occur less frequently than spring, but occasionally birds are noted in late August and throughout September—9/8/66 (Parker) **1** W.

There are two remarkable winter records for the CCC—1/1/70 (Alden, Petersen) **1** C; 12/16/73 (Alden) **1** C.

Louisiana Waterthrush - *Seiurus motacilla*

Status: A rare spring migrant and a rare and local summer resident.

Occurrence: There are only three records of spring migrants—from 4/13/69 (Daltons) **2** to 4/20/65 (Coreys)**1** C.

Hinds observed a chase flight of adults on 4/30/77 in a section of the Estabrook Woods. On 6/25/77 he confirmed the breeding of this species when he discovered a fledged Louisiana Waterthrush. On 5/3/83 the author noted two birds of this species displaying agitated behavior and in chase flight in another area of Estabrook Woods.

Remarks: Observers should note that this is an early spring migrant and is not to be expected after the end of April except on terrritory.

Kentucky Warbler - *Oporornis formosus*

Status: A vagrant.

Records: 5/16/82 to 7/23/82 (Harte) **1,2** C1.

5/25/83 (Hines) **1** W

Connecticut Warbler - *Oporornis agilis*

Status: A rare fall migrant.

Records: Only eleven reports since 1949. From 9/7/66 (Howard) **1** b RH to 10/17/54 (Elkins) **1** C. The only record of more than one bird—maxima: 9/26/64 (J. Baird) **3** b RH.

Mourning Warbler - *Oporornis philadelphia*

Status: A rare migrant.

Occurrence: Only ten records since 1949. Spring migrants are most often observed during the first two weeks of June—6/5/81 (Forster) **1** W.

Fall migrants move through our area during late August and September—9/18/53 (Morgan) **1**.

Common Yellowthroat - *Geothlypis trichas*

Status: A common migrant and summer resident.

Occurrence: Although a few birds are reported in late April, a majority of spring migrants are recorded in May—5/17/82 (Walton) **18**.

Nesting occurs in May, June and July when high counts of residents can be made—6/13/81 (Forster) **32** W.

During late August and throughout September, local birds and migrants gradually move southward—usually with no concentrations noted.

Stragglers in late fall and early winter are noted fairly regularly and this species has been recorded on the CCC on six years since 1960.

Hooded Warbler - *Wilsonia citrina*

Status: A vagrant.

Records: 5/13/51 (Helsher, Whitcomb) **1** C
5/15-19/70 (Bradley) **1** S
5/29/70 (Garrey) **1** S (same bird?)
5/16/62 (Tewksbury) **1** W
5/23-28/82 (Harte) **1** Cl
9/15/59 (Gardler) **1** S

Wilson's Warbler - *Wilsonia pusilla*

Status: An uncommon migrant.

Occurrence: Spring records are all in May and normally involve only one or two birds per report—5/14/80 (Forster) **2** HP.

The fall movement is somewhat more prolonged and this warbler is normally recorded between late August and early October.

An exceptionally late record—12/8/79 (Walton) **1** GM may have been the result of reverse migration.

Canada Warbler - *Wilsonia canadensis*

Status: An uncommon migrant and probable local and rare summer resident.

Occurrence: Spring migrants occur during the month of May. It is unusual to see more than two Canada Warblers per day in this season. An exceptionally high count was made in 1967—maxima: 5/19/67 (Dalton) **20** S.

Hinds observed Canada Warblers in Estabrook Woods in late May and early June of 1977. He noted singing males and several pairs during this period and it is probable that this species has nested in this area.

Fall reports, most often single birds, are scattered between mid-August and the latter part of September—maxima: 8/22/82 (Walton) **7**.

Remarks: Griscom reported an increase in summer resident Canada Warblers in the late 1940s. This trend did not continue and there apparently has been a decline in recent years since only a remnant population is present.

Yellow-breasted Chat - *Icteria virens*

Status: A vagrant.

Records: 5/16/81 (Cowperthwaite, Walton) to
6/7/81 (Forster) **1** W
6/2/52 (Floyd) **1** W
9/16/57 (Garrey) **1** W
10/17/54 (Morgan) **1** W

Summer Tanager - *Piranga rubra*

Status: A vagrant.

Records: 5/6/70 (Garrey, Baird) **1** W
5/8/72 (Alden) **1** C

Scarlet Tanager - *Piranga olivacea*

Status: A fairly common migrant and summer resident.

Occurrence: Although the first spring migrants are noted in early May, it is not until mid-month that a general arrival occurs. Normally two or three birds per trip will be seen or heard at this season. Occasionally a large count is made—5/26/56 (Wiggin) **25** C.

Local residents begin nest building towards the end of May and fledged young are reported in the latter half of June.

The fall flight is generally more extended than the spring movement with reports between late August and early October—maxima: 9/18/53 (Morgan) **6.**

Western Tanager - *Piranga ludoviciana*

Status: A vagrant.

Records: 1/21-24/61 (Lee, Cross, Seamans) **1** C

Northern Cardinal - *Cardinalis cardinalis*†

Status: A common permanent resident.

Occurrence: This species was first recorded in the Valley in 1953—10/24/53 (Stackpole) **1** W. By 1962 it was being reported regularly and it was apparent that this species was extending its range northward. The first nesting confirmation was made in 1966—7/12/66 (Nazor) **2** ad., **3** young C. The Northern Cardinal has gradually increased its population both locally and throughout the state since the early 1960s. A record of the local increase appears in the CCC data: 1960, **0**; 1965, **9**; 1970, **87**; 1975, **195**; 1980, **354**. (27)

Remarks: The concurrent increase in bird feeding has, no doubt, accelerated the range expansion of this species.

†formerly Cardinal

Rose-breasted Grosbeak - *Pheucticus ludovicianus*

Status: A fairly common migrant and summer resident.

Occurrence: Although late April birds are occasionally noted—4/30/81 (L. Taylor) **1** GM, a general arrival can be expected after the first week of May—5/13/82 (Walton) **5**.

Nesting occurs in late May and throughout June.

Fall migrants are recorded in September. A large count was made in 1966—9/3/66 (Morgan) **20** W.

Black-headed Grosbeak - *Pheucticus melanocephalus*

Status: A vagrant.

Records: 12/15/74 to 3/21/75 (Leahy, Forster, Neiffer) **1** C.

Indigo Bunting - *Passerina cyanea*

Status: An uncommon migrant and summer resident.

Occurrence: Residents arrive in our area around mid-May—5/13/80 (Warner) **2** W.

Nesting occurs in June and sometimes continues into early July.

The number of fall migrants between mid-August and late September usually exceeds spring counts—maxima: 9/20/82 (Walton) **15** C.

Painted Bunting - *Passerina ciris*

Status: A vagrant.

Records: Early May - 1961 (Mrs. Ralph A. Parker, *fide* C. Smith) **1** W.

Remarks: The details of this record are convincing. There are two other reports of this species from Cape Cod in late April of 1961.

Dickcissel - *Spiza americana*

Status: A very rare fall migrant with a few records of overwintering birds.

Occurrence: Twenty-seven reports in all—only four in the last fifteen years. Prior to 1967, this species was noted eight times in late winter or early spring (on dates that indicate overwintering birds). Most reports come from the period between late August and the end of October—9/20/76 (Hamilton) **1** S; 10/23/83 (Walton) **1** NAC.

Remarks: The occurrence of this species has decreased markedly in the last twenty years.

Rufous-sided Towhee - *Pipilo erythrophthalmus*

Status: A fairly common spring and uncommon fall migrant; an uncommon summer resident; regularly overwintering in small numbers.

Occurrence: A few birds will be observed in April each year but it is not until May that a general arrival occurs—5/14/66 (Seamans *et al.*) **20** C.

Nesting takes place in late May and June.

This species begins moving southward in late August and September although pronounced waves are seldom encountered in our area—9/9-30/64 (J. Baird) **11** b RH.

Winter stragglers are fairly regular and between one and sixteen birds have been recorded on twenty-one of twenty-four CCC.

American Tree Sparrow - *Spizella arborea*†

Status: A common fall migrant and winter resident; an uncommon spring migrant.

Occurrence: The vanguard of this species appears in the latter part of October—10/26/82 (Walton) **2** GM. Peak numbers often occur in November—11/10/82 (Walton) **80**. Winter flocks of these sparrows begin to thin out during March as the movement northward begins. The highest April total was—4/13/57 (BBC) **25** GM; the latest: 5/6/56 (Bolton, Jr.) **1** S.

Remarks: The winter abundance of American Tree Sparrow is a feature of the Sudbury River Valley. CCC maxima: 1980, **1486.**

†formerly Tree Sparrow

Chipping Sparrow - *Spizella passerina*

Status: An uncommon spring and fairly common fall migrant; a common summer resident.

Occurrence: The spring movement into our area occurs between mid-April and mid-May—5/15/65 (Seamans *et al.*) **20** C. Often the first birds to arrive are local residents.

Nesting takes place throughout June and into July.

The fall movement occurs between late August and mid-October when small groups, seldom large flocks, are seen—10/8/55 (Talbot) **20**; maxima: 9/28/50 (Wellman) **75**.

Winter stragglers have been recorded on seven out of twenty-four Christmas Counts.

Clay-colored Sparrow - *Spizella pallida*

Status: A vagrant.

Records: 12/26/71 to 1/1/72 (Forster) **1** S
1/5/71 (Forster) **1** L

Field Sparrow - *Spizella pusilla*

Status: An uncommon migrant and summer resident; a few birds overwinter.

Occurrence: Spring migrants arrive between April and mid-May—maxima: 5/6/61 (Seamans) **17** C.

Nesting occurs in late May and throughout June.

During the period from late September to late October, small groups of migrants are recorded—10/10/81 (Walton) **3** C.

This species regularly overwinters in small numbers—maxima: 11/25/80 (Forster) **18** S. It has been recorded in every year of the CCC—maxima: 1/2/83, **39**.

Vesper Sparrow - *Pooecetes gramineus*

Status: A rare migrant.

Occurrence: At the present time, it is unusual to see more than one or two birds per season. Spring records occur in April and fall reports between late September and late October—4/29/79 (Walton) **1** GM; 10/24/82 (Walton) **1** Cl. One December record—12/10/83 (Walton) **1** GM.

Remarks: This species was a common summer resident during the period of maximum clearing (1830-1890). As the woodlands increased this species decreased locally. By 1930, Griscom mentions only "two males". Since 1950, development on agricultural lands has further decreased habitat. The last May record that I can find is 5/19/54 (Drew) **2** S; the last sizable count of fall migrants is 9/29/55 (Campbell, Corey) **30** W.

Lark Sparrow - *Chondestes grammacus*

Status: A fall vagrant.

Records: Five fall records—from 9/10/65 (Kelly) **1** GM to 10/18/66 (Garrey) **1** GM.

One winter record—12/23/70 to 1/23/71 (Lavrakas, D'Entremont) **1** C.

Lark Bunting - *Calamospiza melanocorys*

Status: A vagrant.

Records: Only one record—11/11/47 (Cottrells, Griscom, Mrs. H. Parker) **1** W. See *TBOC* for a rather amusing account.

Savannah Sparrow - *Passerculus sandwichensis*

Status: A fairly common spring and common fall migrant; a rare summer resident with a few individuals overwintering on an irregular basis.

Occurrence: Although a few birds arrive in early April, most spring migrants are seen between mid-April and mid-May—4/28/79 (Walton) **17** C.

Nesting occurs in late May and June in only one or two locations in this area.

Fall migrants are most often noted between mid-September and late October—maxima: 9/26/81 (Walton) **150 +** C.

Overwintering Savannah Sparrows have been recorded on eleven out of twenty-four CCC—maxima: 1961 and 1983, **5.**

Remarks: The large, pale coastal race (*P.s. princeps*) has occured in the Valley only once—10/10/66 (Garrey) **1** GM.

Grasshopper Sparrow - *Ammodramus savannarum*

Status: A very rare migrant.

Occurrence: Only five spring records since 1959 —the most recent: 5/20/72 (Bemis) **1** C.

The last summer record—June/July 1952 (Hayden) **2** C (see Remarks).

The most recent fall record was in 1976—10/19-22/76 (Hines) **1** W.

Remarks: This species was a common summer resident in the latter part of the nineteenth century. Armstrong located "12 singing males" in the Concord area in 1943. Since that time this species has essentially been absent from our area although during the 1984 nesting season several pairs were located at Hanscom Field.

Henslow's Sparrow - *Ammodramus henslowii*

Status: A vagrant.

Records: Six records between 1949 and 1959, from 5/14/49 (Griscom) **1** to 8/9/59 (Smith, Jr.) **1** C; only two since 1959—1/1/83 (Hines) **1** W and 9/27/83 (Hines) **1** W.

Remarks: Griscom described this species as an erratic summer resident and his account implies that nesting perhaps occurred as recently as 1948.

Sharp-tailed Sparrow - *Ammodramus caudacutus*

Status: A rare migrant.

Occurrence: Only three spring records since 1949—5/30/52 (Morgan, J. Baird) **1** W; 6/3/51 (Caldwell) **1** C; 6/13/76 (Hines) **1** W.

Twelve fall records—from 9/23/50 (Pratt) **1** W to 11/1/58 (Eliot) **1** C; maxima: 10/6/57 (Morgan) **3** C.

Remarks: Although not recorded annually, this species most likely moves through our area each spring and fall in small numbers. Its secretive nature results in it being overlooked. (31)

Seaside Sparrow - *Ammodramus maritimus*

Status: A vagrant.

Records: 9/5-7/81 (Walton) **1** GM.

Remarks: Because of this species' close association with salt marshes, inland records are rare—this being the only one for Massachusetts. (32)

Fox Sparrow - *Passerella iliaca*

Status: A regular migrant in variable numbers.

Occurrence: Spring migrants move through our area between mid-March and mid-April. Reports for most years involve between five and twenty-five individuals observed—3/31/65 (Parker) **15** W. Occasionally flocks of fifty birds are reported and rarely large waves—maxima: 3/22/59 (Morgan) **700**.

Fall migrants are noted between mid-October and mid-November—11/4/78 (Forster) **18** S.

Fox Sparrow has been missed on only two CCC—maxima: 1969, **39**.

Song Sparrow - *Melospiza melodia*

Status: A common permanent resident and migrant.

Occurrence: Spring migrants are noted between early March and mid-May—4/3/82 (Walton) **37**.

Some local residents are nesting by late April and the nesting season continues into July.

Fall migrants are noted between mid-September and late October—10/5/81 (Hines) **40** W.

The local winter population is variable. CCC minima: 1962, **20**; maxima: 1976, **321**.

Remarks: Griscom indicated that this species was just beginning to winter in our area in 1949.

Lincoln's Sparrow - *Melospiza lincolnii*

Status: A rare spring and uncommon fall migrant.

Occurrence: Less than ten spring records—all in the second half of May—5/23/73 (Scott) **2** GM.

Fall migrants occur between mid-September and late October —10/1-6/81 (Hines) **8** W.

Remarks: It is interesting to note that Griscom considered this species to be less common in fall. This has definitely not been the case since 1949.

Swamp Sparrow - *Melospiza georgiana*

Status: A fairly common migrant and common summer resident; a regular winter straggler in suitable habitat.

Occurrence: Spring migrants usually arrive during the latter part of April—4/24/49 (Morgan) **40**.

Nesting occurs from May through July.

Most fall migrants are recorded between mid-September and late October —10/5/81 (Hines) **80+** W.

Overwintering birds are regularly recorded in the cattail marshes. CCC minima: 1968, **2**; maxima: 1969, **58**.

White-throated Sparrow - *Zonotrichia albicollis*

Status: A common migrant and regular winter resident in variable numbers; possibly a few summer residents.

Occurrence: Most spring migrants are noted between late April and mid-May.

Although not a confirmed nester, there are a few reports of singing White-throated Sparrows from several locations in our area during June and July.

The fall movement begins in the second half of September and is generally over by early November—maxima: 10/13/82 (Walton) **67**.

Numbers of winter residents are variable. CCC minima: 1960, **4**; maxima: 1976, **831**.

White-crowned Sparrow - *Zonotrichia leucophrys*

Status: An uncommon migrant.

Occurrence: Most spring migrants are reported in May—5/8/64 (Howard) **2** C.

Fall migrants occur between late September and early November. Reports are typically of one to five birds—maxima: 10/15/80 (Ewer) **25** C.

One to three individuals of this species have been recorded on six Christmas Counts.

Dark-eyed Junco - *Junco hyemalis*

Status: A common migrant and winter resident; a rare and irregular summer resident.

Occurrence: Migrants move through our area between late March and mid-April—4/11/64 (Alden) **30** C.

Nesting in our area is unusual and there are only three confirmations since 1949: 1952, 1963 and 1964.

In fall, migrants are observed between mid-September and mid-November—10/1-10/68 (Howard) **60** b RH.

Winter numbers are highly variable. CCC minima: 1960, **147**; maxima: 1970, **2118**.

Lapland Longspur - *Calcarius lapponicus*

Status: A rare winter visitor.

Occurrence: Fifteen records have been published since 1949. From 9/10-11/75 (Baird, Miliotis) **1** GM to 3/1/59 (Drury) **3** C; maxima: 12/16/73 (CCC) **6**.

Snow Bunting - *Plectrophenax hyperboreus*

Status: An uncommon migrant and irregular winter visitor.

Occurrence: Migrants are recorded during the latter part of October through mid-November. These are most often groups of one to ten birds—maxima: 11/6/77 (Claytons) **30** GM.

Flocks of winter visitors or spring migrants are recorded between mid-December and late March—maxima: 2/11/56 (Bolton) **125** NAC.

Bobolink - *Dolichonyx oryzivorus*

Status: A fairly common spring and common fall migrant; an uncommon summer resident.

Occurrence; Spring migrants move through in May—earliest: 4/30/56 (Stackpole) **1** S; 5/14/82 (Porter) **50** GM.

A remnant population of summer residents nest during June and July.

Fall migrants are noted from late July through the end of September—8/30/78 (Perkins) **65** C.

An extraordinary late bird was located at the Concord sewer beds in 1983—12/11-17/83 (Hines, Walton) **1**.

Remarks: The status of summer residents has changed from common to uncommon in the last hundred years. Most of the hay fields and upland meadows that once supported this species have been developed or grown up to shrub communities. The few suitable areas that remain are usually cut so early that the nesting Bobolinks are driven off.

Red-winged Blackbird - *Agelaius phoeniceus*

Status: An abundant migrant and summer resident.

Occurrence: The first flocks of spring migrants are sometimes reported in the third week of February—2/18/81 (Walton) **31** C. Numbers begin to build during the first part of March—3/5/80 (J. Baird) **400** S, and peak towards the end of March or the beginning of April—maxima: 3/22/71 (Swift) **5,000** NAC.

Nesting begins during May and continues through June and July.

By mid-July aggregations of local birds are noted—7/11/82 (Walton) **53** S. Fall migrants are most noticeable during September and October when large groups roam about the Valley or fly to roost—maxima: 10/24/67 (Mazzarese) **20,000** at roost W. This species often remains abundant into November.

A few birds are to be expected in our area throughout the winter months—CCC maxima: 1976, **66**.

Eastern Meadowlark - *Sturnella magna*

Status: An uncommon migrant and summer resident; a few birds overwinter in most years.

Occurrence: Spring migrants are reported in late March and April—4/2/66 (BBC) **3** S.

Nesting occurs in May and June.

A few migrants are reported during September and October—10/12/66 (BBC) **3** W.

Small groups of overwintering meadowlarks are reported sporadically between November and February. The highest Christmas Count total was in 1963 when **34** birds were reported.

Remarks: This species suffers locally from basically the same factors that affect the Bobolink population.

Western Meadowlark - *Sturnella neglecta*

Status: A vagrant.

Records: 5/5/69 (McAllester, *fide* C. Smith) **1**

Yellow-headed Blackbird - *Xanthocephalus xanthocephalus*

Status: A vagrant.

Records: 6/25/76 (Hines) **1** W
8/24/59 (Gardler) **1** GM

Rusty Blackbird - *Euphagus carolinus*

Status: A fairly common migrant.

Occurrence: Spring migrants sometimes occur in two movements. The first birds are noted during early March—3/9/80 (Forster) **2** W and this part of the flight continues through the first week in April. Towards the end of April a second flight may be noted which continues through the first week of May—5/2/81 (Forster) **15** W.

Most fall migrants are noted between the latter part of September and mid-October. Normally, groups of between five and fifteen birds are reported although larger flocks are recorded as birds move to roosts—10/11/81 (Petersen) **300** C.

Rusty Blackbirds have been recorded on fourteen CCC—maxima: 1976, **13**.

Common Grackle-*Quiscalus quiscalus*

Status: A common spring migrant and summer resident, abundant at times in fall; the number of overwintering birds is variable.

Occurrence: The vanguard of spring migrants may appear in late February—often in association with Red-winged Blackbirds —2/17/81 (Forster) **50** C. The main flight occurs between mid-March and April. An extraordinary number was recorded in the spring of 1950—maxima: 4/1/50 (Parker) **13,000.**

Nesting occurs in May and June.

Fall congregations are noted from late July through mid-November. A peak is usually reached in late October when tremendous flocks of grackles are noted—particularly at roosts—maxima: 10/26/52 (Wellman, *et al.*) **500,000** C.

Common Grackles have been missed on only one Christmas Count—the first one—maxima: 1977, **164.**

Brown-headed Cowbird - *Molothrus ater*

Status: A common migrant and summer resident; overwintering birds are regular but numbers are highly variable.

Occurrence: Spring migrants are noted between late February and early May—3/30/67 (Elkins) **35** C.

"Nesting" of this brood parasite commences in late May and continues through July at the expense of host species.

Fall migrants are noted between mid-July and early November. An unusually high count was made in 1967 at a roost—maxima: 10/24/67 (Mazzarese) **30,000** W. Flocks of 25 to 150 birds are usual.

Brown-headed Cowbird has not been missed on the Christmas Count —minima: 1962, **2**; maxima: 1973, **549.**

Orchard Oriole - *Icterus spurius*

Status: A rare migrant and summer resident.

Occurrence: The first spring reports are in early May. The majority of sightings are, however, during the third week of the month—5/16/80 (Heil) **3** W.

Nesting occurs in June—6/16/84 (Forster *et al.*) **2** ad. feeding young W.

This species departs soon after nesting is complete and it is rare to see Orchard Orioles after late July—latest: 8/20/52 (Gardler) **2** W. (33)

Northern Oriole - *Icterus galbula*

Status: A common spring migrant, fairly common summer resident, and uncommon fall migrant.

Occurrence: The first spring migrants arrive in early May, although it is mid-May before a general arrival occurs—5/22/82 (Walton) **12**.

Nesting takes place from late May through early July.

The fall migration is underway by the end of August and continues through September; rarely into October.

Northern Orioles are reported on approximately one in three Christmas Counts—maxima: 1967, **3**.

Pine Grosbeak - *Pinicola enucleator*

Status: An irregular winter visitor.

Occurrence: This species has visited our area in fifteen of the last twenty-four winter seasons. Most reports occur from November through March although the earliest record is—10/17/57 (Mott) **1** C and the latest—5/7/66 (Delaney) **2** W. Usual counts range from five to twenty birds. An unprecedented flight took place in 1978—maxima: 1/15/78 (Hamilton, Forster, Walton) **400 +** . (34)

Purple Finch - *Carpodacus purpureus*

Status: An uncommon migrant and summer resident; flocks of winter visitors appear irregularly and in variable numbers.

Occurrence: Residents arrive in April. At times their occurrence coincides with the presence of lingering winter flocks and/or northbound migrants.

By mid-May singing adult, male Purple Finches noted in our area are good evidence that a nest is nearby. Nesting continues throughout June.

Fall migrants are noted from mid-September through October—maxima: 10/12/64 (Rhome) **140** C.

Flocks of winter visitors are usually noted between December and late March—maxima: 12/23/82 (Walton) **63**. The variable nature of winter flocks is reflected in the CCC data—minima: 1966, **6**; maxima: 1982, **612**.

Remarks: The flight of 1982-1983 was an outstanding one. Christmas Count totals were four times as great as the previous high. Other significant flight years were: 1883-1884, 1939, 1941, and 1950-1951.

House Finch - *Carpodacus mexicanus*

Status: A fairly common permanent resident.

Occurrence: Individuals and flocks of varying size may be found near town centers and farm buildings in the Valley at any season.

Remarks: A native of the western states, this species was introduced in the New York City area in the early 1940s, and is now found throughout the East and Midwest from southern Canada south to Georgia and Alabama. The first Massachusetts record was in 1957. The first record for the Valley was in 1964—11/thru/64 (Corey) **1** C. Judging from the House Finch's past success, we may assume that this species is here to stay and will become even more common. CCC maxima: 1983, **844**. (35)

Red Crossbill - *Loxia curvirostra*

Status: An irregular winter and spring visitor.

Occurrence: Most reports (17 out of 21) occur between February and May—maxima: 5/10/70 (Morgan) **75-100** W.

White-winged Crossbill - *Loxia leucoptera*

Status: An irregular winter visitor.

Occurrence: A total of fifteen records in six years since 1949—from 11/3/63 (Morgan) **9** to 4/3/63 (Teich) **1** W. Most reports are between January and March—2/5/82 (Hines) **12** W; maxima: 2/thru/53 (A. Peterson) **40** C.

Common Redpoll - *Carduelis flammea*

Status: An irregular winter visitor.

Occurrence: Records occur between mid-November and April—from 11/15/52 (Morgan) **2** to 4/19/56 (McCarthy) **1** W. Most reports are of between five and fifty birds—maxima: 3/9/76 (Claflin) **200** C. This species has been recorded on nine of the twenty-four Christmas Counts—maxima: 1968, **157**.

Remarks: Redpolls may be common in our area during periods which are characterized as "flight years". These erratic irruptions southward may be tied to food source cycles in the normal (northern) range of this species.

Hoary Redpoll - *Carduelis hornemanni*

Status: A rare and irregular winter visitor.

Records: Eight records in five different years: 1949, 1953, 1958, 1966, and 1982. Reports are of one to three birds in the January through March period—most recent: 3/1-12/82 (Walton) **2** C.

Remarks: This species is invariably found with Common Redpolls in flight years.

Pine Siskin - *Carduelis pinus*

Status: An irregular migrant and winter visitor; some indications of sporadic nesting.

Occurrence: In flight years, reports of Pine Siskins on the move occur in October and November—10/11/80 (Komars) **60** GM. Following such flights, siskins are often observed in small flocks throughout the winter—maxima: 2/15/78 (Long) **100** W. In some years a few birds remain into spring and rarely nesting may occur. Morgan reported a singing siskin in Wayland on 7/21/49.

This species has been recorded on seventeen of the Christmas Counts—maxima: 1977, **1258**.

American Goldfinch - *Carduelis tristis*

Status: A permanent resident; common summer resident and migrant; irregularly common in winter.

Occurrence: Spring migrants are reported from late March through mid-May and are, at times, common—4/24/64 (Rau) **40** W.

Summer residents are late nesters and begin nest building in mid-July. Fledged young are noted in August.

Southbound migrants are recorded from September through mid-November—10/29/67 (Thornton) **50** C.

The winter population varies from year to year. CCC minima: 1960, **48**; maxima: 1972, **1425**.

Evening Grosbeak - *Coccothraustes vespertinus*

Status: A migrant and winter resident in variable numbers.

Occurrence: The fall movement of birds into our area occurs between late September—earliest: 9/16/57 (Stackpole) **1** W, and early December.

Mid-winter records of ten to fifty birds at feeding stations and around trees with persistent seeds and fruit occur regularly. Christmas Count maxima: 1983, **1672**.

The spring flight during the latter part of April through mid-May sometimes produces counts in excess of 100 birds—4/29/83 (Walton) **125**; latest: 6/10/66 (C.E. Smith) **1 W**.

Remarks: The first record for Evening Grosbeak in Massachusetts was in the winter of 1889-1890. For the next sixty years it appeared during some winters but was absent in others. By the late 1940s this species began to visit the state regularly each winter. Griscom described its status in the Concord Region as "now present four winters out of five". It is now to be expected each winter.

*House Sparrow - *Passer domesticus*

Status: An abundant permanent resident.

Records: CCC—minima: 1960, **840**; maxima: 1980, **2419**. These counts are possibly suspect in that observers are loath to count this species carefully. Suffice it to say that there are numerous House Sparrows in the Valley.

Remarks: The House or English Sparrow was brought from Europe and Britain during the 1850s and 1860s and introduced in several New York and New England communities. The House Sparrow was established in the Boston area by 1869 and was common in our area by the 1880s. During the past hundred years it has gradually spread throughout North America—often in close association with man.

It is probable that this species reached its peak several decades ago. Although its numbers are declining, it is still abundant.

Appendix A

Valley Birdlife: Seasons and Habitats

The most productive birding habitats in the Valley are the rivers, the cattail marshes, certain of the Red Maple swamps, the remaining field and agricultural plots, and a few of the maturing, second growth forests. The most frequently visited spots, which contain a combination of several of the above mentioned habitats, are the Heard's Pond area in Wayland, Nine Acre Corner at Route 117 and the Great Meadows National Wildlife impoundments off Monsen Road in Concord. The river is best viewed from the various bridges—most notably the Pelham Island, Route 27 and Sherman bridges in Wayland, the Route 117 bridge and Heath Bridge in Concord, and the Route 225 bridge in Carlisle.

The Sudbury River Valley is a good area to observe the early spring (early March through April) migration of blackbirds and waterfowl. Flocks of redwings and grackles are often noted in the agricultural areas while Rusty Blackbirds are common at times in the Red Maple swamps. Both the diving and the surface-feeding ducks can be numerous along the rivers as well as at Heard's Pond, Wash Brook, Nine Acre Corner and the Great Meadows impoundments. Ring-necked Duck, Common Goldeneye, Common and Hooded Mergansers are regular features of the early spring migration. Wood Duck, both teal species, American Black Duck, Northern Pintail and American Wigeon are commonly noted along with fairly regular sightings of Northern Shoveler and Gadwall. The early spring can also be a good time to observe migrant Common Snipe in many of the flooded fields.

During late April and May, the most advantageous spot to observe the migration is the Heard's Pond locale. Inclement weather often produces both variety and numbers of swallows over the pond and river. Griscom Woods, the area between Heard's Pond and Wash Brook, as well as Heard Farm are two of the better places in the Valley to see migrant warblers and other landbirds. Round Hill, an area of second growth woodlands, agricultural fields and community gardens also attracts spring migrants. Although the number of hawks is usually small, the top of Round Hill is a good vantage point for the spring flight.

Summer resident rails and bitterns are also a feature of the Valley. The extensive cattail marsh areas of Wash Brook and the Great Meadows impoundments are the places to observe the various species. Although numbers are variable from year to year, both the Sora and the Virginia Rail can be found at these spots. In the same locales, the American Bittern is a regular but uncommon resident while there may be no more than one or two pairs of Least Bittern in any given year. Common Moorhen, Marsh Wren and Swamp Sparrow also nest in these marsh habitats. The Wood Duck population is a feature of this area with many birds taking advantage of the nesting boxes located at various places along the rivers. Red-winged Blackbirds, Yellow Warblers, Willow Flycatchers and Warbling Vireos can commonly be found nesting in the flood plain. Productive areas of maturing, wooded uplands include Castle Hill in Wayland, Mt. Misery in Lincoln and Estabrook Woods in Concord and Carlisle.

One of the best places in the Valley to observe the fall migration is at the Great Meadows impoundments. Herons and waterfowl as well as shorebirds (in years of low water) are the predominant groups. By late July, post-breeding birds, including Great Blue Herons and Black-crowned Night-Herons, move into this area. By late August the Green-backed Heron and the American Bittern are seen regularly. Resident and migrant rails (Sora and Virginia) are, at times, numerous in fall at Great Meadows. While the diving ducks are rare in this season, the dabblers move into this staging area in impressive numbers. Species which are often abundant include American Wigeon, Green-winged Teal and Wood Duck. American Black Duck, Northern Pintail, Gadwall, Blue-winged Teal and Northern Shoveler are also seen regularly. In late fall, American Coot can be found feeding along with the ducks. Least Sandpiper, Killdeer, Common Snipe, Spotted Sandpiper, Solitary Sandpiper, Lesser Yellowlegs and Pectoral Sandpiper are among the regular fall migrants which are recorded at Great Meadows. The Lesser Golden Plover is another species which occurs regularly at the impoundments. These plovers are also recorded on the fields at Nine Acre Corner during October. Another fall feature of the Valley is the Water Pipit—a species which favors the same open fields as the golden plover. The Nine Acre Corner area as well as other weed-field habitats are often ideal locales to search for migrating sparrows. Savannah, Swamp and Song Sparrow are often numerous while other species including Lincoln's and White-crowned Sparrows are regular transients. Large flocks of migrating and foraging blackbirds are also typcial of the fall season. Although the fall hawk flight is rarely spectacular in the Valley, the observer can expect to find many of Massachusetts' transient hawks during this season. Ospreys and Broad-winged Hawks are observed frequently.

The scarcity of winter birdlife stands in stark contrast to the relative abundance of fall. Resident Red-tailed Hawks can be found with regularity along the river-bottom land. American Crows and Blue Jays are often highly visible, with the latter species sometimes wintering in very large numbers. The Valley is a good place to look for Northern Shrike; wintering Tree Sparrow flocks are also noteworthy. At the Sudbury-Wayland landfills a few white-winged gulls are occasionally found with the more common species but the winter birdwatcher is more apt to be rewarded by the numerous Fish Crows in this area. In flight years, the various irregular winter vistors may be well represented in the Sudbury River Valley. Large numbers of Pine Grosbeaks, Purple Finches, Common Redpolls and Pine Siskins have been recorded.

Appendix B

Concord Christmas Count

The Concord Christmas Count is one of approximately 1500 bird counts held annually during the period December 17 - January 2. This census is supervised by the National Audubon Society which publishes the results in its journal - *American Birds* (formerly *Audubon Field Notes)*. Each count involves a group of observers who attempt to census as many of the birds as possible in their area (a circle with a fifteen mile diameter) during one calendar day.

The center of the Concord Christmas Count area is the junction of Concord, Sudbury, Maynard and Acton. Twenty-four counts have been held here since 1960. The following tables give the results of these counts. See annual Christmas Count issues of *American Birds* for other details.

CONCORD CHRISTMAS COUNT 1960-1983

SPECIES	1960 1961	1962 1963	1964 1965	1966 1967	1968 1969	1970 1971	1972 1973	1974 1975	1976 1977	1978 1979	1980 1981	1982 1983
Pied-billed Grebe	0 0	0 0	1 0	0 1	1 1	1 1	1 5	0 0	0 1	1 4	2 0	0 1
Great Cormorant	0 0	0 0	0 1	0 0	0 0	0 0	0 0	0 0	0 0	0 0	0 0	0 0
American Bittern	0 0	0 0	0 0	0 0	0 0	0 0	0 0	0 0	0 0	0 1	0 0	0 0
Great Blue Heron	0 1	0 0	0 0	0 0	0 1	0 0	1 2	2 0	1 2	0 1	5 2	1 1
Green-backed Heron	0 0	0 0	0 0	0 0	0 0	0 0	0 0	0 0	0 0	0 1	0 0	0 0
Mute Swan	0 0	0 0	0 0	0 0	0 0	0 0	1 0	0 0	0 0	0 0	0 0	2 0
Snow Goose	0 0	0 0	0 0	0 0	0 0	0 0	0 1	0 0	0 0	0 0	0 0	0 0
Canada Goose	165 232	40 388	208 187	246 175	230 165	168 174	150 1086	581 370	631 521	985 1649	1513 908	3044 1798
Wood Duck	0 1	4 0	0 0	0 0	0 0	0 0	1 1	0 1	1 0	0 0	5 2	1 0
Green-winged Teal	1 0	0 0	0 1	0 1	0 1	0 0	1 10	4 1	4 2	3 1	0 1	2 1

SPECIES	1960 1961	1962 1963	1964 1965	1966 1967	1968 1969	1970 1971	1972 1973	1974 1975	1976 1977	1978 1979	1980 1981	1982 1983
American Black Duck	20 / 8	11 / 52	28 / 104	120 / 46	103 / 205	147 / 153	84 / 508	269 / 195	274 / 123	173 / 281	205 / 84	236 / 222
Mallard	2 / 2	0 / 40	27 / 57	167 / 125	234 / 311	266 / 89	384 / 791	349 / 376	829 / 386	594 / 1223	569 / 560	593 / 539
Northern Pintail	0 / 0	0 / 0	0 / 0	0 / 0	0 / 0	0 / 0	0 / 18	4 / 1	0 / 0	0 / 0	0 / 0	2 / 0
Blue-winged Teal	0 / 0	0 / 0	0 / 0	0 / 0	0 / 0	0 / 0	0 / 0	1 / 0	0 / 0	0 / 0	0 / 0	0 / 0
Northern Shoveler	0 / 0	0 / 0	0 / 0	0 / 0	0 / 0	0 / 0	0 / 0	1 / 0	0 / 0	0 / 0	0 / 0	0 / 0
Gadwall	0 / 0	0 / 0	0 / 0	0 / 0	0 / 0	0 / 0	0 / 65	40 / 0	0 / 0	0 / 0	0 / 0	5 / 0
American Wigeon	0 / 0	0 / 0	0 / 0	0 / 0	0 / 0	0 / 0	0 / 154	12 / 0	1 / 0	0 / 0	0 / 1	1 / 0
Canvasback	0 / 0	0 / 0	0 / 0	0 / 0	0 / 0	0 / 0	0 / 0	0 / 0	0 / 0	0 / 1	0 / 0	9 / 0
Redhead	0 / 0	0 / 0	0 / 0	0 / 0	0 / 0	0 / 0	0 / 0	0 / 1	0 / 0	0 / 0	0 / 0	0 / 0
Ring-necked Duck	0 / 1	0 / 0	0 / 0	0 / 0	0 / 1	0 / 0	0 / 1	5 / 2	0 / 2	2 / 20	0 / 2	17 / 0
Greater Scaup	0 / 0	0 / 0	0 / 0	0 / 0	0 / 0	0 / 0	0 / 0	0 / 0	0 / 0	0 / 0	1 / 0	0 / 0

SPECIES	1960 1961	1962 1963	1964 1965	1966 1967	1968 1969	1970 1971	1972 1973	1974 1975	1976 1977	1978 1979	1980 1981	1982 1983
Lesser Scaup	0 0	0 0	0 0	0 0	0 0	0 0	0 0	0 0	0 1	0 0	0 0	0 0
Scaup species	0 0	0 0	0 0	0 0	0 0	0 0	0 0	0 0	0 0	0 0	0 0	1 0
Common Goldeneye	5 0	0 0	0 4	0 1	0 0	1 0	2 18	10 0	0 0	1 3	1 0	7 0
Bufflehead	0 0	0 0	0 0	0 0	0 0	0 0	0 0	2 0	0 0	0 3	0 0	8 0
Hooded Merganser	0 0	0 0	0 0	0 0	0 0	0 0	0 34	27 0	0 2	4 1	2 0	2 0
Common Merganser	5 1	0 3	0 0	0 0	0 0	0 2	0 47	68 0	9 1	0 15	7 0	56 0
Ruddy Duck	0 0	0 0	0 0	0 0	0 0	0 0	0 0	0 0	0 0	0 0	0 0	34 0
Northern Harrier	0 0	1 1	0 0	0 0	0 0	0 0	0 2	0 0	0 0	0 0.	2 0	0 1
Sharp-shinned Hawk	0 0	0 0	0 1	0 0	1 0	1 4	2 0	0 3	3 6	2 5	2 3	3 7
Cooper's Hawk	0 0	1 2	0 2	0 1	1 1	0 0	1 0	0 0	1 2	3 0	0 0	0 0
Northern Goshawk	0 0	1 0	0 1	0 0	1 1	3 5	8 7	0 2	2 6	2 2	4 3	2 3

SPECIES	1960 1961	1962 1963	1964 1965	1966 1967	1968 1969	1970 1971	1972 1973	1974 1975	1976 1977	1978 1979	1980 1981	1982 1983
Red-shouldered Hawk	2 2	1 2	0 1	0 0	0 0	0 0	1 0	0 0	0 0	0 0	0 1	0 0
Red-tailed Hawk	2 5	2 7	6 5	12 5	8 12	15 34	12 21	34 34	31 56	38 49	91 42	59 74
Rough-legged Hawk	0 0	1 2	10 7	3 1	3 3	5 4	2 0	0 1	2 3	3 1	4 5	0 1
American Kestrel	3 4	6 3	4 4	5 2	2 7	6 17	6 17	12 15	17 13	13 12	19 15	12 15
Peregrine Falcon	0 0	0 1	0 0	0 0	0 0	0 0	0 0	0 0	0 0	0 0	0 0	0 0
Ring-necked Pheasant	94 138	131 198	101 129	346 191	220 474	289 287	257 109	116 124	114 92	104 139	111 190	60 56
Ruffed Grouse	23 19	11 21	9 11	52 11	8 16	15 10	6 3	17 3	12 2	29 4	11 29	15 37
Northern Bobwhite	0 0	0 0	0 1	1 0	0 18	4 0	0 3	0 4	0 0	0 0	0 0	10 2
Virginia Rail	0 0	0 0	0 0	0 0	0 5	1 6	0 3	5 4	1 5	2 2	2 0	1 0
Sora	0 0	0 0	0 1	0 0	0 1	1 3	0 0	0 0	0 1	1 0	0 0	0 0
American Coot	1 0	0 0	1 0	3 0	0 3	1 1	0 127	43 4	0 0	0 13	0 0	0 0

SPECIES	1960 1961	1962 1963	1964 1965	1966 1967	1968 1969	1970 1971	1972 1973	1974 1975	1976 1977	1978 1979	1980 1981	1982 1983
Killdeer	0 / 0	0 / 0	0 / 0	0 / 0	0 / 1	0 / 0	0 / 3	4 / 0	0 / 0	0 / 1	0 / 0	0 / 0
Common Snipe	0 / 0	1 / 1	1 / 0	1 / 0	0 / 2	4 / 1	0 / 3	6 / 4	8 / 3	0 / 2	3 / 0	1 / 2
American Woodcock	0 / 0	0 / 0	0 / 0	0 / 0	0 / 0	0 / 1	1 / 0	0 / 0	0 / 0	0 / 0	0 / 0	1 / 0
Ring-billed Gull	0 / 0	0 / 0	0 / 2	0 / 1	0 / 0	0 / 5	4 / 0	0 / 0	0 / 0	12 / 0	0 / 0	21 / 3
Herring Gull	123 / 92	415 / 1960	1213 / 921	867 / 741	685 / 1497	1987 / 3293	2587 / 1282	1875 / 1770	1367 / 2371	670 / 1407	1621 / 3300	2905 / 1120
Iceland Gull	0 / 0	0 / 1	3 / 1	1 / 3	1 / 5	1 / 3	3 / 0	0 / 0	2 / 0	1 / 0	1 / 0	0 / 0
Lesser Black-backed Gull	0 / 0	0 / 0	0 / 0	0 / 0	0 / 0	0 / 0	0 / 0	0 / 0	0 / 0	0 / 0	0 / 0	1 / 0
Glaucous Gull	0 / 0	0 / 0	1 / 0	0 / 0	0 / 1	0 / 3	0 / 1	0 / 0	0 / 0	0 / 0	0 / 1	0 / 0
Great Black-backed Gull	1 / 2	2 / 45	19 / 2	12 / 38	27 / 150	152 / 592	456 / 68	86 / 504	130 / 284	86 / 209	208 / 1100	276 / 167
Rock Dove	0 / 0	0 / 0	0 / 0	0 / 0	0 / 0	0 / 0	0 / 500	750 / 1032	839 / 628	1129 / 678	1390 / 938	1214 / 959
Mourning Dove	79 / 149	211 / 320	191 / 341	341 / 246	469 / 798	987 / 1187	936 / 863	788 / 876	1188 / 658	929 / 1098	1422 / 985	1290 / 2091

195

SPECIES	1960/1961	1962/1963	1964/1965	1966/1967	1968/1969	1970/1971	1972/1973	1974/1975	1976/1977	1978/1979	1980/1981	1982/1983
Eastern Screech-Owl	1/0	0/1	0/0	6/2	1/2	1/3	4/3	3/12	11/25	24/24	10/18	21/22
Great Horned Owl	4/3	1/2	3/1	1/0	3/0	1/1	4/1	8/3	5/2	7/7	8/9	20/13
Snowy Owl	0/0	0/0	0/0	0/0	0/0	0/0	0/0	0/0	0/0	0/0	0/1	0/0
Barred Owl	0/0	0/1	2/2	0/0	0/2	1/0	0/1	1/2	2/3	0/0	1/4	2/2
Long-eared Owl	0/0	0/0	0/0	0/0	0/0	3/0	0/0	0/1	0/0	0/2	0/0	0/0
Short-eared Owl	0/1	0/0	0/0	0/0	0/0	0/0	0/0	1/0	0/0	1/0	0/0	0/2
Belted Kingfisher	0/0	0/1	0/0	1/0	0/2	0/1	0/4	12/7	1/0	3/9	6/5	6/5
Red-headed Woodpecker	0/0	1/0	0/0	0/0	0/0	0/0	0/0	0/0	0/0	2/0	0/0	0/0
Red-bellied Woodpecker	0/0	0/0	0/0	0/0	1/0	0/0	0/0	0/0	0/0	0/1	0/0	0/1
Downy Woodpecker	34/80	77/110	107/154	129/91	164/303	251/342	274/313	293/231	314/309	260/377	458/399	395/538
Hairy Woodpecker	16/45	32/66	45/90	39/48	58/146	81/116	111/121	120/95	115/118	100/106	161/151	152/213

SPECIES	1960 1961	1962 1963	1964 1965	1966 1967	1968 1969	1970 1971	1972 1973	1974 1975	1976 1977	1978 1979	1980 1981	1982 1983
Black-backed Woodpecker	0	0	0	0	0	0	0	2	0	0	0	0
	0	1	0	0	0	1	0	0	0	0	0	0
Northern Flicker	1	0	1	2	2	4	2	5	6	3	5	6
	0	0	2	4	7	6	6	6	2	7	3	14
Pileated Woodpecker	1	0	0	2	1	1	2	2	5	3	3	2
	2	1	0	0	0	0	0	1	4	5	4	5
Eastern Phoebe	0	0	0	0	0	0	0	0	0	0	0	0
	0	0	0	1	0	0	0	0	0	0	0	0
Say's Phoebe	0	0	0	0	0	0	0	0	0	0	0	1
	0	0	0	0	0	0	0	0	0	0	0	0
Horned Lark	2	0	7	20	77	20	18	44	34	28	61	0
	15	20	0	0	72	22	35	14	104	0	0	55
Blue Jay	100	575	671	1008	1405	2431	737	1443	2054	281	2042	242
	225	995	1153	1362	1133	2837	2082	1162	1874	1174	351	1683
American Crow	130	416	656	677	345	979	1237	997	1537	1357	1705	2343
	247	346	907	473	617	680	1125	852	1326	1599	3048	1834
Fish Crow	0	0	0	0	0	0	0	0	0	2	12	43
	0	0	0	0	0	0	0	0	1	6	58	19
Black-capped Chickadee	230	613	946	1040	1083	1330	1495	1994	2149	2070	3220	2885
	668	789	1213	711	1884	2271	2053	1757	1915	2578	2407	3441
Boreal Chickadee	0	0	0	0	0	0	0	0	0	0	1	0
	0	0	0	0	2	0	0	0	0	0	0	0

SPECIES	1960 1961	1962 1963	1964 1965	1966 1967	1968 1969	1970 1971	1972 1973	1974 1975	1976 1977	1978 1979	1980 1981	1982 1983
Tufted Titmouse	0 6	2 2	10 9	18 23	37 125	115 265	203 251	409 288	502 569	378 497	604 505	554 636
Red-breasted Nuthatch	0 35	0 3	1 3	2 16	1 8	9 69	10 32	13 12	12 142	8 10	68 15	5 73
White-breasted Nuthatch	43 100	68 156	131 188	169 128	128 365	231 411	242 321	382 242	315 325	288 364	408 298	406 515
Brown Creeper	6 16	10 7	17 22	13 11	8 51	28 27	54 64	48 29	33 30	13 43	44 32	59 58
Carolina Wren	1 0	0 0	0 0	0 0	0 0	2 0	0 2	3 2	2 0	0 0	1 3	0 0
Winter Wren	0 0	0 0	1 0	4 1	0 1	2 0	2 1	0 4	0 1	0 2	0 1	0 1
Marsh Wren	0 2	0 1	2 1	1 0	0 0	0 0	0 0	0 0	0 0	0 2	1 0	1 0
Golden-crowned Kinglet	11 19	4 4	8 0	25 11	5 45	24 13	101 273	64 32	36 2	8 14	17 9	110 50
Ruby-crowned Kinglet	0 0	0 0	1 2	1 0	0 1	0 0	3 4	0 0	0 0	0 1	0 0	1 1
Eastern Bluebird	0 0	0 0	0 4	2 0	0 4	0 0	0 0	0 0	0 0	0 0	0 0	0 0
Hermit Thrush	0 0	0 0	1 1	2 1	0 0	1 1	0 1	0 1	5 0	0 1	3 0	0 1

SPECIES	1960 1961	1962 1963	1964 1965	1966 1967	1968 1969	1970 1971	1972 1973	1974 1975	1976 1977	1978 1979	1980 1981	1982 1983
Wood Thrush	0 0	0 0	0 0	0 0	0 0	0 1	0 0	0 0	0 0	0 0	0 0	0 0
American Robin	4 13	3 39	22 54	10 102	32 32	19 74	55 168	46 80	229 86	18 219	116 23	65 123
Varied Thrush	0 0	0 0	0 0	0 0	0 0	0 0	0 0	0 0	0 0	0 0	0 1	0 0
Gray Catbird	0 0	1 0	0 0	0 0	0 1	1 0	2 1	2 0	0 0	0 0	1 0	3 1
Northern Mockingbird	0 1	0 0	1 4	5 3	4 12	24 36	26 64	77 139	171 120	171 144	314 224	157 247
Brown Thrasher	0 0	1 0	0 0	2 0	0 3	6 0	0 1	1 1	0 1	0 0	0 1	0 2
Bohemian Waxwing	0 0	0 0	0 0	0 0	0 1	0 0	0 0	0 0	2 0	2 0	1 0	0 0
Cedar Waxwing	0 11	2 2	18 6	0 25	6 8	10 20	40 5	2 41	10 47	175 36	153 13	283 105
Northern Shrike	0 0	0 0	1 0	0 0	1 1	4 0	1 4	0 1	1 5	10 2	4 1	3 3
Loggerhead Shrike	0 0	0 0	0 0	0 0	0 0	0 0	0 0	0 0	1 0	0 0	0 0	0 0
+European Starling	1248 973	664 1584	3919 9999	7316 3328	6593 3107	3825 9999	9999 3146	3174 3495	4491 3183	6787 3668	5342 3296	5623 5517

SPECIES	1960 1961	1962 1963	1964 1965	1966 1967	1968 1969	1970 1971	1972 1973	1974 1975	1976 1977	1978 1979	1980 1981	1982 1983
Yellow-rumped Warbler	0 0	0 0	0 0	0 0	0 0	0 0	0 1	0 0	2 0	0 12	4 0	35 1
Ovenbird	0 0	0 0	0 0	0 0	0 0	0 0	0 0	0 0	0 0	0 0	1 0	0 0
Northern Waterthrush	0 0	0 0	0 0	0 0	0 1	0 0	0 1	0 0	0 0	0 0	0 0	0 0
Common Yellowthroat	0 0	0 0	0 0	0 0	0 0	0 3	0 2	2 0	0 0	1 2	0 0	0 3
Yellow-breasted Chat	0 0	0 0	0 0	0 0	0 0	0 1	0 0	0 0	0 0	0 0	0 0	0 0
Northern Cardinal	0 3	3 4	5 9	21 26	43 56	87 92	93 140	127 195	260 316	193 232	354 386	266 425
Rose-breasted Grosbeak	0 0	0 0	0 0	1 0	0 0	0 0	0 0	1 0	1 0	0 0	0 0	0 0
Black-headed Grosbeak	0 0	0 0	0 0	0 0	0 0	0 0	0 0	1 1	0 0	0 0	0 0	0 0
Dickcissel	0 1	1 1	0 0	0 0	2 0	0 0	0 0	0 0	0 0	0 0	0 0	0 0
Rufous-sided Towhee	0 0	6 2	2 1	1 4	6 10	16 3	1 6	2 3	6 3	0 1	5 1	2 4
American Tree Sparrow	240 227	197 310	501 533	588 585	878 1015	1231 987	615 953	527 674	1021 1130	608 551	1486 786	1001 1140

SPECIES	1960 1961	1962 1963	1964 1965	1966 1967	1968 1969	1970 1971	1972 1973	1974 1975	1976 1977	1978 1979	1980 1981	1982 1983
Chipping Sparrow	0 0	0 0	0 0	0 0	0 3	1 0	0 1	0 3	0 0	0 0	0 3	3 5
Clay-colored Sparrow	0 0	0 0	0 0	0 0	0 0	0 1	0 0	0 0	0 0	0 0	0 0	0 0
Field Sparrow	3 2	1 1	7 5	10 15	4 18	8 6	13 22	13 10	19 14	16 23	25 10	39 29
Vesper Sparrow	0 0	0 0	0 0	0 0	0 1	0 0	0 0	0 0	1 0	0 0	0 0	0 0
Lark Sparrow	0 0	0 0	0 0	0 0	0 0	1 0	0 0	0 0	0 0	0 0	0 0	0 0
Savannah Sparrow	0 5	0 0	0 0	4 0	0 3	0 2	0 4	0 1	1 0	0 1	3 0	4 5
Fox Sparrow	1 0	4 2	4 12	4 9	16 39	23 10	13 12	3 4	23 1	0 2	16 3	1 5
Song Sparrow	55 79	20 52	56 51	99 108	65 256	260 220	118 216	128 155	321 172	127 195	269 200	225 266
Swamp Sparrow	45 23	13 6	21 3	9 4	2 58	37 53	18 47	36 17	25 28	17 34	21 41	15 26
White-throated Sparrow	4 13	10 24	17 29	9 101	46 138	326 98	80 324	117 177	831 243	66 192	263 80	111 299
White-crowned Sparrow	0 0	0 0	0 0	0 0	0 0	0 0	1 0	0 1	0 0	1 1	3 0	1 0

SPECIES	1960	1961	1962	1963	1964	1965	1966	1967	1968	1969	1970	1971	1972	1973	1974	1975	1976	1977	1978	1979	1980	1981	1982	1983
Dark-eyed Junco	147	271	327	633	790	526	600	1113	776	1388	2118	1025	1110	897	565	997	1470	1424	374	749	1248	1273	1120	1698
*Oregon Junco	0	0	0	0	2	0	2	0	0	1	0	1	0	0	0	0	0	0	0	0	0	0	0	0
Lapland Longspur	0	0	0	0	0	0	0	0	0	0	0	1	0	6	0	0	0	2	0	0	0	0	0	0
Snow Bunting	0	7	0	0	1	0	10	1	0	0	33	1	32	0	1	1	22	124	0	0	31	26	0	17
Red-winged Blackbird	0	0	0	63	0	30	10	1	1	6	8	8	2	28	33	6	66	2	3	58	61	7	25	25
Eastern Meadowlark	1	6	0	34	28	7	8	1	2	5	1	0	0	0	3	6	0	0	0	8	9	1	1	0
Rusty Blackbird	0	0	0	0	9	8	0	3	0	1	0	1	1	0	5	8	13	3	9	4	1	0	3	0
Common Grackle	0	1	1	33	4	16	14	4	5	4	39	25	3	18	36	7	11	164	11	8	13	16	5	21
Brown-headed Cowbird	11	3	2	137	100	148	37	193	13	355	162	18	12	549	86	20	79	28	3	153	4	42	25	73
Northern Oriole	0	0	0	0	0	0	1	3	0	1	1	1	0	0	1	1	0	1	0	0	0	0	0	0
Pine Grosbeak	0	49	0	0	0	82	0	1	128	0	0	5	524	0	0	0	0	46	0	0	33	58	0	0
Purple Finch	12	21	39	43	89	29	6	97	179	105	39	74	101	33	41	88	120	87	85	97	123	162	612	114

SPECIES	1960 1961	1962 1963	1964 1965	1966 1967	1968 1969	1970 1971	1972 1973	1974 1975	1976 1977	1978 1979	1980 1981	1982 1983
House Finch	0 0	0 0	1 0	0 0	0 2	10 2	12 12	3 10	70 150	33 44	228 110	546 844
Red Crossbill	0 0	0 1	0 0	0 0	0 11	0 5	0 0	0 1	0 10	0 0	0 0	0 0
White-winged Crossbill	0 0	0 0	0 0	0 0	0 1	0 9	0 0	0 4	0 15	0 0	0 0	0 0
Common Redpoll	0 1	0 0	0 0	0 0	157 73	6 136	0 0	0 0	0 6	0 0	95 9	0 1
Pine Siskin	1 0	0 77	0 0	0 3	605 359	3 794	5 127	4 375	9 1258	0 0	74 150	4 141
American Goldfinch	48 119	232 241	328 472	323 571	916 886	704 1165	1425 936	825 666	1073 1187	766 702	1007 710	899 1156
Evening Grosbeak	26 233	2 463	138 366	1 95	396 1442	110 1036	551 148	209 524	496 548	600 676	915 507	691 1672
House Sparrow	840 977	1180 1573	1799 1754	1262 897	847 1746	2081 1792	1692 1626	3171 1455	1222 1218	1535 2855	2419 1712	1593 2012
Total Birds	3792 5160	5347 10878	12296 19680	15692 11765	17036 19599	20764 30646	25952 21943	20197 19247	24672 23545	21234 24324	30682 25345	30472 32262
Total Species	45 53	48 59	59 61	62 58	58 81	72 76	70 81	78 78	73 75	67 79	81 71	84 75
Party Hours	42 64	89 119	101 142	137 89	90 179	154 172	171 305	191 213	209 192	161 225	312 236	300 310

+Starling count exceeded 10,000 thus "Total Birds" number for these years is below actual count total.

*Now a Sub-species

PART I

Notes and Sources

For a detailed look at the SuAsCo river basin see Laurence Richardson's *Concord River* (1964) and Ann Swinger and Edwin Way Teale's *A Conscious Stillness (1982).*

Chapter I

Page   1   John Locke, *An Essay Concerning the True Original, Extent and End of Civil Government* (1690).

1   It is clear that the language group affiliation of the local Indian tribes was Algonquian. Although some authors have suggested that the Indians living in this area were members of the Nipmuck tribe, most research indicates that the Pawtuckett was the correct local affiliation. This case is made by Shirley Blanke in *Analysis of Variation In Point Morphology As A Strategy In The Reconstruction Of The Culture History Of An Archaeologically Disturbed Area* (1978) Concord Free Public Library - Special Collections.

1   "Act of Incorporation - September 2, 1635," *Records of the General Court.*

1-2   Edward Johnson, *Wonder-working Providence* (1651). This narrative provides an insight into the Puritan perspective of the wilderness and those "resolved servants of Christ" with salvation on their minds. Shattuck remarked that "This account may, therefore, be received with more implicit faith, than some of the author's statements of fact; and, for its curiosity . . ."

2   William Woods' *New England's Prospect* (1634) has a touch of Madison Avenue and the language of glossy travel brochures in its accounts. Wood did, however, visit the area now known as the Sudbury River Valley and provided early first-hand descriptions of the territory.

4   Roderick Nash, *Wilderness and the American Mind* (1967). This excellent work traces the origins and evolution of the concept of wilderness in America.

4   Lemuel Shattuck's *The History of the Town of Concord* (1835) was published on the town's bicentennial. It was the first comprehensive history for the town and contains a wealth of source material, narrative accounts and municipal statistics.

Page   4-5   Alfred Hudson's *The History of Sudbury, Massachusetts* (1889) is similar in conception to Shattuck's work and offers many accounts of the early history and conditions in Sudbury.

5   Shattuck, *ibid.*

5-6   First-hand accounts of the everyday and commonplace are, unfortunately, often difficult to unearth—particularly those details of life during the first hundred years of colonization. Fortunately the town records which do survive allow us some insights into those matters which concerned the local citizens. *Transcripts of the Ancient Records of Concord* - seven volumes - Concord Free Public Library - Special Collections.

6   Shattuck, *ibid.*

6-7   Robert Gross, *The Minutemen and Their World* (1976); "Culture and Cultivation: Agriculture and Society in Thoreau's Concord," *The Journal of American History* (Vol. 69, No. 1 - June 1982). Gross' research of local tax, valuation reports and property records has resulted in the quantification of land use changes in the eighteenth and nineteenth centuries.

7   Howard Russell, *A Long, Deep Furrow* (1976). This detailed work covers three centuries of agriculture in the New World.

7   Townsend Scudder, *Concord: American Town* (1947).

Chapter II

8   Elijah Wood Jr., "Reclaiming Wet Lands," *Notes of the Concord's Farmers Club* (1852) - Concord Free Public Library - Special Collections.

8   Information on agricultural and economic trends is from Robert Gross' "Culture and Cultivation: Agriculture and Society in Thoreau's Concord," *The Journal of American History* (Vol. 69, No. 1 - June 1982).

8   Wood Jr., *ibid.*

8-9   Henry F. French, *Farm Drainage* (1859).

9   Howard Russell, "Sudbury River meadows . . ." *The Sudbury Town Crier* (August 3, 1978).

9,11   Richardson, *ibid.*

Page 9-11 *The Complaint and Petition of the Inhabitants of Wayland, Sudbury, Concord, Bedford and Carlisle* (1859) - Concord Free Public Library - Special Collections - The complete text includes many interesting first-hand accounts of the history of the river meadows and their subsequent flooding.

11 This characterization of economic and commercial change is drawn from the works of Robert Gross and Laurence Richardson noted above.

Chapter III

12 Henry David Thoreau, *Walking* (1862).

12 Henry David Thoreau, *Walden* (1854).

12 Henry David Thoreau, *Walking* (1862).

12 Nash, *ibid.*

12 Henry David Thoreau, *A Week on the Concord and Merrimac Rivers* (1849).

12-13 Henry David Thoreau, *Journals.*

13 Milton Meltzer and Walter Harding, *A Thoreau Profile* (1962). This work outlines the many facets of Thoreau's life and is, as the authors point out, "drawn largely in his (Thoreau's) own words . . ."

13 Ray Angelo, *Botanical Index to Henry David Thoreau's Journals* (In Print). This is the first comprehensive index to botanical references in the *Journals.*

14 Ralph Waldo Emerson, *Journals:* May 21, 1856.

14 Richard Eaton, *A Flora of Concord* (1974). This book contains detailed descriptions of natural habitats and a history of botanical work in the Concord Region as well as an annotated checklist of the plants of this area.

14 Helen Cruickshank, *Thoreau on Birds* (1964). Selections from Thoreau's writings with comments by the author.

14-19 Thoreau, *ibid.*

17 Aldo Leopold, *A Sand County Almanac* (1949). This classic series of essays presents a "land ethic" whose themes have been influential in raising the environmental conscience of Americans.

18 Emerson, *ibid.*

Chapter IV

Page 20   Henry David Thoreau, *Walden* (1854).

20   John Wilinsky, *The Impact of the Railroad on Concord, Massachusetts 1844-1887* (1975) - Concord Free Public Library - Special Collections.

20   Paul Brooks' *The View from Lincoln Hill* (1976) is a detailed work on the evolution of the town of Lincoln, Massachusetts. Brooks discusses many of the cultural and environmental changes that affected Concord, Sudbury and Wayland.

20,22   Two books that explain the dynamics and history of the land are Betty Flanders Thomson's *The Changing Face of New England* (1958) and Neil Jorgensen's *A Guide to New England's Landscape* (1971).

22   Peter Whitney, *History of the County of Worcester* (1793).

22   Hugh M. Raup and Reynold E. Carlson, "The History of Land Use in the Harvard Forest," *Harvard Forest* (Bulletin No. 20 - 1941). This excellent paper is one of the best histories of land use in eighteenth and nineteenth century America.

22   Gordon G. Whitney and William C. Davis, *Concord, Massachusetts: An Ecological History of its Woodlands from 1620 to the Present* (unpublished).

22   Donald Worster, *Nature's Economy - The Roots of Ecology* (1977).

24   Henry David Thoreau, *Journals:* March 19, 1859.

24   Hudson, *ibid.*

24   "Agricultural Products and Property," *The Census of Massachusetts:* 1845, 1855, 1865, 1875, 1885.

25   The woodland statistics are taken from Robert Gross, *Ibid* and *The Census of Massachusetts:* 1875, 1885, 1895, 1905.

25   Henry Henshaw, "In Memoriam: William Brewster," *The Auk* (January 1920).

25-26   William Brewster, *Journals.*

26   Marian H. Wheeler, *Farming in Concord* (1975) - Concord Free Public Library - Special Collections.

26   Helen Emery, *The Puritan Village Evolves: A History of Wayland, Massachusetts* (1981).

27   Richardson, *ibid.*

27   Henry David Thoreau, *Huckleberries* (1970).

Chapter V

Page 28   Brewster, *ibid.*

28-29   Edward Jarvis, *Traditions and Reminiscenses* (1880) - unpublished manuscript - Concord Free Public Library - Special Collections.

29   Edward Howe Forbush, *A History of Game Birds, Waterfowl and Shorebirds of Massachusetts and Adjacent States* (1920).

29-30   Edward Howe Forbush, *Useful Birds and Their Protection* (1907).

30   Henry David Thoreau, *Journals:* September 12, 1854.

29-30   William Brewster, *The Birds of the Cambridge Region of Massachusetts* (1906).

30   Ludlow Griscom, *The Birds of Concord* (1949).

Chapter VI

Major biographical sources for William Brewster are: Frank Chapman, "William Brewster, 1851-1919," *Bird Lore* (Vol. 21, No. 5, September-October 1919).

Henry Henshaw, "In Memoriam: William Brewster," *The Auk* (January 1920).

Daniel Chester French, "The Introduction," *October Farm* (1936).

31   Brewster, *ibid.*

33   Griscom, *ibid.*

33-37   William Brewster, *Journals.*

35   Charles F. Batchelder, *A Bibliography of William Brewster* (1951).

35   *New York Times.*

Chapter VII

38   "Agriculture, the Fisheries, and Commerce," *The Census of Massachusetts* (Vol. 4 - 1909).

Page 38   William MacConnell and Marcia Cobb, *Remote Sensing 20 Years of Change in Middlesex County Massachusetts,* Massachusetts Agricultural Experiment Station (Bulletin No. 622 - November 1974).

38   Jorgensen, *ibid.*

38   Griscom, *ibid.*

40   Roger Tory Peterson, "In Memoriam: Ludlow Griscom," *The Auk* (Vol. 82 - October 1965).

The following reviews of *The Birds of Concord* are pertinent to the discussion on pages 40-41.

H.I. Fisher, "The Birds of Concord," *The Auk* (Vol. 67 - 1950).

Francis H. Allen, "The Birds of Concord," *The Bulletin* of the Massachusetts Audubon Society (October 1950).

Ralph Palmer, "The Birds of Concord," *Bird-Banding* (Vol. 21 - January 1950).

41   Griscom, *ibid.*

Chapter VIII

43   Griscom, *ibid.*

43   *U.S. Census:* 1900-1980.

45   Building Permits for New Residences, *Town Reports:* Concord, Sudbury, and Wayland (1949-1980).

45-46 MacConnell and Cobb, *ibid.*

45-46 "Agriculture, the Fisheries, and Commerce," *The Census of Massachusetts* (Vol. 4 - 1909).

46   *Open Space Plans:* Concord, Sudbury, and Wayland (1977).

Chapter IX

47   Personal Correspondence - Allen Morgan to C. Russell Mason.

47-49 Allen Morgan, "Barometer of Change," *Massachusetts Audubon* (Vol. I, No. 2 - Winter 1965).

Page   47,49   Personal Correspondence - Allen Morgan.

47,49   Allen Morgan, *Journals:* 1936-1956 (unpublished).

49   Mary Eugenia Meyer, *History of the Sudbury Valley Trustees, Inc. 1953-1978* (1978).

49-50   *Report of the Sudbury Valley Commission* (1950).

50   Personal Correspondence - Allen Morgan.

50   Judge Robert Wolcott, "President's Page," *The Bulletin* of the Massachusetts Audubon Society (April 1956).

53   Allen Morgan, *SVT Newsletter* (October 1956).

53   Meyer, *ibid.*

Chapter X

55   Barbara Robinson *et al., The Big Water Fight* - The League of Women Voters of the United States.

56   Tom Conuel, "Selling the Sudbury," *Sanctuary:* The Bulletin of the Massachusetts Audubon Society (September-October 1982).

56-57   Diane Dumanoski, "US cuts key research on acid rain . . . ," *Boston Globe* (January 16, 1983).

57   "Site Fact Sheets: Nyanza and W.R. Grace," Massachusetts Department of Environmental Quality Engineering (January 1983).

57   Gerard Bertrand, "One Small Step," *Sanctuary:* The Bulletin of the Massachusetts Audubon Society (November 1982).

PART II

Sources for the Journal Accounts

F.B.   Frank Bolles - This account comes from *Land of the Lingering Snow* (1891).

W.B.   William Brewster - The following journal accounts were published in part or entirely in *October Farm* (1936): March 31, 1895; April 2, 1910; April 7, 1899; May 17, 1912; May 28, 1906; June 11, 1898; June 21, 1898; September 9, 1906; October 4, 1897; October 17, 1894; November 21, 1896.

     - The following journal accounts were published in part or entirely in *Concord River* (1937): February 2, 1892; March 19, 1909; April 2, 1893; April 9, 1907; May 3, 1892; June 21, 1892; September 7, 1892; October 8, 1892; November 4, 1902; November 1916; December 30, 1891.

     - The following accounts are published here courtesy of the Museum of Comparative Zoology, Harvard University: February 2, 1892; April 2, 1893; May 16, 1900; June 16, 1886; September 9, 1906; October 27, 1891.

R.P.E.   Ruth P. Emery - Journals (unpublished).

R.A.F.   Richard A. Forster - Journals (unpublished); the January 14, 1978 account was published in *Massachusetts Audubon,* April 1978 - Vol. 17, No. 8.

D.L.G.   David L. Garrison - Journals (unpublished).

L.G.   Ludlow Griscom - Journal accounts are published here courtesy of the Peabody Museum of Salem, Massachusetts.

A.H.M.   Allen H. Morgan - Journals (unpublished).

W.R.P.   Wayne R. Petersen - Journals (unpublished).

E.B.P.   Betty Porter - Journals (unpublished).

E.W.T.   Edwin Way Teale - This account appears in *A Conscious Stillness* by Edwin Way Teale and Ann Zwinger (1982).

H.D.T.   Henry David Thoreau - All the journal accounts are from *Thoreau's Bird Lore - Notes on New England Birds,* edited by Francis H. Allen (1910).

R.K.W.   Richard K. Walton - Journals (unpublished).

PART III

References

1. Jeremy Hatch, "The Cormorants of Boston Harbor and Massachusetts Bay," *Bird Observer of Eastern Massachusetts* (*BOEM*) (Vol. 10, No. 2 - April 1982).

2. Wayne R. Petersen, "Massachusetts Waders: Past and Present," *BOEM* (Vol. 10, No. 3 - June 1982).

3. G.W. Cottrell, Jr., "The Southern Heron Flight of 1948," *The Bulletin* of the Massachusetts Audubon Society (Vol. 33, Nos. 3 and 4 - April and May 1949).

4. William H. Drury Jr., Allen H. Morgan, and Richard Stackpole, "Occurrence of an African Cattle Egret (*Ardeola ibis ibis*) in Massachusetts," *The Auk* (Vol. 70, No. 3 - July 1953).

5. Wayne Hanley, "Mute Swans," *BOEM* (Vol. 2, No. 2 - March/April 1974).

6. John K. Terres, *The Audubon Society Encyclopedia of North American Birds* p. 194 (1980).

7. James J. Pottie and H. W. Heusmann, "Taxonomy of Resident Geese in Massachusetts," *Transactions of the Northeast Section, The Wildlife Society* (1979).

8. H. W. Heusmann and Robert Belville, "Wood Duck Research in Massachusetts," Research Bulletin 19 - Massachusetts Division of Fisheries and Wildlife (1982).

9. Paul A. Johnsgard, *Waterfowl of North America* (1975).

10. Richard Borden and H. A. Hochbaum, "General Notes - The Establishment of a Breeding Population of Gadwall in Massachusetts," *Records of New England Birds* (March 1966).

11. Ludlow Griscom, *The Birds of Concord* (*TBOC*) p. 195 (1949).

12. Philip Martin, "What Future for the Osprey," *BOEM* (Vol. 2, No. 2 - March/April 1974).

13. Donna Finley, "The Incredible Peregrine - On the Rebound?," *Endangered Species Technical Bulletin* - Department of the Interior, U.S. Fish and Wildlife Serice (Vol. 5, No. 8 - August 1980).

14. "The Autumn Migration - Hudson-Delaware Region," *American Birds* (Vol. 37, No. 2 - March/April 1983).

15. Ludlow Griscom, *TBOC* p. 124-127.

16. James E. Cardoza, "The Wild Turkey in Massachusetts," *BOEM* (Vol. 5, No. 3 - May/June 1977).

17. Edward Howe Forbush, *Birds of Massachusetts And Other New England States* (Vol. II, 1927).

18. Wayne R. Petersen, "Massachusetts Rallidae - A Summary," *BOEM* (Vol. 9, No. 4 - August 1981).

Ludlow Griscom, "Massachusetts Rails," *The Bulletin* of the Massachusetts Audubon Society (1945).

19. Ludlow Griscom, *TBOC* p. 211-213.

Tim Manolis, "The Kicker Song," *American Birds* (Vol. 35, No. 3).

20. Ludlow Griscom, *TBOC* p. 152-155.

21. Edward Howe Forbush, *ibid. (Vol. I, 1925).*

R. M. Erwin, Costal Waterbird Colonies: Cape Elizabeth, Maine to Virginia - U.S. Fish and Wildlife Service, Biological Services Program (1979).

22. W. Earl Godfrey, "A Possible Shortcut Spring Migration Route of the Arctic Tern to James Bay, Canada," *Canadian Field-Naturalist* (Vol. 87, No. 1 - January/March 1973).

23. *Audubon Field Notes,* Northeastern Maritime Region (Vol. 17, No. 3 - June 1963).

24. Michael J. Brazauskas, "The Mourning Dove in Massachusetts," *BOEM* (Vol. 7, No. 3 - June 1979).

25. Trevor Lloyd-Evans, "Chickadee Invasion," *BOEM* (Vol. 9, No. 6 -December 1981).

26. Bruce A. Sorrie, "Boreal Chickadee Invasion," *BOEM* (Vol. 3, No. 5 - September/October 1975).

27. "Results of the 1982 Cardinal, Tufted Titmouse, Mockingbird Census," Massachusetts Audubon Society - Department of Natural History.

28. John Bull, *Birds of New York State* (1974).

29. Christopher W. Leahy, "The Rise and Fall of *Sialia sialis,*" *Sanctuary:* The Bulletin of the Massachusetts Audubon Society (Vol. 21, No. 3 - November 1981).

30. Robert H. MacArthur, "Population Ecology of Some Warblers of North-Eastern Coniferous Forests," *Ecology* (Vol. 39, No. 4 October 1958).

31. Norman P. Hill, "Sharp-tailed Sparrows in Massachusetts," *BOEM* (Vol. 4, No. 2 - March/April 1976).

32. Richard K. Walton, "Inland Record of Seaside Sparrow," *BOEM* (Vol. 9, No. 6 - December 1981).

33. Richard A. Forster, "Orchard Orioles in Massachusetts," *BOEM* (Vol. 3, No. 3 - May/June 1975).

34. Richard A. Forster, "Pine Grosbeak Invasion," *Massachusetts Audubon* (Vol. 17, No. 8 - April 1978).

35. Bruce A. Sorrie, "The House Finch in Massachusetts," *BOEM* (Vol. 3, No. 6 - November/December 1975.)

INDEX

The index references Parts I and III of this volume. I have also designed the index so that it enables the reader to cross reference bird names which are out of use or have recently been changed. As such, the index will help the reader determine contemporary terminology for "older" bird names as these occur frequently in the journal accounts. The index does not, however, reference specific information in Part II. The species accounts in Part III are listed in boldface type.

Acid Rain, 56-57
Acton, town of, viii, 11
Agassiz, Louis, 13
Agriculture (see Land, agricultural)
Agricultural Preservation Restriction, 55
Allen, Arthur A., 40
American Museum of Natural History, 40
American Ornithologists' Union 36, 42
Angelo, Ray, 13-14
Ashland, town of, viii
Assabet Village, 11
Audubon, John James, 33
Baird, James, 53
Baldpate (see Wigeon, American)
Ball's Hill, 29, 34, 35
Batchelder, Charles, 35
Bedford, town of, viii
Bent Company, 26
Bergstrom, Alexander, 47
Bertrand, Gerard, 57
Billerica, town of, viii, 9
Bittern, American, **102**, 190
    Green (see Heron, Green-backed)
    Least, **102**
Blackbird, Red-winged, 5, 34, **180**, 201
    Rusty, 41, **181**, 201
    Yellow-headed, **181**
Bluebird, Eastern, 34, **156**, 197
Bobolink, 37, **180**
Bobwhite (see Bobwhite, Northern)
Bobwhite, Northern, 30, **123**, 193
Bolles, Frank, 67-68
Boston, city of, 9, 27, 43

Boston Society of Natural History, 42
Brant, **107**
Brewster, William, 25, 28-37, 40
Bufflehead, **115**, 192
Bunting, Indigo, **173**
    Lark, **176**
    Painted, **173**
    Snow, **180**, 201
Cambridge, town of, 31, 36
Canal, Erie, 20
    Middlesex, 9
Canvasback, **111-112**, 191
Cardinal (see Cardinal, Northern)
Cardinal, Northern, **172-173**, 199
Carlisle, town of, viii, 24, 35
Carlisle State Forest, 26
Catbird, Gray, **158**, 198
Chapman, Frank, 35, 40
Chat, Yellow-breasted, **172**, 199
Chelmsford, town of, viii, 11
Chickadee, Black-capped, 15, **151-152**, 196
    Boreal, **152**, 196
Chicken, Prairie, 30
Clean Water Act, 55
Concord, town of, viii,, 1, 4-7, 11, 24, 38, 43-45
Concord Farmers Club, 8
Coot, American, **125-126**, 193
Cordaville, town of, viii
Cormorant, Double-crested, **101**
    Great, **101**, 190
Cowbird, Brown-headed, **182**, 201
Crane, Sandhill, **126**
Creeper, black and white (see Warbler, Black-and-white)
Creeper, Brown, 15, **153**, 197
Crossbill, Red, **184**, 202
    White-winged, **184**, 202

Crow, American, 5, **151**, 196
  Common (see Crow, American)
  Fish, **151**, 196
Cruickshank, Helen, 14
Cuckoo, Black-billed, **139**
  Yellow-billed, **139**
Damon Mill, 26
Dana, Richard, 31
Davis' Hill, 25, 35
Dickcissel, **174**, 199
Dove, Carolina (see Dove,
  Mourning)
  Mourning, **138**, 194
  Rock, 5, **138**, 194
Dovekie, 137
Dowitcher, Long-billed, **133**
  Short-billed, **133**
Drury, Jr., William H., 53
Duck, American Black, **108-109**,
  191
  Black (see Duck, American
  Black)
  Harlequin, **113**
  Ring-necked, **112**, 191
  Ruddy, **116**, 192
  Summer (see Duck, Wood)
  Wood, **107-108**, 190
Dunlin, **132**
Eagle, Bald, **117**
  Golden, **121**
Eaton, Richard, 14, 49
Egret, American (see Egret, Great)
  Cattle, **104**
  Great, **103**
  Snowy, **103**, 104
Emerson, George, 22
  Ralph Waldo, 14, 18
F. hyemalis (see Junco, Dark-eyed)
F. linaria (see Redpoll, Common)
Fairhaven Bay (Pond), 18, 35
Falcon, Peregrine, 47, **122**, 193
Farming (see Land, agricultural)
Finch, House, **184**, 202
  Purple, 37, **183**, 201
Fisher, H.I., 40
Flicker, Common (see Flicker,
  Northern)
  Northern, 28, **145**, 196
  Yellow-shafted (see Flicker,

  Northern)
Flycatcher, Alder, **146**
  Great-crested, 36, **147**
  Least, **147**
  Olive-sided, **145**
  Scissor-tailed, **148**
  Willow, **146**
  Yellow-bellied, **146**
Forbush, Edward Howe, 29, 35
Forest, (see Land, forest)
Foster, Charles H.W., 53
Framingham, town of, viii,, 44, 53
French, Daniel Chester, 8, 31, 34
  Henry F., 8-9
Fresh Pond, Cambridge, 31, 36
Fringilla linaria (see Redpoll,
  Common)
Gadwall, **110-111**, 191
Gallinule, Common (see Moorhen,
  Common)
  Purple, **125**
Gannet (see Gannet, Northern)
Gannet, Northern, **101**
Garrison, David, 47
Gnatcatcher, Blue-gray, **155**
Godwit, Hudsonian, **129**
Goldeneye, American (see
  Goldeneye, Common)
  Barrow's, **115**
  Common, **114**, 192
Goldfinch, American, 33, **185**, 202
Goose, Canada, 2, 17, **107**, 190
  Greater White-fronted, **106**
  Snow, **106-107**, 190
Goshawk (see Goshawk, North-
  ern)
Goshawk, Northern, **118-119**, 192
Grackle, Common, **182**, 201
Great Meadows, 4, 25, 34
Great Meadows National Wildlife
  Refuge, 53
Grebe, Horned, **100**
  Pied-billed, **100-101**, 190
  Red-necked, **101**
Griscom, Ludlow, 14, 30, 33,
  38-42, 43, 47, 49
Grosbeak, Black-headed, **173**, 199
  Evening, **185-186**, 202
  Pine, **183**, 201

Grosbeak, *continued*
  Rose-breasted, **173**, 199
Gross, Robert A., 6-7
Grouse, Ruffed, 5, 7, 28, 29. **122**, 193
Gull, Bonaparte's, **134**
  Glaucous, **136**, 194
  Great Black-backed, **136**, 194
  Herring, **135**, 194
  Iceland, **136**, 194
  Lesser Black-backed, 194
  Ring-billed, **135**, 194
Gyrfalcon, **122**
Hanley, Wayne, 53
Harrier, Northern, 35, **117-118**, 192
Hawk, Broad-winged, **119-120**
  Cooper's, 35, **118**, 192
  Duck (see Falcon, Peregrine)
  Fish (see Osprey)
  Frog (see Harrier, Northern)
  Marsh (see Harrier, Northern)
  Pigeon (see Merlin)
  Red-shouldered, 35, **119**, 193
  Red-tailed, 35, **120**, 193
  Rough-legged, **120-121**, 193
  Sharp-shinned, 15, 35, **118**, 192
  Sparrow (see Kestrel, American)
  Swainson's, **120**
Heard's Pond, 41, 47
Hen-hawk, 13
Hen, meadow or mud (see Rail, Virginia)
Henshaw, Henry, 33, 34
Heron, Great Blue, **102-103**, 190
  Green (see Heron, Green-backed)
  Green-backed, **104**, 190
  Little Blue, **103-104**
Hudson, town of, viii
Hudson, Alfred S., 4-5, 7, 24
Hummingbird, Ruby-throated, 34, **143**
Hunting, 4, 5, 7, 28-30, 31, 33
Ibis, Glossy, **105**
Indians (see Pawtuckett)
Jarvis, Edward, 28-29
Jay, Blue, 5, **150-151**, 196
Johnson, Edward, 1-2
Junco, Dark-eyed, **179**, 201

Oregon, 201
Kestrel, American, **121**, 193
Kicker (see Rail, Virginia)
Killdeer, **127**, 194
Kingbird, Eastern, **148**
  Western, **148**
Kingfisher, Belted, **143**, 195
Kinglet, Golden-crowned, **155**, 197
  Ruby-crowned, **155**, 197
Kite, American Swallow-tailed, **117**
Knight, W.H., 11
Knot, Red, **130**
Lake Umbagog, Maine, 36
Land, agricultural, 1-7, 8-11, 20, 22, 26, 28, 38, 43, 46, 55
  clearing of, 4-7, 8, 11, 15, 22, 24-25
  forest, 4, 7, 20-26, 28, 36, 38 43, 45-46, 55-57
  reclamation of, 4, 8, 11, 36, 46, 47, 50
  (see also, Uplands, Wetlands)
Lark, Horned, **148**, 196
Leopold, Aldo, 17
Lincoln, town of, viii
Linnaean Society, 40
Longspur, Lapland, **179**, 201
Loon, Common, 19, **100**
  Red-throated, **100**
Lowell, town of, viii
Mallard, **109**, 191
Marlboro, town of, viii
Martin, Purple, **149**
Massachusetts Audubon Society, 36, 42, 50, 53, 57
Massachusetts Department of Environmental Quality Engineering, 57
Massachusetts Fish and Game Commission, 36
Maynard, town of, viii
Maynard, A., 11
McConnell-Cobb Map-Down Project, 45-46
Meadowlark, Eastern, **181**, 201
  Western, **181**
Merganser, American (see Merganser, Common)
  Common, 17, **115**, 192

Merganser, *continued*
  Hooded, 41, **115**, 192
  Red-breasted, **116**
Merlin, 35, **121**
Metropolitan District Commission, 56
Milldam Company, 11
Mockingbird (see Mockingbird, Northern)
Mockingbird, Northern, **158**, 198
Moorhen, Common, **125**
Morgan, Allen H., 47-54, 55
Murre, Thick-billed, **138**
Museum of Comparative Zoology, 40
Musketaquid, 1, 4-5
Nash, Roderick, 4
National Audubon Society, 42
National Environmental Policy Act, 55
New England Rivers Center, 55
Nighthawk, Common, **142**
Night-Heron, Black-crowned, **105**
  Yellow-crowned, **105**
Night Warbler (see Ovenbird)
Nine Acre Corner, 29
Northborough, town of, viii
Nuclear War, 57
Nuthatch, Red-breasted, **152-153**, 197
  White-breasted, 33, **153**, 197
Nuttall Ornithological Club, 36, 42
Nuttall, Thomas, 33
October Farm, 35, 36
Old Colony Bird Club, 41
Oldsquaw, **113**
Oriole, Northern, 37, **183**, 201
  Orchard, **182**
Osprey, **116-117**
Ovenbird, 34, **169**, 199
Owl, Barn (see Owl, Common Barn-)
  Barred, **141**, 195
  Boreal, **142**
  Common Barn-, **139**
  Eastern Screech-, 31, **140**, 195
  Great Gray, **141**
  Great Horned, **140**, 195

Hawk (see Owl, Northern Hawk-)
  Long-eared, **141**, 195
  Northern Hawk-, 42, 47, **140-141**
  Northern Saw-whet, **142**
  Saw-whet (see Owl, Northern Saw-whet)
  Short-eared, **141**, 195
  Snowy, **140**, 195
Pantry Brook, 53
Partridge (see Grouse, Ruffed)
Parula, Northern, 34, **163**
Pawtuckett Indians, 1-2, 5-6, 22
Pesticides, 57
Petersham, town of, 22
Peterson, Roger Tory, 14, 40
Pewee (see Wood-Pewee, Eastern)
Phalarope, Northern (see Phalarope, Red-necked)
  Red, **134**
  Red-necked, **134**
  Wilson's, **134**
Pheasant, Ring-necked, **122**, 193
Phoebe, Eastern, 37, 47, **147**, 196
  Say's, 196
Pigeon (see Dove, Rock)
Pigeon, Passenger, 30, **138**
Pintail (see Pintail, Northern)
Pintail, Northern, **109**, 191
Pipit, Water, **159**
Plover, American Golden (see Plover, Lesser Golden-)
  Black-bellied, **126**
  Lesser Golden-, **126**
  Piping, **127**
  Semipalmated, **127**
  Upland (see Sandpiper, Upland)
Pumper (see Bittern, American)
Quail (see Bobwhite, Northern)
Rail, Carolina (see Sora)
  Clapper, 124
  King, **123-124**
  Virginia, **124**, 193
  Yellow, **123**
Railroad, Boston & Albany, 20
  Fitchburg, 20
  Framingham & Lowell, 20
Reading, town of, 30

Redhead, **112**, 191
Redpoll, Common, **184**, 202
  Hoary, **185**
Redstart, American, **168**
Richardson, Laurence, 9, 27
River, Assabet, viii, 11, 26, 27, 50
  53, 57
  Concord, viii, 6, 9, 25, 29, 35
  diversion, 27, 56
  meadows (see Wetlands)
  Merrimack, viii
  Sudbury, viii, 9, 27, 50, 53, 56,
  57
Robin, American, 28, **157**, 198
  Gold (see Oriole, Northern)
Ruff, **132**
Russell, Howard, 7, 9
Sanderling, **130**
Sandpiper, Baird's **131**
  Buff-breasted, **132**
  Least, **131**
  Pectoral, **131-132**
  Semipalmated, **130**
  Solitary, **128**
  Spotted, 14-15, 31, **129**
  Stilt, **132**
  Upland, **129**
  Western, **131**
  White-rumped, **131**
Sapsucker, Yellow-bellied, **144**
Saxonville, town of, viii, 24, 27
Scaup, Greater, **113**, 191
  Lesser, **113**, 192
Scoter, Black, **114**
  Surf, **114**
  White-winged, **114**
Scudder, Townsend, 7
Self-Help Act of 1960, 55
Shattuck, Lemuel, 4, 5, 7
Sheldrake (see Merganser,
  Common)
Shoveler, Northern, **110**, 191
Shrike, Loggerhead, **160**, 198
  Northern, **160**, 198
Sierra Club, Thoreau Group, 55
Siskin, Pine, **185**, 202
Snipe, Common, 29, 31, **133**, 194
  Wilson's (see Snipe, Common)
Snyder, Dorothy, 42

Sora, **124-125**, 193
Southborough, town of, viii
Sparrow, American Tree, **174**, 199
  Chipping, **174-175**, 200
  Clay-colored, **175**, 200
  English (see Sparrow, House)
  Field, 17, 28, **175**, 200
  Fox, **177**, 200
  Grasshopper, **176**
  Henslow's, **177**
  House, **186**, 202
  Lark, **176**, 200
  Lincoln's, **178**
  Savannah, **176**, 200
  Seaside, **177**
  Sharp-tailed, **177**
  Song, 28, 31, **178**, 200
  Swamp, 31, **178**, 200
  Tree (see Sparrow, American
    Tree)
  Vesper, **175**, 200
  White-crowned, **179**, 200
  White-throated, **179**, 200
Stakedriver (see Bittern,
  American)
Starling (see Starling, European)
Starling, European, **160**, 198
Storm-Petrel, Leach's, **101**
Stow, town of, viii
SUASCO Corporation, 50
SuAsCo River Basin Group, 53
SuAsCo Watershed Association,
  55
SuAsCo Watershed Work Plan,
  53
Sudbury, town, of, viii, 4-5, 11,
  24, 25, 38, 43-45
Sudbury Valley Commission,
  Report of, 49-50
Sudbury Valley Trustees, 49-53
Swallow, Bank, 17, **150**
  Barn, **150**
  Cliff, **150**
  Northern Rough-winged, **149**
  Rough-winged (see Swallow,
    Northern Rough-winged)
  Tree, **149**
Swan, Mute, **106**, 190
  Tundra, **106**

Swan, *continued*
  Whistling (see Swan, Tundra)
Swift, Chimney, **143**
Tanager, Scarlet, 29, **172**
  Summer, **172**
  Western, **172**
Teal, Blue-winged, **110**, 191
  Green-winged, **108**, 190
Tern, Arctic, **137**
  Black, **137**
  Caspian, **136**
  Common, **137**
  Least, **137**
Tewksbury, town of, viii
Thoreau, Henry David, 12-19, 20,
  24, 27, 35-36, 43
Thrasher, Brown, 28, **159**, 198
Thrush, Gray-cheeked, **156**
  Hermit, **157**, 197
  Olive-backed (see Thrush,
    Swainson's)
  Swainson's, **156**
  Varied, **158**, 198
  Wilson's (see Veery)
  Wood, 36-37, **157**, 198
Titlark (see Pipit, Water)
Titmouse, Tufted, **152**, 197
Towhee, Rufous-sided, 28, **174**,
  199
Toxic Waste, 57
Turkey, Wild, 4, 7, 29, **123**
Turner Plan, 50
Turnstone, Ruddy, **130**
Uplands, 4, 11, 28
Veery, **156**
Vireo, Philadelphia, **162**
  Red-eyed, **162**
  Solitary, 34, **161**
  Warbling, **161**
  White-eyed, **161**
  Yellow-throated, **161**
Vulture, Turkey, **116**
Wakefield, town of, 31
Walcott, Judge Robert, 50
Walden Pond, 13, 17, 19
Warbler, Bay-breasted, **167**
  Black-and-white, 13, 28, **168**
  Blackburnian, 34, **166**
  Blackpoll, **168**

Black-throated Blue, **165**
Black-throated Green, **165-166**
Blue-winged, **162**
Canada, **171**
Cape May, **165**
Cerulean, **168**
Chestnut-sided, 28, **164**
Connecticut, **170**
Golden-winged, 28, **162**
Hooded, **171**
Kentucky, **170**
Magnolia, **164**
Mourning, **170**
Myrtle (see Warbler, Yellow-
  rumped)
Nashville, **163**
Night (see Ovenbird)
Orange-crowned, **163**
Palm, **167**
Parula (see Parula, Northern)
Pine, **166**
Prairie, **167**
Prothonotary, 47, **169**
Tennessee, **163**
Wilson's, **171**
Worm-eating, **169**
Yellow, **164**
Yellow-rumped, 33, **165**, 199
Yellow-throated, **166**
Waring Hat Factory, 26
Waterthrush, Louisiana, **170**
  Northern, **169**, 199
Waxwing, Bohemian, **159**, 198
  Cedar, **159-160**, 198
Wayland, town of, viii, 11, 24, 26
  38, 43-45, 47, 49
Westborough, town of, viii, 53
Wetlands, 4-6, 8-11, 27, 46, 47,
  49-54, 55-57
Wetlands Protection Act (1963),
  55
Wetlands Restriction Act, 55
Whimbrel, **129**
Whip-poor-will, **142**
Whitney, Peter, 22
Widgeon (see Wigeon)
Wigeon, American, **111**, 191
  Eurasian, **111**
  European (see Wigeon, Eurasian)

Willet, **128**
Wilson, Alexander, 15
Wood, William, 2
Wood, Jr., Elijah, 8
Woodcock, American, 29,
   133-134, 194
Woodlands (see Land, forest)
Woodpecker, Black-backed, **145**,
   196
  Black-backed Three-toed (see
    Woodpecker, Black-backed)
  Downy, 28, 33, **144**, 195
  Hairy, **144**, 195
  Pigeon (see Flicker, Northern)
  Pileated, **145**, 196
  Red-bellied, **144**, 195
  Red-headed, **143**, 195
Wood-Pewee, Eastern, **146**
Worster, Donald, 22
Wren, Carolina, **153**, 197
  House, **154**
  Long-billed Marsh (see Wren,
    Marsh)
  Marsh, **154-155**, 197
  Sedge, **154**
  Short-billed Marsh (see Wren,
    Sedge)
  Winter, **154**, 197
Yellowlegs, Greater, **127-128**
  Lesser, **128**
Yellowthroat, Common, **170-171**,
   199
  Maryland (see Yellowthroat,
    Common)